Cradled In Sweden

Carl-Erik Johansson

By

Everton Publishers, Inc.
P. O. Box 368
LOGAN, UTAH 84321

PRINTED BY

Keith W. Watkins & Sons
5 SOUTH MAIN
PROVIDENCE, UTAH 84332

A Practical Help to Genealogical Research In Swedish Records

CARL-ERIK JOHANSSON

To My Beloved Maja

and Children

PREFACE

This book is written mainly for those who desire to search the millions of pages of Swedish genealogical records that are available on microfilm at the Genealogical Society Library in Salt Lake City, but who do not master the language of the records.

May it serve its eternal purpose.

My thanks to all those who through the years have made it possible — teachers, students, and friends; but above all to the untold thousands who through the centuries so painstakingly filled page after page with careful notes about our progenitors. Little did they dream of our joy over them.

May that joy be their unseen reward.

Salt Lake City in June 1967

CARL-ERIK JOHANSSON

Table of Contents

Chapter 1

The Language

The single greatest obstacle for a foreigner to a study of the Swedish genealogical sources would probably be the unfamiliarity with the language used in those records. They were mostly kept in Swedish, but the farther back in time we go the greater the chance of finding more and more Latin, being the universal language of most of the Christian clergy.

It it not our purpose here to teach you how to speak these languages, only to give you some working knowledge in using maps, encyclopedical works, and the many original records that are extant.

You would, however, do well to study the language somewhat, as the records and its people will come much more alive to you, and you will be able to pick out and understand those certain small notes in margins etc., that add so much to our knowledge of the people in the records, and are like gravy on the meat or spice in the cake.

We will only talk briefly about three main points of the language and its sound values, the knowledge of which is a necessity in studying the records. They are:

1. There are three more letters after Z in the Swedish alphabet, all three being vowels — Åå, Ää and Öö. In English text we often find these letters without the rings or dots, making them plain a's or o's. Sometimes we find them spelled AA, AE and OE or Ø. But just do not forget that they are individual, distinct letters in the alphabet, being the last three. The ring over the A was originally an O, and the dots over A and O represented an E. The W is not a special letter, but stands for V and is pronounced as a V.

2. The letters have a different sound value in Swedish than in English.

3. A spelling reform took place in 1906, simplifying the spelling.

Values of the Sounds

Let us start with the nine vowels. They are divided into two groups — a, å, o, u, called the hard vowels, and e, ä, i, y, ö called the soft vowels. Each vowel has at least two sound values, the long and the short, and we will try to give an example of each.

a — long — sounds like A in car
fader (father)   stad (city)

a — short — sounds like U in much (**not** like A in match)
kall (cold or calling)   hall (hall)

å — long — sounds like O in hole
Skåne   Håkan

å — short — sounds like O in rock
lång (long)   ålder (age)

o — long — as OO in food
moder (mother)   bo (live)

o — short — is pronounced exactly like short å
dotter (daughter)   och (and)

o — is also pronounced exactly like long å in some cases
son (son)   kol (coal)

u — long — the exact sound would not be found in English, however, the closest sound would be U in fluke with lips rounded
hus (house)   ute (outside)

u — short — pronounced like U in pull
rum (room)   ljung (heather) (lj pronounced like Y in yield)

e — long — like A in lake
lek (play, game)   de (they)

e — short — like E in bet
svensk (Swedish)   sex (six)

e — in ends of words with two or more syllables — sounds like E in mother
gosse (boy)   broder (brother)

ä — long — like AI in fair
äga (own)   räkna (count, figure)

ä — short — is pronounced exactly like short e
bägge (both) änka (widow)

i — long — like EE in deed
ni (you) liten (little, small)

i — short — like I in into
inne (inside) icke (not)

y — there is no similar sound in English. The closest would be I in into. The French U in lune or the German Ü in Frühstück are the correct sounds.

y — long — would be like Ü in Früh in Frühstück
by (village) ny (new)

y — short — would be like Ü in stück in Frühstück
hydda (cottage) bygd (countryside)

ö — long — there is no similar sound in English, however, a more open mouth than at the short ö will produce an acceptable sound
öga (eye) öra (ear)

ö — short — very similar to U in fur
dött (died) rött (red)

The Consonants

The consonants sound like their English equivalents in most cases, However, there are a few exceptions:

j is pronounced like y in year
jord (earth) juni (June)

k is always sounded before N
knä (knee) Knivsta

w is pronounced like V and is not a special letter or sound

Sounds by Letter Combinations

Some sounds are produced by different letters or combination of letters. As a researcher it is quite important to keep this in mind as in olden days (and also today) the same sound may be spelled in a different way than we are used to, and we may be fooled by this difference in spelling, in looking up indexes etc., for various times and places.

The more common of these sounds are:

J — sound (pronounced like y in year). It may be spelled in the following ways:

j — jag (I), jul (Christmas)
g — gift (married or poison), älg (elk)
gj — gjorde (did or made), gjort (done or made)
hj — hjon (pauper), hjälte (hero)
lj — ljung (heather), ljus (candle, light)
dj — djup (deep), djur (animal)
i — Bielke

K — sound may be spelled in the following ways:

k — karl (man), tak (ceiling or roof)
ch — och (and)
ck — också (also)
g — högt (high)
gg — byggt (built)
c — Carl
q — quinna or qvinna, old fashioned for kvinna (woman)

S — sound may be spelled in the following ways:

s — sak (thing)
ss — pussel (puzzle)
c — december (December)
z — Zander
x — Xerxes

T — sound may be spelled in the following ways:

t — stor (large, big, great)
tt — smått (small)
dt — Annerstedt
th — Theorell

V — sound may be spelled in the following ways:

v — hav (sea, ocean)
hv — Hven
fv — hafva (have - old fashioned)
fw — hafwa (have - old fashioned)
f — Lagerlöf

Tje — sound (pronounced like ch in cherry) may be spelled in the following ways:

k — (in front of soft vowels — e, ä, i, y, ö —) **kyrka** (church)
tj — tjugo (twenty)

kj — kjusa (narrow valley)
ch — Cherstin

Sje — sound (pronounced something like sh in shall, but with a more pointed and close mouth) may be spelled in the following ways:
sj — sju (seven)
sk — sky (sky)
skj — skjul (shed, shelter)
stj — stjärna (star)
sch — scharlakansfeber (scarlet fever)
ssi — mission (mission)

Äng — sound (pronounced like ng in song) may be spelled in the following ways:
ng — kung (king)
n — änka (widow)
g — regn (rain)

Some of the main points in the 1906 spelling reform were (from our point of view as genealogists):

1) f, fv, fw, hv, and hw as signs of the V-sound were replaced by V

2) The DT was changed to T or TT

3) The C was in most places replaced by K and is used today mostly to make a double k, which always is written ck.

It is well to realize that the people who wrote our genealogical records were as prone to misspelling, or I would prefer — spell words their unique way — as we are today! Thus we must not be surprised at any spelling of a word. Not long ago I saw the month of December spelled "DÄSÄMBRE" in a birth record. Let us enjoy these unusual spellings as a good joke in our research, which keeps us on our toes and removes all dullness and consistency and only leaves life, change, joy, problems and inconsistency.

With some understanding of sound values, of differences in alphabets, of different letter combinations for certain sounds, and of spelling reforms we are ready to look at some specific problems.

1) We find the name of a parish given as Hvällinge. However, we cannot find it on our map of the landskap (province) of Skåne, where it is supposed to be located. May the name possibly be spelled in a different way? What can it be? The spelling reform did away with H in front of V, and thus we may suspect that the

first letter of the name may be V. Also realizing that the short e and ä are pronounced the same way we may try Ve as the first letters. We are right! The parish is called Vellinge, located in Skåne and the county (län) of Malmöhus. Grandpa's Hwällinge is his grandchildren's Vellinge.

2) We find the word Encka mentioned in a record from 1850 and would like to know what it means by looking it up in a dictionary. We do not find any word spelled as above. Let us now think! What may it be? Knowing that C and K stand for the same sound we try the spelling ENKA. No success. Why not try ÄNKA? That's it! We found it. It means widow, just as we thought!

Let these two examples suffice to bring out the point, that a word may be spelled in many different ways — depending on part of the country, period, speller's background, dialect spoken, etc. It may seem confusing — and is at times — but a little moving here and there of letters may help us find our goal. Remember O and Å are pronounced alike sometimes, and so are Ä and E! The double spelling of the consonants — the F in the old spelling may be V in the modern — the N may be NG, yes, and several more to try out our detective instincts.

Before we close this chapter, something ought to be said about the spelling of Swedish names, places and words by record keepers in this country. Very often they heard a Swedish word like SKÅNE, and then tried to write it down, but using English spelling they came up with something like SCONA, or they heard the old soldier name HJÄLTE (hero) and when finished it looked something like YELTE in the records. How confused must the poor recorder have been, when he spelled the name of the city of Gothenburg (Göteborg) in the following manner UTABREA, or his companion who a couple of days later solved the same problem by a GATOBURG. Better luck for us it was, when we found the province of DALSLAND spelled DOLLSLAND, or that most Swedish of all provinces DALARNA written DALLENE. Think both languages when trying to solve this kind of problems.

The Latin in Swedish genealogical records is found only to a small degree, wherefore a textbook of genealogical terms will suffice in most cases. Most of the Latin words used in the Swedish parish records are found in the word list at the back of this book.

If you desire to study the Swedish language as a help to your genealogical research, I suggest that the study include the language before the spelling reform of 1906.

Chapter 2

The Country

In this chapter we will discuss the ecclesiastical and civil jurisdictions that kept or preserved records of genealogical value.

The Ecclesiastical Jurisdictions

The head of the Church of Sweden since the Reformation in the sixteenth century is the king. Under him the realm is divided into dioceses (stift) with a bishop (biskop) as the presiding authority. Each diocese is made up of rural deaneries (kontrakt) with a dean (kontraktsprost) as the head. The deanery in its turn is divided into a number of smaller units, called benefices or districts (pastorat) with a rector or vicar (kyrkoherde) as the presiding official. The benefice is made up of one and sometimes two or a few more parishes. In the latter case the parish in which the vicar resides is named the mother parish (moderförsamling), while the other parish(es) is called annex parish (annexförsamling). Sometimes the records of the whole benefice would be kept as one, wherefore it is well to check the records of the mother parish for persons living in the annex parishes.

Only the diocese and the parish kept records of genealogical value.

The Diocese (Stiftet)

Sweden is at the present time divided into thirteen dioceses. The oldest go back to pre-reformation days, and as need arose new ones were added, the latest in the capital of Stockholm in 1942.

The bishop (biskopen) is the head of the diocese. At his side is found a council or consistory (domkapitel), which meets regularly to judge in matters of church discipline and appointments. The consistory or cathedral chapter, as it sometimes is called, also heard family marital matters, such as infidelity, separation and divorces. Records of these meetings are preserved and some are available on microfilm at the Genealogical Society libraries. There they are called Consistory minutes* or church records.

The following table shows the name of each diocese, its year of coming into being and geographical boundaries, and also the

* For a sample of consistory minutes, see **Thus They Wrote,** page 121. (Carl-Erik Johansson, BYU Press, Provo, Utah.)

earliest year from which records are available on microfilm at the Genealogical Society.

Diocese	Year of Organization	Area
Göteborg	1665	Göteborg och Bohus county, the western part of Älvsborg county, Halland county
Härnösand from Uppsala arch diocese	1772	Västernorrland and Jämtland counties
Kalmar	1602-1915	See Växjö
Karlstad	1646	Provinces of Värmland and Dalsland
Linköping	Pre-reformation	Östergötland county, northeastern part of Jönköping county, northern part of Kalmar county
Luleå from Härnösand diocese	1904	Norrbotten and Västerbotten counties
Lund	Pre-reformation	Provinces of Skåne and Blekinge
Skara	Pre-reformation	Mainly the province of Västergötland
Stockholm	1942	Stockholm city and immediate surroundings
Strängnäs	Pre-reformation	The part of the province of Södermanland located in Stockholm county, Södermanland county, Stockholm county, the part of the province of Närke located in Örebro county
Uppsala Arch diocese (Ärkestift)	Pre-reformation	Uppsala and Gävleborg counties, the part of the province of Uppland located in Stockholm county, Simtuna, Torstuna, and Våla districts (härader) of Västmanland county
Visby	Pre-reformation	Gotland county
Västerås	Pre-reformation	Kopparberg county, the county of Västmanland except the part located in the province of Uppland, the part of the province of Västmanland located in Örebro county
Växjö	Pre-reformation	Kronoberg county, Jönköping county, except northern part, southern part of Kalmar county

The Parish (Socken or församling)

The original word for parish is socken, which indicates both a civil and an ecclesiastical jurisdiction over the same geographical area. Sometimes we find the word "kyrkosocken" used for the ecclesiastical unit. However, in 1862 a stronger division between the civil and ecclesiastical jurisdiction of the parish was made, and the civil administration was called kommun and the ecclesiastical församling. For our purposes we will use the word parish for all three units — socken, kommun, församling.

There are about 2,500 parishes in Sweden. Their bounds were mostly set before the era of recorded history began in that northern land. They remained virtually unchanged until 1952, when in the interest of government efficiency a uniting of certain smaller parishes took place. This, however, has no or little bearing on locating the parish records at the Genealogical Society libraries, as they are listed under the name of the original parish. A listing of all parishes in Sweden is found in Appendix C.

Each parish was subdivided into villages and/or farms. Each village and farm has a name, sometimes also a number, especially in Southern Sweden. Thus we may find a large parish like Västra Vingåker in Södermanland having about 500 smaller units, villages (by, byar) and farms (gård, gårdar, hemman) etc., each with a different name. This is a good thing, or it would be impossible to keep track of each person by the name of ANDERS PERSSON living at the same time in the same parish. Now, we are able to identify him by the farm on which he lives.

The main officials of the ecclesiastical parish were the minister (präst, prost, kyrkoherde) and his assistants, who were called curates (komminister) and chaplain (kaplan, cappelan). These were all members of the clergy. Some offices were held by the laity. The most common of these were parish clerk (klockare), church warden (kyrkovärd) prefect or monitor (sexman), and ward master (rotemästare).

In 1686 a law was passed, which stated that the parish clergy, the ministers in other words, were to keep a record of the ordinances they performed for their parishioners. This was the beginning of the official vital records of Sweden. The clergy was in the service of the government, which controlled the appointment of each minister. Thus the ministers taught the word of God, performed ordinances and, best of all for the genealogist, kept a record of those ordinances.

The responsibility of the lay members on the parish staff varied. The parish clerk (klockaren) was to assist in the actual keeping of the records, to ring the bell in the steeple and to assist in teaching what little of the three R's the children (and also some adults) were taught.

The church warden (kyrkovärden) took care of the property of the church. There were two of them in every parish. They took up collection for the maintenance of the church. In the law of 1763 it was stated that the parish should take special care of its poor, and this responsibility was usually headed by the church wardens. They also assisted with other duties, carrying the wafers and wine to communion, etc. They were considered men of trust and confidence, as they handled money and had to give an account of it.

In the cities the church warden was often called "kyrkoföreståndare."

The prefect or monitor (sexman) was in charge of church discipline. He had quite a variety of civil and ecclesiastical tasks. He was to be a kind of a witness when the inventory of the Church property was taken. He was to assist the nobility, the clergy and the church warden with the maintenance of the infirm in the parish. He, along with the clergy and the most prominent people in the parish, had the right to sentence offenders to sit in stock, and if needed, to assist the sheriff in putting the offender there. He would collect the fine assigned by the parish minister to those who held weddings and other family feasts more than two days. He, together with the parish minister, would investigate mothers who accidently choked their infants to death in bed. In one parish the "sexman" was ordered to sit in the balcony of the church in order to keep track of the youth during the Sunday services. They served as doorkeepers, preventing people from leaving the church out of order. They collected fines from those who did not keep their part of the cemetary wall in good order or who rang the church bells carelessly. They also collected fines for mistreatment of paupers, and fees for wills and biercloth.

The ward master (rotemästare) mainly collected the church tithing within the parish. Some of his duties were similar to that of the prefect, but the offices were kept apart.

The Civil Jurisdictions

Administratively, Sweden is divided into counties (län), districts (härad) and parishes (kommun or socken). To these may be added the old historical units of provinces (landskap) and the three geographical divisions of Götaland, Svealand and Norrland.

The County (län)

For administrative purposes on a larger scale the country is divided into 24 län, which term is translated county by the Genealogical Society libraries and which also is used in this book. A law of 1634 established the counties and its borders. In order to find most genealogical records at the Genealogical Society libraries we must know in what county our place of interest is located. The borders of the counties have changed so little since they were established in 1634, that it is of no consequence in our search. For the name and location of each county see map on page. 38.

The county is divided into subdivisions called "fögderier" and "landsfiskalsdistrikt". These units do not keep any records that are of value to the researcher.

The Province (Landskap)

The provinces (landskap) are the old historical units of Sweden from pre-record time. There are 25 of them today. They are not being used in the jurisdiction or administration of records for our purpose. Because they are natural, cultural, and geographical units with deep roots, they play an important role in the daily lives of the Swedish people. The dialects spoken — and there are many — are mostly named after the provinces and so are the people, not after the county of origin. This makes it imperative for us to know the difference between the provinces and the counties. Some counties and provinces cover the same geographical area, like Blekinge, while others are just different, like Småland, being divided into three counties, Kronoberg, Kalmar and Jönköping.

Historically Sweden is also divided into three main geographical parts — Götaland in the south, Svealand in the middle and Norrland covering the northern half of the realm.

The District (Härad, Tingslag, Skeppslag)

The districts are subdivisions under the county, each consisting of 2-20 parishes. They are judicial units governed by a district chief (häradshövding) and a council (nämnd) of twelve trusted and reliable men of honor and stability (nämndeman.) The borders of the districts, numbering about 300 in all, are of very old and historical origin, and few changes have taken place during the last few centuries. The common expression for this unit is "härad", but in the northern half of Sweden the word "tingslag" may be

*See Thus They Wrote, p. 117.

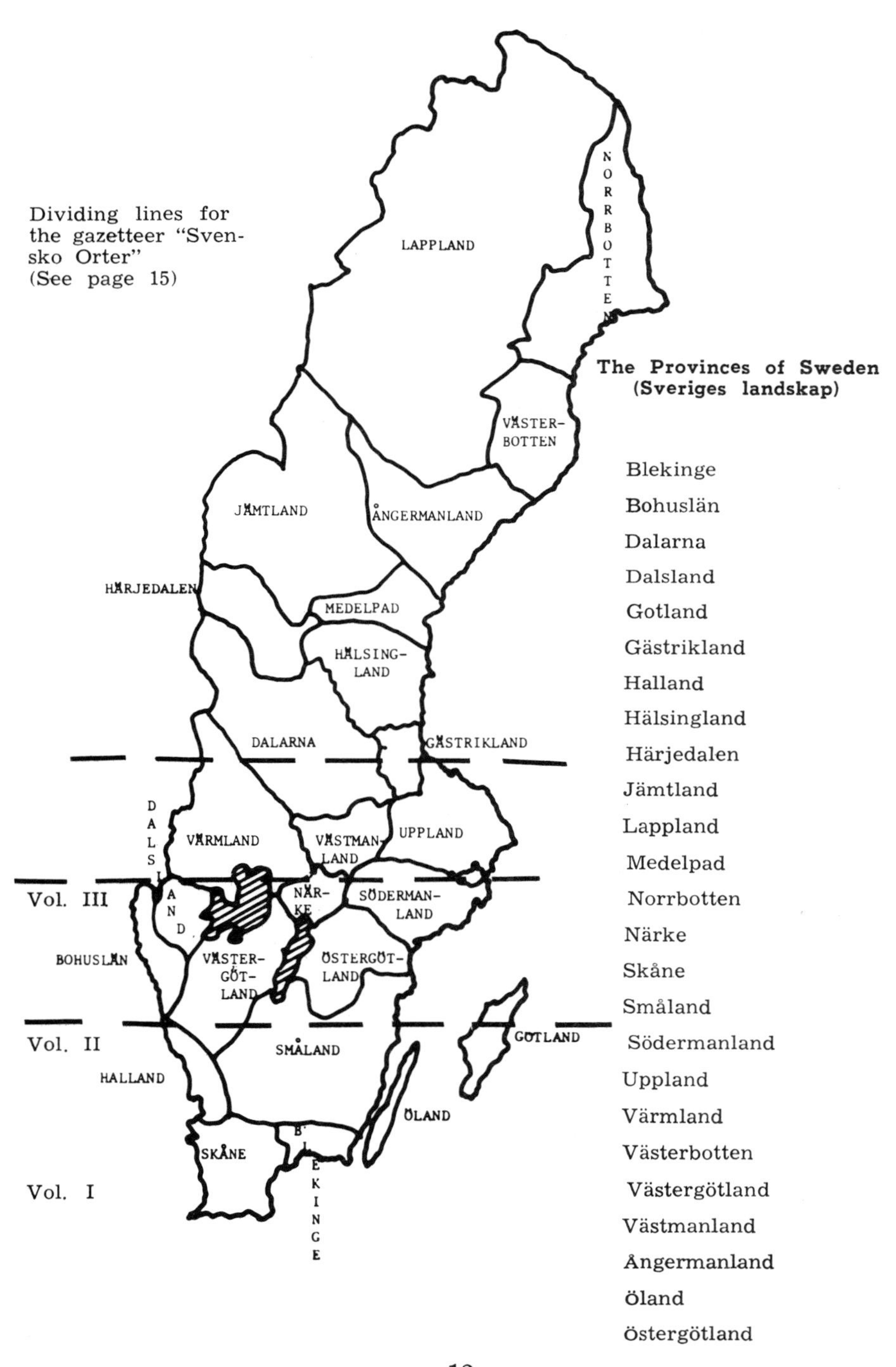

The Provinces of Sweden (Sveriges landskap)

Blekinge
Bohuslän
Dalarna
Dalsland
Gotland
Gästrikland
Halland
Hälsingland
Härjedalen
Jämtland
Lappland
Medelpad
Norrbotten
Närke
Skåne
Småland
Södermanland
Uppland
Värmland
Västerbotten
Västergötland
Västmanland
Ångermanland
Öland
Östergötland

used. In some coastal areas the word "skeppslag" may be found. All three words and areas indicate the same judicial unit, where court proceedings were instituted and death estates probated.

Below are listed the names of each province, the counties within its borders, and the names of the natives there (needed for study of military records, among others).

Landskap	Län	Name of natives
A. GÖTALAND		
Skåne	Malmöhus län	Skåning
Blekinge	Blekinge län	Bleking
Halland	Hallands län	Hallänning
Småland	Kronobergs län	Smålänning
	Kalmar län	
	Jönköpings län	
Öland	Kalmar län	Ölänning
Got(t)land	Got(t)lands län	Gottlänning, gut(e)
Östergötland	Östergötlands län	Östgöte
Västergötland	Skaraborgs län	Västgöte, (knalle)
	Älvsborgs län	
	Göteborgs och Bohus län	
Dalsland	Älvsborgs län	Dalslänning, dalbo
Bohuslän	Göteborgs och Bohus län	
B. SVEALAND		
Uppland	Uppsala län	Upplänning
	Stockholms län	
	Västmanlands län	
Södermanland	Södermanlands län	Sörmlänning
	Västmanlands län	
	Stockholms län	
	Östergötlands län	
Västmanland	Västmanlands län	Västmanlänning
	Örebro län	
Närke	Örebro län	Närking
	Värmlands län	
Värmland	Värmlands län	Värmlänning
	Örebro län	
Dalarna	Kopparbergs län	Dalmas, dalkarl for male
	Värmlands län	Dalkulla for female
	Gävleborgs län	
C. NORRLAND		Norrlänning
Gästrikland	Gävleborgs län	Gästrike
Hälsingland	Gävleborgs län	Hälsing(e)
	Jämtlands län	
Medelpad	Västernorrlands län	Medelpading
Härjedalen	Jämtlands län	Härjedaling, härdaling or härjing
Jämtland	Jämtlands län	Jämte or jämtlänning
Ångermanland	Västernorrlands län	Ångermanlänning
	Västerbottens län	
Västerbotten	Västerbottens län	Västerbottning
Norrbotten	Norrbottens län	Norrbottning
Lappland	Västerbottens län	Lapplänning or lapp
	Norrbottens län	

Chapter 3

The Names of Places

As we go about our research we find it absolutely necessary to know the names of places and where they are located. In fact, before we undertake research in the original records we ought to spend some time studying our particular area in books and maps as to names of places and topographical features. It makes it so much easier to understand and read the old handwriting if we know some of the geographical names, especially if we are not familiar with the Swedish language. It also saves us a lot of time in the long run. So let us look at some available tools. They may be divided into five main groups for our purpose:

1. Name lists
2. Geographical encyclopedias
3. General encyclopedias
4. County directories (länskalender)
5. Maps

1. Name Lists

In this classification we find two that are especially valuable as they are extensive, compact, and available for a reasonable price. They are "Svensk Ortförteckning" and "Sweden, Gazetteer number 72."

Svensk Ortförteckning (List of Swedish places) is published by the Royal Boards of the Post Office, the Rail Roads and the Tele-communications for the use by these government departments and "their customers". The latest edition was published in 1970, containing about 130,000 names of places in Sweden on a little more than 1,000 pages. The places are listed in strictly alphabetical order, with the exception of names starting with the words:

Norra (N:a), North	Mellersta, Middle
Södra (S:a), South	Nedre, Lower
Ostra (O:a), East	Ovre, Upper
Västra (V:a), West	Nya, New
Lilla (L:a), Little, Small	Gamla, Old
Stora (St:a), Large, Great	Inre, Inner
	Yttre, Outer

These words follow the main part of the name. Example: Södra Fagerskog is found under the entry of Fagerskog, S:a.

Each name occupies about one line on the double columned page. That single line tells the story we want to know. It looks something like this:

BRÅNE by Glava Vrml P Glava Tf 0570 Ks Glava tu 4 J Arvika 35. I think we had better try to translate this for you. It reads:

The village (by) BRÅNE is located within Glava parish (kommun) in the county (län) of Värmland (Vrml). Postal address is Glava, Telephone (Tf) area number is 0570 and the individual telephone numbers are found in the Karlstad directory. Telegrams should be sent through Glava 4 kilometers away. Nearest railway station is Arvika 3 kilometers away.

Thus, in this book, Svensk Ortförteckning, we find the parish and the county (län) of a place (from the smallest farm to the largest city). However, we do not find the district (härad), which we need to know in order to find many of the records kept by the civil authorities, such as land, tax, court and probate records. Also, some of the records kept by the ecclesiastical powers are catalogued according to the civil districts.

With it comes inserted a map book, with a folded map in 7 sections in the scale 1:1,000,000, showing the outlines of every county (län) and containing the names of about 6,000 post offices.

Sweden, Gazetteer number 72, was published in English in 1963 by the U. S. Department of Interior, and within its 1,000 double columned pages are found about 75,000 geographical names, each described in only one word, as farm, populated place, lake, stream, etc. The location of each place is indicated in latitude and longitude coordinates to the nearest minute (ex: 56 50 N 15 25 E) and in number code to county (län).

The one great advantage this book has for many researchers is, of course, that it is written in English. There is, however, no accompanying map for the convenience of the user.

2. Geographical Encyclopedias

In this class we also find two works. They are the most valuable and extensive of all mentioned in this chapter, "Svenska Orter" (Swedish place names) and "Geografiskt-Statistiskt Handlexikon" (Geographical-Statistical Encyclopedia).

Svenska Orter was published in 1932 by "Generalstabens Litografiska Anstalt, Stockholm", the official publisher of all government maps, etc. in Sweden. It contains a discription of each geographical name and place in Sweden at time of publishing. Originally it was planned to be published in six volumes, but the second world war stopped the project after the third volume, and there are no plans at the present to finish it. Each volume is divided into three parts, thus there are nine books altogether in this work.

Volume One covers the southern part of the country as far north as an east-westerly line just south of Göteborg (Gothenburg)

Volume Two covers the area immediately to the north of Volume One as far north as just south of the capital Stockholm.

Volume Three covers the area just north of this line as far north as just south of the city of Gävle. See dividing lines on map on page 12.

Of the three parts of each volume, one contains the maps in scale 1:300,000, one all the names starting with the letters A-K and one L-Ö. With every name goes a description of the place, be it a small farm (gård, hemman, etc.) rating a line, or a large parish (kommun) rating a paragraph or more. There are, however, only a few key words and things to be read for our purpose so, even if you do not read Swedish, you will still be able to use this most excellent reference work by learning the following key words and phrases:

a) Reference to the corresponding map
b) Name of county (län)
c) Name of district (härad)
d) Name of parish (kommun, socken, församling)
e) Name of smaller units within the parish

The names are listed in alphabetical order. However, as in Gazetteer number 72, some compounded names follow after the main word or name. They are:

Norra,	(North)	Inre,	(Inner)
Södra,	(South)	Yttre,	(Outer)
Ostra,	(East)	Lilla,	(Little, small)
Västra,	(West)	Stora,	(Large, great)
Gamla,	(Old)	Mellan,	(Middle)
Nya,	(New)	Mellersta	(Middle)
Nedre,	(Lower)	Sankt,	(S:t) (Saint)
Ovre,	(Upper)		

Thus we find Södra Råda recorded under Råda, Södra.

Let us now take a look at the entry of Stora Mölleberga. (It is found on page 837, Vol. I, pt. 3.) We read: Mölleberga, Stora, by i Malm, län, Mölleberga. kn. (This is all we need to understand for our purpose, even though there are 23 more lines under this entry.) In translation it reads: Mölleberga, Stora (or Stora Mölleberga), village in Malmöhus county (län), Mölleberga parish (kommun, abbreviated kn). Now we know that our place is located in Mölleberga parish, so we look up this word in order to get the name of the district (härad). We find the entry of Mölleberga on the preceding page:

Mölleberga, 111 g 2. Kommun i Malm. län, Bara hd . . . Byar: Lilla och Stora, Mölleberga samt Önsvala . . .

This is all we need to know. In translation it reads:

Mölleberga, map 111, square g2. Parish in Malmöhus county (län), Bara district (härad, which is abbreviated hd) . . . Villages: Lilla and Stora Mölleberga and Önsvala.

You understood most of it anyway — you are on your way to read the records!

In the above entry we find, as stated before in this chapter, the five things we want to know,

a) reference to map — number 111 in the map part, and to square 2g on that map
b) county — Malmöhus
c) district — Bara
d) parish — Mölleberga
e) smaller units — Lilla and Stora Mölleberga, Önsvala.

The smaller units within the parish are divided into five different headings: byar (villages), hemman (farms), samhälle (communities — without own jurisdiction), herrgårdar (manorial estates), and fisklägen (fishing villages). Thus we look for any or all of these headings after the little rectangle in the entry. There may be only a few as in the case above or close to 100 as in Västra Vingåker parish.

This reference work has the advantage of covering every geographical name within its area at time of compilation, which no other work does.

Geografiskt-Statistiskt Handlexikon by C. M. Rosenberg was printed 50 years before "Svenska Orter" and thus is using the old spelling (see Chapter 1). It covers the whole country, however, not in as great detail as "Svenska Orter", but all parishes and most villages and some larger farms are included. It is published in two parts, A-K and L-Ö plus a supplement in the latter part. The names in this work appear in strictly alphabetical order and there are, contrary to "Svenska Orter" and "Svensk Ortförteckning", no exceptions for compounded names.

How do we read the book? Very easily, if we just remember the old spelling. Let us show by using the word Almesåkra as an example. We find it in part 1 on page 18:

Sn i Vestra och Tveta hd af Jönköpings län.

Translated it means: Parish (Sn is an abbreviation of socken, meaning parish) in Västra and Tveta districts of Jönköping county.

This work is also very excellent, covering as it does all of Sweden in great detail and giving us the three main jurisdictions, parish, district and county. There are no references to any map, however.

3. General Encyclopedias

In this category we also would like to refer you to two good works, both in Swedish, in the same class and style as Encyclopedia Americana:

a) Nordisk Familjebok in 20 volumes

b) Svensk Uppslagsbok in 32 volumes (not available at Genealogical Society Library in Salt Lake City.)

Each contains a description of all parishes and larger units with a very brief history of each and very often a picture of some outstanding feature like a church.

4. County Directories

These are published more or less regularly since the middle of the 1800's, containing the names of the different administrations and jurisdictions within the county borders. Often we find the names of all parishes and other jurisdictions and all the officials within these jurisdictions.

5. Maps

The interest and fancy of the researcher will decide what kind of map to use. There are many different kinds available, but we will only bring the reader's attention to a few. They are all published by "Generalstabens Litografiska Anstalt, Stockholm".

a) Kommunkarta över Sverige (Map of parishes in Sweden), published in 1952, scale 1:700,000. It contains the names and borders of every parish, district, and county. It is printed in two colors, black and red. The black print indicates the names and borders of parishes as they were before 1952, the red print as they are now after the reform. The map itself is divided into two parts, the northern and the southern, each being the size of about 4 x 6 feet and folded within heavy covers.

b) KAKs bilatlas (road map) in book form. It is the best road map of Sweden; however, it does not show the borders between the parishes. There is an excellent index with references to map and square number, but the individual places are not identified as to parish and district. Scale 1:500,000.

c) Generalstabens kartblad. These maps were originally for military in the scale 1:100,000 for the southern part of the country and 1:200,000 for the northern part. There are 103 different sheets for the southern part, most of them measuring 23 x 17 inches and including an area of about 36 x 27 miles. For the northern part there are a total of 171 sheets, about half of them in the scale 1:200,000, all of them 11 inches in height and 12 to 16 inches wide. All these sheets are based on field surveys. They show the borders of parishes, districts, counties and provinces. They are very detailed, showing the terrain and even many small farms and their names can be seen. Excellent for our purpose.

d) County and province maps. (Län or landskapskarta). These maps cover one or two counties or provinces in scale 1:200,000 for most of them. They vary in size from 38 x 40 inches for Skåne to 20 x 27 for Värmland. They show the borders of the parish both before and after the reform of 1952, but do not show the borders of the district.

Some Common Names

As many geographical names are made up of some basic word components, as stream, hill and town, we will give you some of these with the knowledge that they are just a few in the long list of our forefathers' inventive genius.

backe	hill	by	village	fjärd	bay, inlet
bank	bank	bäck	stream	fors	rapid
berg	mountain	dal	valley	gruva	mine
bo	place	damm	dam	gård	farm
borg	castle	djup	deep	göl	lake, pool
bro	bridge	fall	waterfall	hed	heath

hem	home	ljung	heather	ström	stream
holm(e)	island	lund	grove	vik	bay, gulf
hög	mound, high	mosse	bog	äng	meadow
kron(o)	crown	näs	point, peninsula		
kulle	mound, hill	sjö	lake, sea		
kärr	lake, swamp	skog	forest, woods		

Chapter 4

The Names of Persons

The earliest known Swedish names appear about 500 A.D. on some 2000 Runic stones scattered around the realm. Usually the given names were given to describe a quality or characteristic, or resemble an occurrence or occasion that was desired in the new-born babe, such as Ragnvald, which means "He who is mighty with power."

Later most of the names were formed from parts of the father's name, or that of the mother, grandfather or other close ancestor or relative. For example, Ingemund may have named a son, Ingemar or Agmund. Torulf and his wife Gunhild, who had an ancestor Torsten, had children with such names as Guntor, Gunnulf, Gunsten, Hildulf, Torgun, Torhild, Stenhild, Ulfhild.

Later on, the full given name of a deceased ancestor was given to a descendant in order that the ancestor might be remembered. This practice eventually gave way to present day custom of naming a child after his parents and grandparents etc., which preserved the old Swedish names from generation to generation to our day, fortunately.

At the turn of the first millenium of the Christian era all Sweden was christianized, and a conscious effort was undertaken by the clergy to substitute the names of the Christian saints for the old Swedish names. Thus the apostolic names of Peter, Andrew, John, and Paul took on their present day forms of:

Petrus, Peter, Peder, Pehr, Pär

Andreas, Anders

Johannes, Johan, Jan, Jaen, Jean, Joen, Jon, Jöns

Paulus, Paul, Påfvel, Påfwel, Pål, Påhl

Given or Christian Names

Some of the more common given names used in Sweden during the last four centuries are listed below:

Male Names

Adils
Adolf
Agne
Alf
Al(f)vin
Algot
Alvar
Ambjörn
Amund
Anders
Andreas
Arne
Arnvald
Arvid
Asmund
Assar
Asser
Astrad
August
Axel
Bengt
Birger
Björn
Björnvid
Bo
Bodel
Bonde
Botvid
Bror
Bryngel
Börje
Christer
Clemens
Carl
David
Ebbe
Elof
Enar
Enevald
Engelbrekt
Erik
Erland
Erngisle
Ernst
Esbjörn
Eskil
Evert
Folke
Frans
Fredrik
Frenne
Fridmund
Frände
Georg
Germund
Gregor
Gudmund
Gumme
Gunnar
Gunne
Gustaf
Göran
Gösta
Göte
Halvar(d)
Hans
Harald
Helge
Hemming
Henning
Herbert
Hilding
Hjalmar
Holger
Hufvud
Hugo
Håkan
Inge
Ingemar
Ingvar
Isak
Ivar
Jeppe
Johan
Jon
Jöns
Jörgen
Jan
Karl
Kjell
Klas
Klemens
Knut
Kolbjörn
Lars
Lennart
Magnus
Matts
Matthias
Måns
Mårten
Nicolaus
Niklas
Nils
Olaus
Ola
Olof
Oscar
Otto
Paul
Per
Peter
Petrus
Povel
Pål
Påvel
Pär
Ragnar
Rune
Sibbe
Sigfrid
Sigmund
Sigurd
Sigvald
Sigvard
Sjunne
Sone
Staffan
Stefan
Sten
Sture
Sune
Svante
Sven
Svenning
Svennung
Sören
Tomas
Tor(e)
Torkil
Torsten
Trued
Tue
Tuve
Truls
Tyr
Ulrik
Valdemar
Vaste
Wollmar
Åke
Östen

Female Names

Anna
Astrid
Bengta
Birgitta
Bodil
Boel
Brita
Börta
Christina
Cissela
Clarissa
Dagny
Dordi
Dorotea
Ebba
Elena
Elin
Elisa(bet)
Ella
Elna
Elsa
Estrid
Frida
Gerda
Gertrud
Greta
Gudrun
Gunnil
Gunnela
Gyda
Hanna
Helena
Helga
Inga
Ingeborg
Ingegerd
Inger
Ingrid
Johanna
Kajsa
Karin
Karna
Katarina
Kerstin
Kristina
Lisa
Lisken
Lotta
Lotten
Lovisa
Maja
Malena
Margareta
Margit
Marit
Marna
Marta
Mat(h)ilda
Metta
Märeta
Nilla
Olu
Olug
Pernilla
Petronella
Rangela
Signe
Sigrid
Sissa
Sissela
Sofia
Stina
Troen
Ulla
Ulrika
Vilhelmina

Interchangeable First Names

In Sweden it has always been common to call a person by an affectionate form of his given name (cf, William - Bill). This may be confusing in research, where for example someone is called Kjerstin in the birth records but later on is called Stina in another record. It really is not much of a problem once we have learned to recognize these names. Some of the more common ones are listed below:

Anders
- Andreas

Johan
- Jaen
- Jan
- Janne
- Jean
- Joen
- Johannes
- John
- Jon
- Jonas
- Jöns

Hans
- Hasse

Lars
- Lasse

Magnus
- Måns

Nils
- Nicolaus
- Niklas
- Nisse

Olof
- Ola
- Olle
- Oluf

Per
- Peder
- Pehr
- Pelle
- Peter
- Petrus
- Petter
- Päder
- Pähr
- Pär

Pål
- Paul
- Pofwel
- Povel

Anna
- Annicka
- Anika

Catrina
- Cajsa
- Kajsa

Christina
- Stina

Charlotta
- Lotta
- Lotten

Cherstin
- Stina

Elisabet

Elisa	Elin	Cajsa	**Magdalena**
Lisa	Ellen	Kajsa	Lena
Lisbet	Helen	**Katrina**	Maja
Lisken	Lena	Cajsa	**Margareta**
Eljena	**Johanna**	Kajsa	Greta
Elna	Hanna	**Kristina**	**Maria**
Helena	**Karin**	Stina	Maja

These names and others are used interchangeably within their own group. We must be very careful, however, before accepting such a change. Not all girls by the name of Catharina, for example, are called Cajsa or Kajsa. If we suspect a change like this, we must prove it to be sure that "our Catharina Magnusdotter" in the birth record is the same girl, who is called Cajsa Månsdotter in the marriage record some twenty years later.

The Surnames

It may be stated with authority that family names were hardly used in Sweden until after the Middle Ages. In the seventeenth century they became more common and by the end of that century the nobility had firmly established their family names. Also, the burghers or townsmen in the cities and the merchants and tradesmen adopted the use of family names in the same century. The latter group very often constructed their names in a way that made them uniquely Swedish, as Dalberg, Bergström, Strömberg and Lindberg clearly indicate.

The Latinizing of names began to be employed several hundred years earlier by the clergy and other learned men. Thus, Eric Karlsson became Ericus Caroli, and Abraham, from the landskap Ångermanland, called himself Abrahamus Ångermannus. When family names began to be used by this group during the seventeenth century, it was very often in a latinized form of the place of origin, as illustrated by Arosenius, meaning from Västerås (West Arós), or Montander, (mons = mountain) meaning from the mountain. The tracing of the families of these three groups — nobility, clergy and burghers — has been done to a large extent and their genealogies are available in printed form, especially is this true of the nobility and clergy.

Moreover, these three groups or estates of people are, naturally, better known to us historically than those of the fourth estate — the farmers — who made up the largest part of the population. The names of the former were created in a more "poetic" way than the farmer's too! During the period of the last 300 years or so, which is the period when original genealogical records are available, the farmers used the more "prosaic" patronymic system of naming.

The Patronymics

The patronymic system simply means that a child was known as the son or daughter of a certain man. The son of a person with the first name of Anders, for example, would have as his last name, ANDERSSON, and the daughter would be known as ANDERSDOTTER. The son of Nils would become NILSSON and the daughter NILSDOTTER, the son of Erik would be ERIKSSON or ERSSON and the daughter ERIKSDOTTER or ERSDOTTER. It is understood of course, that all of these children were given a first or christian name to precede the patronymic surname. Patronymics were consistently used in rural Sweden and among day laborers in urban centers until 1860, when it became more fashionable to adopt a "frozen" or permanent family surname. In some quarters patronymics persisted for another two or three generations. Gradually, however, people began to substitute their patronymic surname with their father's patronymic surname as a permanent fixture. The children of a family wouldn't necessarily all change at the same time. Thus, some sons in the family of ANDERS OLSSON would call themselves ANDERSSON and others OLSSON, while some daughters would adopt the surname of ANDERSDOTTER and some OLSSON. It should be pointed out that there were no rules or laws governing names prior to 1901, when the first name law to protect family names was passed in Sweden. It has taken a long time for people to conform and even today the old practice is still in use in some areas of the country (especially Dalarna).

One must read the available records (especially from about 1860 to 1901) very carefully to see if a clue as to what last name a person was known by in the official records can be picked up. The minister may not even have known what last name a person used. Very often in birth records for this period entries like the following are found:

> Lars, född 16/8 1889 i Osteråker, Söd. 1. son till torparen Eric Persson o h h Cajsa Olofsdotter
>
> Lars, born 16 Aug. at Osteråker parish, Södermanland län, the son of the crofter Eric.

Persson and his wife (och hans hustru) Cajsa Olofsdotter. What is the last name of Lars? Is it Ersson or Persson? Only research or information supplied by the family will tell.

Soldier Names

Soldiers often assumed different surnames upon entering military service in order to avoid the inevitable mix-up that would follow, when a typical company consisting of 10 Andersson, 10 Ersson, 10 Johansson, 10 Jönsson, 10 Larsson, 10 Olofsson, etc. would be formed; and the problem is compounded when it is remembered that their given names were similarly divided between Anders, Erik, Johan, Jöns, Lars, Olof, Sven, Pär and Petter. To avoid the confusion, the troups were issued along with clothing and weapons, new names, which smack of military prowess such as Modig (Courageous), Tapper (Brave), Munter (Happy), and Stark (Strong) or by some armament like Svärd (Sword), Spjut (Spear), Lans (Lance), and Sköld (Shield). They may also have been called by some derivation of the name of the area from which they came, such as Täpp from Stora Täppe, or Ekberg from Ekeby.

Not until the last few generations did the children of soldiers retain their father's military name. They preferred instead the regular patronymic name. Then, Anna and Eric, children of Anders Modig, would have been known in most cases as Anna ANDERSDOTTER and Eric ANDERSSON.

The following is a list of some surnames with their translations as used by army personnel:

Ahl — Alder tree
Ask — Ash tree
Asp — Aspen tree
Björk — Birch tree
Blixt — Lightning
Blomster — Flower
Borg — Stronghold, Bulwark
Brask — Crisp
Brax — Carp
Brink — Steep hill
Bäck — Brook
Dahl — Valley
Dristig — Bold, daring
Elf — River
Fager — Fair
Flod — River
Fors — Rapids
Frimodig — Fearless, frank
Frisk — Fresh
Fröjd — Joy
Fyr — Spark
Glad — Happy
Granat — Grenade
Grip — Griffin
Hassel — Hazel tree
Hed — Moor, heath
Hjelm — Helmet
Hjelte — Hero
Hjort — Deer
Holm — Island
Hult — Grove
Hård — Hard
Häger — Heron
Hägg — Cherry tree
Hög — Tall
Kihl — Wedge
Klint — Clift

Kraft — Strength
Krans — Wreath
Kron — Crown
Kull — Hill
Kämpe — Fighter
Käck — Dashing
Lans — Lance
Lilja — Lily
Lind — Linden tree
Ljung — Heather
Lod — Bullet
Lund — Grove
Lång — Tall
Löf — Leaf
Malm — Ore
Mod — Courage
Modig — Courageous
Munter — Happy
Nord — North
Nöjd — Satisfied
Orre — Grouse
Palm — Palm
Pihl — Arrow
Quist — Branch, twig
Rapp — Instant
Rask — Swift
Rehn — Reindeer
Ros — Rose
Roth — Root
Sabel — Saber
Seger — Victory
Skans — Redoubt
Skarp — Sharp
Skepp — Ship
Skog — Forest
Sköld — Shield
Snäll — Fast, kind
Spjut — Spear
Spång — Bridge
Staf — Staff, Cane
Stark — Strong
Sten — Stone, rock
Stolt — Proud
Storck — Stork
Strand — Shore
Strid — Battle
Sträng — String, strict
Ström — Stream
Styf — Stiff
Stål — Steel
Sund — Healthy
Svan — Swan
Svärd — Sword
Tapper — Brave
Torn — Tower
Trygg — Confident
Vred — Angry
Värn — Guard
Äng — Meadow
Örn — Eagle
Öst — East

Following is a list of some surnames with their translations used by naval personnel:

Abbore — Perch
Ankar — Anchor
And — Duck
Block — Pulley
Boglina — Bowline
Blomster — Flower
Blå — Blue
Blåsa — Bubble
Båtshake — Boat-hook
Bössa — Gun
Dragg — Grapnel
Dansare — Dancer
Dykare — Diver
Fisk — Fish
Fyr — Lighthouse
Fyrtopp — Top of lighthouse
Fribytare — Freebooter
Granat — Grenade
Godvilling — Voluntary
Gök — Cuckoo

Hake — Hook
Hummer — Lobster
Hök — Hawk
Klack — Heel
Knop — Knot
Klockare — Bell ringer
Krabbe — Crab
Lax — Salmon
Liten — Small
Lärcka — Lark
Menlös — Innocent
Rolig — Funny
Sexpunning — Six Pounder
Sjöman — Sailor, Seaman
Skaffare — Procurer
Skeppare — Skipper
Skuta — Ship
Spansk — Spanish
Spelare — Player
Stor — Tall
Storm — Wind storm
Strand — Shore
Strömming — Herring
Sund — Healthy, Sound
Svala — Swallow
Söder — South
Timglas — Hour glass
Tross —Hawser
Vind — Wind
Väster — West
Yxa — Ax

Names of Tradesmen

It was also common among country folk, who were skilled craftsmen, to exchange their patronymic surname with something else. This was especially true when they learned a trade or accepted a position as parish tailor, cobbler, saddle-maker, carpenter etc. This new name would just suddenly appear in the record, as in the case of Gustaf Persson from Norberg (Västmanland), where the minister wrote in the margin of the clerical survey record: "Wants to call himself Gustaf Persson NORMAN." No legal or other action was needed. It was only necessary to let the record-keeping minister know of the new name to get it into the records!

Names of Illegitimate Children

No set rules were followed in surnaming children born out of wedlock. In most cases, no name or mention of the father was made in the birth record, just the very discouraging note unknown "okänd". If a last name was not given to such a child at the time of birth, eventually, in nearly all cases, a last name will be found in the records; however, sometimes not before leaving home or getting married.

A child born out of wedlock was usually named in one of four ways:

1) the patronymic name after its father's first name like any other child
2) the father's surname

3) the matronymic name after its mother's first name; i.e. Eric LENASSON, Anna Brita ANNAEDOTTER (ANNASDOTTER), Stina ELINSDOTTER.

4) the mother's surname

Names of Emigrants

When a person emigrated from Sweden to the United States, he normally kept his surname even though the spelling would be anglicized, making Johansson into Johnson or Jensen (Sic!), Nilsson into Nielson, etc. Some translated their names, such as Sjöstrand to Seashore. Others, however, completely changed their identity by assuming completely unrelated names like Duke, Wilson, Rogers, etc. This last category, obviously, will cause a lot of trouble, unless one is lucky enough to know the facts in the case.

Special Practices

The age old custom of preceding the name with the name of the farm, still exists in the province of Dalarna. Nils Olsson from the farm of Täppe, for example, would call himself Täpp Nils Olsson, and Lars Persson from Sars would be known by Sars Lars Persson. In a similar fashion, a schoolteacher named Anders Ingemarsson, would be called Skol Anders Ingemarsson. If a person moved, he would drop the name of the old farm and take that of the new one. Our above mentioned Täpp Nils Olsson, in moving to a new farm named Sars, became Sars Nils Olsson. Conversely, on the large island of Gotland, "the Baltic Pearl", the name of the farm or residence was often added at the end of the patronymic surname. Thus, Hans Olsson living at the farm Svie, would be called Hans Olsson Svie in the records.

In Skåne there was an old and peculiar custom of recording names of wives. The record says in one place: Hust (ru) Arna Jöns Pärs, which simply means Jöns Pärsson's wife Arna. We are not informed of her last name. It may also read: Ellse Åke Måns, which is Åke Månsson's wife Ellse.

List of Family Names

We will close this chapter by listing in frequency order the more common family names that do not end in "son". It may be of interest to know that the 19 most common surnames in Sweden end in "son" with Andersson leading the list (5.4%) and Johansson

(5.2%) and Karlsson following next.

Lindberg (.3%)	Holmberg (.2%)	Åberg (.1%)	Nygren (.09%)
Lindström	Bergkvist	Öberg	Lindholm
Lindkvist	Bergman	Hellström	Bäckström
Lindgren	Söderberg	Blom	Västerlund
Lundberg	Lövgren	Hedlund	Borg
Bergström	Blomkvist	Söderström	Norrman
Lundgren	Björk	Dalberg	Holmström
Lundkvist	Lundström	Sundkvist	Nyman
Berg	Nyberg	Strömberg	Dal
Berglund	Nordström	Sundström	Hedberg
Sandberg	Ström	Holmkvist	Skog
Lind	Berggren	Norberg	Höglund
Forsberg	Vi(c)klund	Ek	Söderlund
Engström	Sundberg	Palm	Boman
Sjöberg	Björklund	Möller	Östlund
Vallin	Nordin	Englund	Skoglund
Eklund	Holmgren	Öman	Björkman
Lundin	Sjögren	Falk	Lindholm
Holm	Sandström	Sjöström	Val(l)ström
Nyström	Ekström	Boström	Törnkvist
Vi(c)kström	Lund	Hallberg	Friberg (0.08%)

Chapter 5

The Archives

Sweden has a very orderly and well organized archive system to preserve its official civil and ecclesiastical records. The main archive is the National Archives and under it are found regional archives, city archives, the Royal War Archives, the Central Bureau of Statistics, the Archives of the House of Nobility, the Archives of the Foreign Office, the emigration archives and some miscellaneous archives.

The National Archives (Riksarkivet)

The National Archives keep the records and documents of the central government from earliest days until today. It also contains well over 200 genealogical and many biographical collections, most of them indexed, and several private archives. Also on file is found a copy of every roll of microfilm the Church of Jesus Christ of Latter-day Saints has filmed in Sweden.

The Exchequer Archives (Kammararkivet) are a part of the National Archives and preserve the records of government accounts, and house the land records (jordebok) and tax lists (mantalslängd.)

In 1968 the National Archives moved into its beautiful new building in Stockholm on the shore of the historic Lake Mälaren. The archive is built underground in solid granite which makes it one of the finest, safest and most efficient National Archives in the world. All collections are housed in the many mountain vaults, blasted out of the hard granite, while the researcher enjoys the lofty halls above ground.

Often overlooked is the collection of maps available, consisting of several tens of thousands of maps and pictures, which certainly are of both value and interest to the genealogist, especially as many of them are from earlier centuries.

The Provincial Archives (Landsarkiven)

These archives are regional repositories under the National Archives. They are the most important archives for the researcher in our field and are located in Östersund, Härnösand, Uppsala, Vadstena, Göteborg, Visby and Lund. Respective jurisdictions are listed on the map on page 38, and a table with addresses is found at the end of this chapter.

The city archives (stadsarkiven) of Stockholm, Göteborg, and Malmö are equal with the provincial archives in jurisdiction, being the repositories of their respective city records. What is said about the provincial archives also holds true of these three city archives.

In the provincial archives are found the original records — parish registers and clerical survey records — that are more than 100 years old from each parish within its region. There are also located the court records, including the probate records, for the same period and region — and duplicate copies of the land records (jordeböcker) and taxlists (mantalslängder) mentioned in connection with the Exchequer Archives (Kammararkivet) on the previous page.

At the present time the provincial archives have on file the parish records up to 1870, and according to plans the records for the ten year period 1870-1880 will be delivered to the provincial archives in 1980 and so on every ten years. If we thus want an extract of a birth, marriage or death record from a parish in Kristianstad county (län) for the year 1845 we will have to get it from the provincial archives (landsarkivet) in Lund, as it keeps the records for that county up to 1870. If we want the same for the year 1898 we have to write to the parish, as it keeps its records until they are 100 years old. It may be well to mention here that letters may be written in English both to the archives and parishes. The address to a parish is simply:

Pastorsämbetet
N.N. församling
N.N.
Sweden

Sometimes parish records before 1870 are not found in respective provincial archives. There may be two main reasons for this:

1. The records may be partly or fully destroyed by fire or some other cause, or

2. The parish is exempt from delivery of the records to the provincial archives and keeps them all in its own parish. There are only a few of them, and their numbers are diminishing. The latest list shows the following exempt parishes and the jurisdiction they serve:

Provincial Archive in Vadstena: Jönköping Kristine and Ljungarum parishes;

Provincial Archive in Uppsala: Kjura, Edsberg, Ekeby (Örebro county), Ervalla, Falun Kristine and Kopparberg, Floda (Kopparberg county), Folkärna, Gagnef, Grangärde, Gräve, Gällersta, Hackvad, Hidinge, Jäder, Karlskoga, Kil (Örebro county), Knista, Leksand, Lima, Linde, Lindesberg, Ludvika, Malung, Mockfjärd, Mora, Näs, Näsby, Ore, Orsa, Rättvik, Sollerö, Stora Skedvi, Stora Tuna, Strängnäs, Svartnäs, Svärdsjö, Västra Vingåker, Älvdalen.

It is well to note that the records of most — if not all — of these exempt parishes are available on microfilm at the Genealogical Society libraries.

The military muster rolls from most regiments are also deposited with the provincial archives.

The Royal War Archives (Kungliga Krigsarkivet)

Kept in this archive are the army and navy muster rolls for the many Swedish regiments through the last three centuries. Included are also many records of the Finnish and German regiments that served under the blue and yellow banners of the Swedish realm. A very large biographical collection concerning officers and the military men in the civilian branches of the army and navy are also housed here as are military accounts and discharge lists.

The Archives of the Royal Central Bureau of Statistics (Statistiska Centralbyrån)

In this archive are filed four kinds of records that are of special interest to our readers.

1. Extracts of the parish registers 1860-1947. At the end of every year starting with 1860 the parish minister had to extract information on every birth, marriage and death in his parish and submit it to the Central Bureau of Statistics. This practice was discontinued in 1947 when the personal record act took effect (see below.) The birth extracts contain the full name of the

person, his sex, birth date, birth place within the parish, his father's full name and occupation, his mother's full maiden name, if legitimate or illegitimate birth, if birth was attended by a registered nurse or not, and if of nobility. Sometimes the age of the mother and the number of the child in the family are included even though not officially called for. The extracts are sorted according to year and county, with an index of the order in which the parishes appear within the county. The order is the same through every year. No christening is recorded, however.

The marriage record contains the names of the bride and groom, their residence and marriage date.

The death record indicates the name of the deceased, age, residence and cause of death.

These records have been microfilmed and are available at the Genealogical Society in Salt Lake City for the years 1860-1897. At present the 70 year rule of secrecy prevents any later filming of these records. It seems, however, as if microfilming of these records is done about every five years.

2. Clerical survey extracts. In 1860 and every ten years afterwards an extract was made of the clerical survey records (husförhörslängden) of each parish and deposited with this archive. The records are filed according to the same system as the extracts of the parish registers. They contain a list of every person in the parish, his birth year and birth place. Microfilms for the years 1860, 1870, 1880 and 1890 are available at the Genealogical Society.

3. Emigration records 1860-1947. An extract was made every year on a special printed form from the parish registers of every person moving to a foreign country and moving into the parish from a foreign country. They are catalogued according to the same system used for point 1 and 2 above. They have all been microfilmed and are available for all years at the Genealogical Society. Recent research has shown that about ten percent more people emigrated from the parishes than are recorded on these lists. If a person is not found in them, it may be well to go into the parish clerical survey record to check.

4. Personal record (personakt) of deceased or emigrated people. In 1946 a reform in keeping parish registers was enacted, establishing a personal record in addition to the traditional parish registers. In it is found an extract of all pertinent information or data of the parish register. This record follows the person whenever he moves from one parish to another within the realm.

In case of death or emigration the record is sent to the Central Bureau of Statistics (Statistiska Centralbyrån) for permanent safe keeping.

The Archives of the House of Nobility (Riddarhusets arkiv)

Here are preserved the records of the families introduced into the House of Nobility, but no other information ought to be expected from this archive. Most of its information is available in published books.

The Archives of the Ministry for Foreign Affairs (Utrikesdepartementets arkiv)

These archives keep the departmental records for 50 years, after which they are deposited with the National Archive. Information about diplomatic personnel and Swedes who reside in foreign countries may be had from this archive.

Miscellaneous Archives

The three largest cities of the Swedish Kingdom, Stockholm, Göteborg, and Malmö, have city archives, which in function and records are equal to a provincial archive. Some other cities are exempt from depositing their records with the respective provincial archive. Among them are Arboga, Borås, Jönköping, Karlstad, Norrköping, Nyköping, Söderköping, Strängnäs, Västerås. The mailing address to any of these archives is simply: Stadsarkivet, name of city, Sweden.

Established archives are also found within labor, cooperative, temperance, religious and other organizations, at the universities (especially in Uppsala and Lund), schools and institutions and with older industries and larger manors.

The largest emigration archives are located in Växjö and Karlstad. The one in Växjö is called "The Emigrant Institute, The House of Emigrants." (Emigrantsinstitutet, Utvandrarnas Hus). It houses diaries written by emigrants to the U.S.A., excerpts from Swedish newspapers concerning emigration and also from parish records in Sweden. Among the most valuable genealogical records must be counted several hundred rolls of microfilm of the membership of the Swedish congregations in the U.S.A., mainly from the three states of Illinois, Minnesota and Wisconsin.

The Karlstad emigrant archive contains information gathered on both sides of the Atlantic concerning most of the 100,000 emigrants that left their home province of Värmland for greener pastures on the sunset side of the big ocean.

The Genealogical Society in Salt Lake City

Within the walls of this unique institution are housed most of the original records of primary value in genealogical research found in all the archives of Sweden discussed above. This has been made possible through the microfilming of all these records in Sweden. There are three main sources of assistance in Swedish genealogical research available at this institution, the archives, the library and the staff personnel.

a) The archive houses the records of completed research for individuals and families. Here are probably found more complete family units of the common people in Sweden—the farmer (bonde, åbo, torpare, statare, dräng, etc.) — than at any other place in the world. However, no figures are available on how many are recorded but it must be in the hundreds of thousands.

b) The library holds (1) a reference section with all the reference works mentioned in earlier chapters with the exception of some of the maps; (2) all the parish registers and court, military, land and census records found in the provincial archives, the extracts of parish registers from all of Sweden 1860-1897, the extracts of the clerical survey records from all of Sweden 1860, 1870, 1880, 1890; (3) the emigration records 1860 (1855) - 1940 deposited at the Archive of the Royal Central Bureau of Statistics; (4) the clerical survey records from every parish in Sweden 1860-1895; (5) miscellaneous other records, indexes, etc; (6) a large section of Swedish printed books, magazines, periodicals, etc.

c) Certain staff members at the library are trained specialists in Swedish research and material and provide great service to patrons — experienced or inexperienced — in Swedish research.

NOTE: Take time to thumb through the catalogues of Swedish sources and material before doing any research in the actual records — and once in a while later on, too. It will pay great dividends! You must become acquainted with the material available — so thumb and browse, THUMB and BROWSE!

Addresses of Some Swedish Archives

Riksarkivet

Fyrverkarbacken 13-17, Fack 100 26, S-112 60 Stockholm, Sweden

Landsarkivet at Göteborg
Geijersgatan 1, Postbox 3009, S-400 10 Göteborg 3, Sweden
Landsarkivet at Härnösand
Nybrogatan 17, S-871 00 Härnösand, Sweden
Landsarkivet at Lund
Dalbyvägen 4, S-223 60 Lund, Sweden
Landsarkivet at Uppsala
Slottet, Box 135, S-751 04 Uppsala 1, Sweden
Landsarkivet at Vadstena
Slottet, S-592 00 Vadstena, Sweden
Landsarkivet at Visby
Visborgsgatan 1, S-621 00 Visby, Sweden
Landsarkivet at Ostersund
Museiplan, Postfack, S-831 09 Ostersund 1, Sweden
Stockholms Stadsarkiv
Kungsklippan 6, S-112 25 Stockholm, Sweden
Göteborgs Stadsarkiv
(Same as Göteborgs landsarkiv)
Malmö Stadsarkiv
Kyrkogatan 6, S-211 22 Malmö, Sweden
Borås Stadsarkiv
Stadshuset, S-500 02 Borås, Sweden
Västerås Stadsarkiv
Rådhuset, S-721 87 Västerås, Sweden
Kungliga Utrikesdepartementets arkiv
Gustav Adolfs Torg, S-111 52 Stockholm, Sweden
Kungliga Krigsarkivet
Banergatan 64, S-104 50 Stockholm, Sweden
Statistiska Centralbyråns arkiv
Linnegatan 87, S-115 23 Stockholm, Sweden
Riddarhusets arkiv
Riddarhuset, S-111 28 Stockholm 2, Sweden

Miscellaneous hints

These archives and the parish offices will answer simple questions but not do any extensive research. If that is needed, they will turn it over to a private researcher, very often an employee who will do the search on his own time. Always expect to pay for the service they render. Specify the amount of money you are willing to spend on your particular problem. Pay by money order or cashier's check, as personal checks are very difficult to cash in Sweden. You may write in English and usually your reply will be in that same language. Good luck!

The counties of Sweden
(Sveriges län)

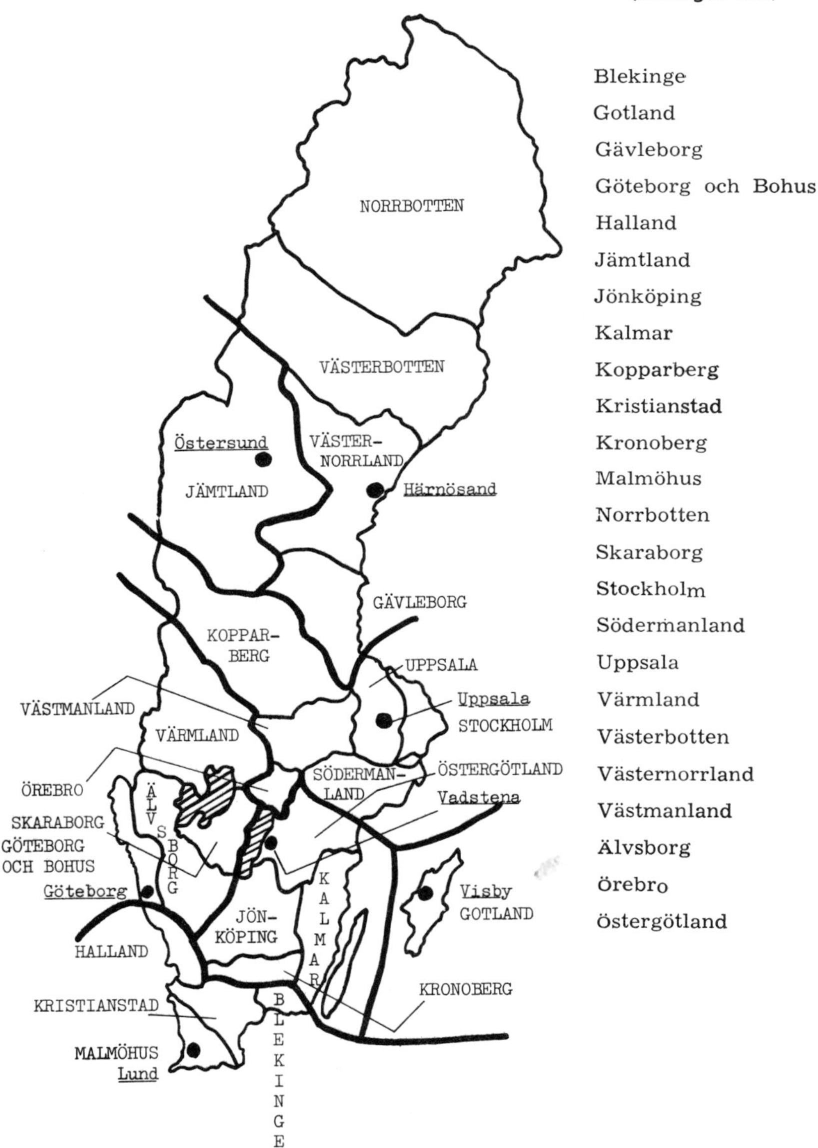

Blekinge
Gotland
Gävleborg
Göteborg och Bohus
Halland
Jämtland
Jönköping
Kalmar
Kopparberg
Kristianstad
Kronoberg
Malmöhus
Norrbotten
Skaraborg
Stockholm
Södermanland
Uppsala
Värmland
Västerbotten
Västernorrland
Västmanland
Älvsborg
örebro
östergötland

Chapter 6

Fixed And Movable Feast Days

Through the Christian era there developed the custom of calling every Sunday of the year by a name of specific religious significance. Many week days were also so named. The ministers very often used the names of these days to indicate a certain date. They were all part of the so-called ecclesiastical year, which started with the first Sunday in Advent, which is the fourth Sunday before Christmas, and not on January 1st. Certain of these days, or feast days as they were called, fell (and fall) on a specific date, like Christmas day on December 25th, and we call them fixed feast days (fasta helgdagar), while others were (and are) movable, like Easter day coming earliest on March 25th and latest on April 25th. The Swedish name for movable feast days is rörliga helgdagar. The ministers very often used the Latin form of the name of the feast day and thus we have to know both the Swedish name and the Latin name for the day. We may find an entry in a birth record reading something like thus: Hans Åkesson was born **Juldagen** (Christmas day) or if the same entry was made in Latin we may find it reads like this: Hans Åkesson was born **Natio Christi** or **Nativitas** or **Nat. X** (Christ).

Fixed Feast Days

Below is listed the names of the fixed feast days, that fall on the same date every year. We list their Swedish, Latin and English names.

Date	Swedish	Latin	English
Jan. 1	Kristi omskärelses dag	Circumcisio Domini	Circumcision of the Lord
	Nyårsdagen		New Years day
Jan. 5	Trettonafton		
Jan. 6	Trettondagen		
	Heliga tre konungars dag	Trium Regum Sanct Rex Tertia	
	Epifania	Epiphania	Epiphany
	Kristi döpelses dag	Baptismus Christi	
Jan. 13	Tjugondag jul		
Feb. 2 or following Sunday	Jungfru Marie kyrkogångsdag	Purificatio B.V. Marie	Purification of the Virgin Mary
	Kyndelsmässodagen		
Mar. 25	Maria Bebådelsedag (not celebrated after 1950)	Annunciato	Annunciation Day

Date	Swedish	Latin	English
May 1	Filippus Jacob		
June 23	Midsommarafton		
June 24	Johannes döparens dag Midsommardagen (since 1950 celebrated on Saturday closest to June 24)	Sct. Hans	John the Baptist
June 29	Petrus och Paulus dag Persmässa		
July 29	Olofsmässa or Olsmässa		
Aug. 24	Bartolomeus		
Sept. 29 or following Sunday	Den helige Mikaels dag	Sct. Michaelis	St. Michael, the Archangel
Nov. 1	Alla helgons dag	Omnium Sanctorum	All Saints Day
Nov 30	Den helige Andreas dag	Sct. Andreas	St. Andrew
Dec. 21	Tomasmässa		
Dec. 24	Julafton		Christmas Eve
Dec. 25	Juldagen Kristi födelses dag	Nativitas Natio Christi Feria Nativ.	Christmas Day
Dec. 26	Annandag jul Den helige Stefanus dag	Stephanus Protomartyr	St. Stephen
Dec. 27	Tredjedag jul (not celebrated after 1772)		3rd day of Christmas
Dec. 28	Fjärdedag jul (not celebrated after 1772)		4th day of Christmas
Dec. 31	Nyårsafton		New Year's Eve

Movable Feast Days

Below we will list the names of the movable feast days in their Swedish, Latin and English names.

Swedish	Latin	English
Första söndagen efter trettondagen		First Sunday after Epiphany
Andra söndagen efter trettondagen		Second Sunday after Epiphany
Tredje, Fjärde, Femte, Sjätte dito		Third, Fourth, Fifth, Sixth dito
Nionde söndagen före påsk	Septuagesima	Ninth Sunday before Easter
Åttonde söndagen före påsk	Sexagesima	Eighth Sunday before Easter
Sjunde söndagen före påsk	Quinquagesima	Seventh Sunday before Easter

Swedish	Latin	English
Fastlagssöndagen	Estomihi Bachantes	Sunday before Lent
Sjätte söndagen före påsk	Quadragesima	Sixth Sunday before Easter
Första söndagen i fastan	Invocavit	First Sunday in Lent
Femte söndagen före påsk Andra söndagen i fastan	Reminiscere	Fifth Sunday before Easter Second Sunday in Lent
Fjärde söndagen före påsk	Oculi	Fourth Sunday before Easter
Tredje söndagen i fastan		Third Sunday in Lent
Tredje söndagen före påsk Fjärde söndagen i fastan	Laetare	Third Sunday before Easter Fourth Sunday in Lent
Midfastosöndagen		Middle fast
Andra söndagen före påsk Femte söndagen i fastan	Judica	Second Sunday before Easter Fifth Sunday in Lent
Palmsöndag	Palmarum Dom. ad Palmas	Palm Sunday
Skärtorsdag	Dies viridium	Maundy Thursday Thursday in Holy Week
Långfredag	Dies Adoratis Passiones	Good Friday
Påskafton		Saturday before Easter
Påskdagen	Pascha	Easter Sunday
Annandag påsk		Monday after Easter
Tredjedag påsk (not celebrated after 1772)		Tuesday after Easter
Fjärdedag påsk (not celebrated after 1772)		Wednesday after Easter
(Första) söndagen efter påsk	Quasimodogeniti	Sunday after Easter
Andra söndagen efter påsk	Misericordia	Second Sunday after Easter
Tredje söndagen efter påsk	Jubilate	Third Sunday after Easter
Fjärde söndagen efter påsk	Cantate	Fourth Sunday after Easter
Femte söndagen efter påsk	Rogate	Fifth Sunday after Easter
Bönsöndagen	Vocem Jucunditatis	Prayer Sunday
Kristi himmelsfärdsdag	Ascensio	Ascension Day (40 days after Easter)
Sjätte söndagen efter påsk	Exaudi	Sixth Sunday after Easter
Pingstsöndagen	Pentecoste	Pentecost
Annandag pingst		Monday after Pentecost

Swedish	Latin	English
Tredjedag pingst (not celebrated after 1772)		Tuesday after Pentecost
Fjärdedag pingst (not celebrated after 1772)		Wednesday after Pentecost
Trefaldighetssöndagen	Trinitatis	Trinity Sunday
Första söndagen efter trefaldigheten	I post Trinitatis	First Sunday after Trinity
Andra söndagen efter trefaldigheten	II post Trinitatis	Second Sunday after Trinity
Tredje, Fjärde, etc. until	the 27th Sunday after Trinity	
Sjunde söndagen efter trefaldigheten	VII past Trinitatis	Seventh Sunday after Trinity
Kristi Förklaringsdag	Festum transfigurationis Christi	Transfiguration Day
Första söndagen i advent	Adventis	Advent Sunday
Andra söndagen i advent	II post Adventis	Second Sunday in Advent
Tredje söndagen i advent	III post Adventis	Third Sunday in Advent
Fjärde söndagen i advent	IV post Adventis	Fourth Sunday in Advent

To establish the exact date of any of the movable feast days in a given year special tables or calendars will have to be used. They may be found in most public libraries. They are also printed in the Genealogical Instruction Manual or in A Guide to Genealogical Research by Archibald F. Bennett (both books published by the Genealogical Society of The Church of Jesus Christ of Latter-day Saints, Inc., Salt Lake City, Utah).

Miscellaneous hints

In using the tables and calendars we should notice that Sweden changed from the Julian to the Gregorian Calendar on February 18, 1753, which date became March 1, 1753 on the new Gregorian Calendar.

Sometimes we find the names of the last four months of the year recorded in the following manners:
VIIber or VIIbris or 7ber or 7bris for September
VIIIber or VIIbris or 8ber or 8bris for October
IXber or IXbris or 9ber or 9bris for November
Xber or Xbris or 10ber or 10bris for December

This custom comes from the old Roman numerals septem for seven, okto (eight), novem (nine) and decem (ten). In early days these months were respectively the seventh, eighth, ninth and tenth — January and February being added later in the beginning of the year.

At times it may be difficult to read the name of a feast day or understand the abbreviation used for it. However, in most cases this can easily be solved, as the entries of the dates usually come in chronological order and you will thus be able to fence in "your date" between two legible or easy-to-understand dates.

Prayer and Penitence Days (Böndag, botdag)

A few days of the year were set aside by the King for fasting, praying and penitence to divert national catastrophies and other great disasters. They fell on any week day and were irregular in numbers for the year. From the 1700's they were combined into four days a year and from 1807 they are held on a Sunday in March, May, July and October, respectively.

Extracts of Dates from Parish Registers

Some actual examples of recording of dates in parish registers are shown below:

Dnica XX post Trinitatis — Dominica (day of the Lord—Sunday) 20th after Trinity

Dominica IV Adventis — Fourth Sunday in Advent

Feria. 4 Nativit. — Feria (day or holiday) The fourth day after birth of Christ or Christmas.

Dnica inter Circumsis et Epiphan — Sunday between January 1st and 6th.

Doca 20: Trinit — Twentieth Sunday after Trinity

Doca: 1. pst festum Circumc: — First Sunday after the feast of Circumcision

Doca: Reminise — Fifth Sunday before Easter

Doca Palmorum — Palm Sunday

The following dates are from the year 1768. Try to figure them out from the tables or calendars. If you get the same result as shown here, be happy as you know how to do it!

Dom 3tia. Epiph — 24 January
Dom Septuagesima — 31 January
Dom Sexagesima — 7 February
Dom Quinquag — 14 February
Dom Invocavit — 21 February
Dom Reminisar — 28 February
Dom Laetare — 13 March

Note: **Eod die** stands for Eodem die, meaning **the same day**

And finally, try the following additional feast days taken from Swedish parish registers:

1712 Feria 4ta Pentecostes — 11 June
1717 Dom. Oculi — 24 March
1754 Dom. III post Trinit. — 30 June
1755 Dom. 3tia Adv. — 14 December

The Change of Calendars in Sweden

The Julian Calendar had been used more than 1600 years when Pope Gregorius XIII made a change and correction in 1582, making October 5 into October 15. Ten days were simply lifted out of the year.

In Sweden an excited debate with both theological and mathematical arguments was carried on for years for and against the Gregorian Calendar. In November 1699 an agreement was reached to switch over from the old to the new calendar by gradually taking away the eleven days that separated them. By taking away only a day a year time would be gained for further discusisons, as the decision for reform was far from unanimous.

A beginning was made by leaving out the leap day in 1700. But the reform was not carried any further.

In January 1711 King Charles XII declared the return to the old way. He stated that the Swedish almanac did not follow that of any other country since the leap day in 1700 was left out. Many mistakes had been made due to this. He also decreed that the month of February should have 30 days in 1712. Sweden was back to the Julian calendar after twelve years of unique dating.

Not until 1753 was Sweden ready for the adoption of the Gregorian calendar. The problem was solved by letting February 17 be followed by March 1. The reform, however, was not joyfully accepted by all, as many held that they had been robbed of 11 days of life.

TABLE D

GUIDE FOR FINDING THE DATES OF MOVABLE FEAST DAYS

Year	No.	Year	No.	Year	No. J	No. G	Year	No. J	No. G	Year	No. J	No. G	Year	No. J	No. G	Year	No. J	No. G	Year	No. J	No. G	Year	No. J	No. G	Year	No.	Year	No.	Year	No.
1528*	22	1555	24	1582	25	25	1609	26	29	1636*	27	2	1663	29	4	1690	30	5	1717	31	7	1744§	4	15	1771	10	1798	18	1825	13
1529	7	1556*	15	1583	10	20	1610	18	21	1637	19	22	1664*	20	23	1691	22	25	1718	23	27	1745	24	28	1772*	29	1799	3	1826	5
1530	27	1257	28	1584*	29	11	1611	3	13	1638	4	14	1665	5	15	1692*	6	16	1719	8	19	1746	9	20	1773	21	1800	23	1827	25
1531	19	1558	20	1585	21	31	1612*	22	32	1639	24	34	1666	25	35	1693	26	1	1720*	27	10	1747	29	12	1774	13	1801	15	1828*	16
1532*	10	1559	5	1586	13	16	1613	14	17	1640*	15	18	1667	17	20	1694	18	21	1721	19	23	1748*	20	24	1775	26	1802	28	1829	29
1533	23	1560*	24	1587	26	8	1614	34	9	1641	35	10	1668*	1	11	1695	3	13	1722	4	15	1749	5	16	1776*	17	1803	20	1830	21
1534	15	1561	16	1588*	17	27	1615	19	29	1642	20	30	1669	21	31	1696*	22	32	1723	24	7	1750	25	8	1777	9	1804*	11	1831	13
1535	7	1562	8	1589	9	12	1616*	10	13	1643	12	15	1670	13	16	1697	14	17	1724*	15	26	1751	17	21	1778	29	1805	24	1832*	32
1536*	26	1563	21	1590	29	32	1617	30	5	1644*	31	6	1671	33	8	1698	34	9	1725	7	11	1752*	8	12	1779	14	1806	16	1833	17
1537	11	1564*	12	1591	14	24	1618	15	25	1645	16	26	1672*	17	27	1699	19	29	1726	20	31	1753	21	32	1780*	5	1807	8	1834	9
1538	31	1565	32	1592*	5	8	1619	7	10	1646	8	11	1673	9	12	1700§	11	21	1727	12	23	1754	13	24	1781	25	1808*	27	1835	29
1539	16	1566	24	1593	25	28	1620*	26	29	1647	28	31	1674	29	4	1701	30	6	1728*	31	7	1755	33	9	1782	10	1809	12	1836	*13
1540*	7	1567	9	1594	10	20	1621	11	21	1648*	12	22	1675	14	24	1702	15	26	1729	16	27	1756*	24	28	1783	30	1810	32	1837	5
1541	27	1568*	28	1595	30	5	1622	31	6	1649	4	14	1676*	5	15	1703	7	18	1730	8	19	1757	9	20	1784*	21	1811	24	1838	25
1542	19	1569	20	1596*	21	24	1623	23	26	1650	24	27	1677	25	28	1704*	26	2	1731	28	4	1758	29	5	1785	6	1812*	8	1839	10
1543	4	1570	5	1597	6	16	1624*	7	17	1651	9	19	1678	10	20	1705	18	22	1732*	19	23	1759	21	25	1786	26	1813	28	1840*	29
1544*	23	1571	25	1598	26	1	1625	27	9	1652*	28	10	1679	30	12	1706	3	14	1733	4	15	1760*	5	16	1787	18	1814	20	1841	21
1545	15	1572*	16	1599	18	21	1626	19	22	1653	20	23	1680	21	31	1707	23	34	1734	24	35	1761	25	1	1788*	2	1815	5	1842	6
1546	35	1573	1	1600*	2	12	1627	4	14	1654	5	15	1681	13	16	1708*	14	18	1735	16	20	1762	17	21	1789	22	1816*	24	1843	26
1547	20	1574	21	1601	22	32	1628*	23	33	1655	25	7	1682	26	8	1709	34	10	1736*	35	11	1763	2	13	1790	14	1817	16	1844*	17
1548*	11	1575	13	1602	14	17	1629	15	25	1656	16	26	1683	18	28	1710	19	30	1737	20	31	1764*	21	32	1791	34	1818	1	1845	2
1549	31	1576*	32	1603	34	9	1630	7	10	1657	8	11	1684*	9	12	1711	11	15	1738	12	16	1765	13	17	1792*	18	1819	21	1846	22
1550	16	1577	17	1604*	18	28	1631	20	30	1658	21	31	1685	29	32	1712*	30	6	1739	32	8	1766	33	9	1793	10	1820*	12	1847	14
1551	8	1578	9	1605	10	20	1632*	11	21	1659	13	23	1686	14	24	1713	15	26	1740*	16	27	1767	18	29	1794	30	1821	32	1848*	33
1552*	27	1579	29	1606	30	5	1633	31	6	1660*	32	7	1687	6	9	1714	7	11	1741	8	12	1768*	9	13	1795	15	1822	17	1849	18
1553	12	1580*	18	1607	15	25	1634	16	26	1661	24	27	1688*	25	28	1715	27	31	1742	28	4	1769	29	5	1796*	6	1823	9	1850	10
1554	4	1581	5	1608*	6	16	1635	8	18	1662	9	19	1689	10	20	1716*	11	22	1743	13	24	1770	14	25	1797	26	1824*	28	1851	30

NOTE: All years followed by an asterisk (*) are leap years.

§—The year 1700 was a leap year only in the localities still using the Julian Calendar.
The year 1744 was a leap year on both the Julian and Gregorian Calendars; however Easter was celebrated a week apart in Germany and Denmark, thus the key for 1744 in Denmark and Norway under the Gregorian Calendar would be "8" instead of "15" as shown in the table above.

(Compiled by Henry E. Christiansen)

TABLE E CALENDAR OF FEAST DAYS

Feast Days	Guide Numbers											
	1	2	3	4	5	6	7	8	9	10	11	12
Septuagesima	18 Jan	19 Jan	20 Jan	21 Jan	22 Jan	23 Jan	24 Jan	25 Jan	26 Jan	27 Jan	28 Jan	29 Jan.
Sexagesima	25 Jan	26 Jan	27 Jan	28 Jan	29 Jan	30 Jan	31 Jan	1 Feb	2 Feb	3 Feb	4 Feb	5 Feb
Quinquagesima	1 Feb	2 Feb	3 Feb	4 Feb	5 Feb	6 Feb	7 Feb	8 Feb	9 Feb	10 Feb	11 Feb	12 Feb
Invocavit	8 Feb	9 Feb	10 Feb	11 Feb	12 Feb	13 Feb	14 Feb	15 Feb	16 Feb	17 Feb	18 Feb	19 Feb
Reminiscere	15 Feb	16 Feb	17 Feb	18 Feb	19 Feb	20 Feb	21 Feb	22 Feb	23 Feb	24 Feb	25 Feb	26 Feb
Oculi	22 Feb	23 Feb	24 Feb	25 Feb	26 Feb	27 Feb	28 Feb	1 Mar	2 Mar	3 Mar	4 Mar	5 Mar
Laetare	1 Mar	2 Mar	3 Mar	4 Mar	5 Mar	6 Mar	7 Mar	8 Mar	9 Mar	10 Mar	11 Mar	12 Mar
Judica	8 Mar	9 Mar	10 Mar	11 Mar	12 Mar	13 Mar	14 Mar	15 Mar	16 Mar	17 Mar	18 Mar	19 Mar
Palmarum (Palm Sunday)	15 Mar	16 Mar	17 Mar	18 Mar	19 Mar	20 Mar	21 Mar	22 Mar	23 Mar	24 Mar	25 Mar	26 Mar
Pascha (Satirious) (Easter)	22 Mar	23 Mar	24 Mar	25 Mar	26 Mar	27 Mar	28 Mar	29 Mar	30 Mar	31 Mar	1 Apr	2 Apr
Quasimodogeniti	29 Mar	30 Mar	31 Mar	1 Apr	2 Apr	3 Apr	4 Apr	5 Apr	6 Apr	7 Apr	8 Apr	9 Apr
Misericordias	5 Apr	6 Apr	7 Apr	8 Apr	9 Apr	10 Apr	11 Apr	12 Apr	13 Apr	14 Apr	15 Apr	16 Apr
Jubilate	12 Apr	13 Apr	14 Apr	15 Apr	16 Apr	17 Apr	18 Apr	19 Apr	20 Apr	21 Apr	22 Apr	23 Apr
Cantate	19 Apr	20 Apr	21 Apr	22 Apr	23 Apr	24 Apr	25 Apr	26 Apr	27 Apr	28 Apr	29 Apr	30 Apr
Rogate	26 Apr	27 Apr	28 Apr	29 Apr	30 Apr	1 May	2 May	3 May	4 May	5 May	6 May	7 May
Exaudi	3 May	4 May	5 May	6 May	7 May	8 May	9 May	10 May	11 May	12 May	13 May	14 May
Pentecoste (Whitsunday)	10 May	11 May	12 May	13 May	14 May	15 May	16 May	17 May	18 May	19 May	20 May	21 May
Trinitatis	17 May	18 May	19 May	20 May	21 May	22 May	23 May	24 May	25 May	26 May	27 May	28 May
Adventis	29 Nov	30 Nov	1 Dec	2 Dec	3 Dec	27 Nov	28 Nov	29 Nov	30 Nov	1 Dec	2 Dec	3 Dec

NOTE: For leap years add one day to all holidays in the months of January and February.

(Compiled by Henry E. Christiansen)

TABLE E CALENDAR OF FEAST DAYS (Continued)

Feast Days	Guide Numbers											
	13	14	15	16	17	18	19	20	21	22	23	24
Septuagesima	30 Jan	31 Jan	1 Feb	2 Feb	3 Feb	4 Feb	5 Feb	6 Feb	7 Feb	8 Feb	9 Feb	10 Feb
Sexagesima	6 Feb	7 Feb	8 Feb	9 Feb	10 Feb	11 Feb	12 Feb	13 Feb	14 Feb	15 Feb	16 Feb	17 Feb
Quinquagesima	13 Feb	14 Feb	15 Feb	16 Feb	17 Feb	18 Feb	19 Feb	20 Feb	21 Feb	22 Feb	23 Feb	24 Feb
Invocavit	20 Feb	21 Feb	22 Feb	23 Feb	24 Feb	25 Feb	26 Feb	27 Feb	28 Feb	1 Mar	2 Mar	3 Mar
Reminiscere	27 Feb	28 Feb	1 Mar	2 Mar	3 Mar	4 Mar	5 Mar	6 Mar	7 Mar	8 Mar	9 Mar	10 Mar
Oculi	6 Mar	7 Mar	8 Mar	9 Mar	10 Mar	11 Mar	12 Mar	13 Mar	14 Mar	15 Mar	16 Mar	17 Mar
Laetare	13 Mar	14 Mar	15 Mar	16 Mar	17 Mar	18 Mar	19 Mar	20 Mar	21 Mar	22 Mar	23 Mar	24 Mar
Judica	20 Mar	21 Mar	22 Mar	23 Mar	24 Mar	25 Mar	26 Mar	27 Mar	28 Mar	29 Mar	30 Mar	31 Mar
Palmarum (Palm Sunday)	27 Mar	28 Mar	29 Mar	30 Mar	31 Mar	1 Apr	2 Apr	3 Apr	4 Apr	5 Apr	6 Apr	7 Apr
Pascha (Satirious) (Easter)	3 Apr	4 Apr	5 Apr	6 Apr	7 Apr	8 Apr	9 Apr	10 Apr	11 Apr	12 Apr	13 Apr	14 Apr
Quasimodogeniti	10 Apr	11 Apr	12 Apr	13 Apr	14 Apr	15 Apr	16 Apr	17 Apr	18 Apr	19 Apr	20 Apr	21 Apr
Misericordias	17 Apr	18 Apr	19 Apr	20 Apr	21 Apr	22 Apr	23 Apr	24 Apr	25 Apr	26 Apr	27 Apr	28 Apr
Jubilate	24 Apr	25 Apr	26 Apr	27 Apr	28 Apr	29 Apr	30 Apr	1 May	2 May	3 May	4 May	5 May
Cantate	1 May	2 May	3 May	4 May	5 May	6 May	7 May	8 May	9 May	10 May	11 May	12 May
Rogate	8 May	9 May	10 May	11 May	12 May	13 May	14 May	15 May	16 May	17 May	18 May	19 May
Exaudi	15 May	16 May	17 May	18 May	19 May	20 May	21 May	22 May	23 May	24 May	25 May	26 May
Pentecoste (Whitsunday)	22 May	23 May	24 May	25 May	26 May	27 May	28 May	29 May	30 May	31 May	1 June	2 June
Trinitatis	29 May	30 May	31 May	1 June	2 June	3 June	4 June	5 June	6 June	7 June	8 June	9 June
Adventis	27 Nov	28 Nov	29 Nov	30 Nov	1 Dec	2 Dec	3 Dec	27 Nov	28 Nov	29 Nov	30 Nov	1 Dec

NOTE: For leap years add one day to all holidays in the months of January and February.

(Compiled by Henry E. Christiansen)

TABLE E CALENDAR OF FEAST DAYS (Continued)

Feast Days	Guide Numbers										
	25	26	27	28	29	30	31	32	33	34	35
Septuagesima	11 Feb	12 Feb	13 Feb	14 Feb	15 Feb	16 Feb	17 Feb	18 Feb	19 Feb	20 Feb	21 Feb
Sexagesima	18 Feb	19 Feb	20 Feb	21 Feb	22 Feb	23 Feb	24 Feb	25 Feb	26 Feb	27 Feb	28 Feb
Quinquagesima	25 Feb	26 Feb	27 Feb	28 Feb	1 Mar	2 Mar	3 Mar	4 Mar	5 Mar	6 Mar	7 Mar
Invocavit	4 Mar	5 Mar	6 Mar	7 Mar	8 Mar	9 Mar	10 Mar	11 Mar	12 Mar	13 Mar	14 Mar
Reminiscere	11 Mar	12 Mar	13 Mar	14 Mar	15 Mar	16 Mar	17 Mar	18 Mar	19 Mar	20 Mar	21 Mar
Oculi	18 Mar	19 Mar	20 Mar	21 Mar	22 Mar	23 Mar	24 Mar	25 Mar	26 Mar	27 Mar	28 Mar
Laetare	25 Mar	26 Mar	27 Mar	28 Mar	29 Mar	30 Mar	31 Mar	1 Apr	2 Apr	3 Apr	4 Apr
Judica	1 Apr	2 Apr	3 Apr	4 Apr	5 Apr	6 Apr	7 Apr	8 Apr	9 Apr	10 Apr	11 Apr
Palmarum (Palm Sunday)	8 Apr	9 Apr	10 Apr	11 Apr	12 Apr	13 Apr	14 Apr	15 Apr	16 Apr	17 Apr	18 Apr
Pascha (Satirious) (Easter)	15 Apr	16 Apr	17 Apr	18 Apr	19 Apr	20 Apr	21 Apr	22 Apr	23 Apr	24 Apr	25 Apr
Quasimodogeniti	22 Apr	23 Apr	24 Apr	25 Apr	26 Apr	27 Apr	28 Apr	29 Apr	30 Apr	1 May	2 May
Misericordias	29 Apr	30 Apr	1 May	2 May	3 May	4 May	5 May	6 May	7 May	8 May	9 May
Jubilate	6 May	7 May	8 May	9 May	10 May	11 May	12 May	13 May	14 May	15 May	16 May
Cantate	13 May	14 May	15 May	16 May	17 May	18 May	19 May	20 May	21 May	22 May	23 May
Rogate	20 May	21 May	22 May	23 May	24 May	25 May	26 May	27 May	28 May	29 May	30 May
Exaudi	27 May	28 May	29 May	30 May	31 May	1 June	2 June	3 June	4 June	5 June	6 June
Pentecoste (Whitsunday)	3 June	4 June	5 June	6 June	7 June	8 June	9 June	10 June	11 June	12 June	13 June
Trinitatis	10 June	11 June	12 June	13 June	14 June	15 June	16 June	17 June	18 June	19 June	20 June
Adventis	2 Dec	3 Dec	27 Nov	28 Nov	29 Nov	30 Nov	1 Dec	2 Dec	3 Dec	27 Nov	28 Nov

NOTE: For leap years add one day to all holidays in the months of January and February.

(Compiled by Henry E. Christiansen)

TABLE F CALENDAR OF WEEKS

	1	2	3	4	5	6	7
	8	9	10	11	12	13	14
MAY*	15	16	17	18	19	20	21
	22	23	24	25	26	27	28
	29	30	31	1	2	3	4
	5	6	7	8	9	10	11
JUNE*	12	13	14	15	16	17	18
	19	20	21	22	23	24	25
	26	27	28	29	30	1	2
	3	4	5	6	7	8	9
	10	11	12	13	14	15	16
JULY	17	18	19	20	21	22	23
	24	25	26	27	28	29	30
	31	1	2	3	4	5	6
	7	8	9	10	11	12	13
AUG	14	15	16	17	18	19	20
	21	22	23	24	25	26	27
	28	29	30	31	1	2	3
	4	5	6	7	8	9	10
SEP	11	12	13	14	15	16	17
	18	19	20	21	22	23	24
	25	26	27	28	29	30	1
	2	3	4	5	6	7	8
	9	10	11	12	13	14	15
OCT	16	17	18	19	20	21	22
	23	24	25	26	27	28	29
	30	31	1	2	3	4	5
	6	7	8	9	10	11	12
NOV	13	14	15	16	17	18	19
	20	21	22	23	24	25	26
	27	28	29	30	1	2	3
	4	5	6	7	8	9	10
	11	12	13	14	15	16	17
DEC	18	19	20	21	22	23	24
	25	26	27	28	29	30	31

**Note* — When finding a movable feast day identified as following Epiphania Domini, use the May and June sections above, respectively, as Jan and Feb. The months of Mar and Apr have been omitted since it is not necessary to use these two months in determining the dates of movable feast days.

How to Use the Calendars

To find the date of a movable feast day in a given year:

1. Determine whether the Julian or the Gregorian calendar was in use. The Julian calendar was used to 18 February 1753, when that day became 1 March 1753 on the Gregorian calendar.

2. Ascertain what calendar number to use. Refer to Table A "Guide for Finding the Dates of Movable Feast Days." Locate on this table the year desired. Let us use the year 1666. Besides it are two numbers: 25 in the "J" (for Julian) column and 35 in the "G" (for Gregorian) column. Since in Sweden in 1666 the Julian calendar was in use, the number of the calendar to be consulted is 25.

3. Find the Date of the Feast Day, by referring to the calendar with guide number 25. It shows that Easter (Pascha) fell on 15 April, Trinity on 10 June and Septuagesima on 11 February.

4. Use Table C "Calendar of Weeks" to find dates following a Feast Day. If the date given in a record is the 7th Sunday after Trinity in the year 1666, first locate the above steps that Trinity that year fell on 10 June. Find 10 June on the table C "Calendar of Weeks." All the remaining Sundays in that year will follow in sequence in vertical line below that date. Count down seven Sundays in that vertical column. This brings you to 29 July, which is the desired date of the seventh Sunday after Trinity in 1666 in Sweden.

Chapter 7

The Handwriting

Some call it the Gothic style, some call it the German style. Whatever the true definition may be, we will only tell you how to read it, as it is the style of handwriting used in the official Swedish records for more than two centuries, the seventeenth, the eighteenth and the early part of the nineteenth. At this latter time the Latin style took over, having been used in names and dates earlier, and it is the style we use today.

It is most frustrating to go into a record and find what you want, and then not be able to read it because of the old-fashioned handwriting. However, it is not more difficult to learn to read this style than it is to learn, say, Hebrew. If we just realize that we deal with a different style, and that the letters look different than they do today, then we have won half the battle.

The Letters

The ideal letters or handwritten alphabet would look as shown here:

Aa ä Bb Ccc Dd Ee Ff Gg Hh Ih

Ii Jj Kk Ll Mm Nn Oo ö Pp

Qq Rr Sss Tt Uu u Vv Ww

X Xx Yy Zz St ss ss sch ch ck

However, in the olden days, as with us today, no two persons formed the letters the same way, and thus in the text they may

For more detailed information about the old handwriting, see THUS THEY WROTE by Carl-Erik Johansson, Brigham Young University Press, Provo, Utah, 1970.

look like the letters copied below:*

CAPITAL LETTERS

A

B

C

D

E

F

G

H

I

J

K

L

*The examples are taken from THUS THEY WROTE, Carl-Erik Johansson, Brigham Young University Press, Provo, Utah, 1970.

M

N

O

P

Q

R

S

T

U

V

W

X

Y

Z

Å

Ä

Æ

Ö

Ø

SMALL LETTERS

a

b

c

d

e

f

g

h

i

j

k

l

m

n

o

p

q

r

s

t

u

v

w

x

y

z

å

ä

æ

ö

ø

1 1, 7, i, j 5 v, b, v

2 ü, ij, ÿ 6 vj, bi, bj

3 iü, üj, ÿj 10 x, e, [illegible]

½ f 1½ [illegible] 10½ x f

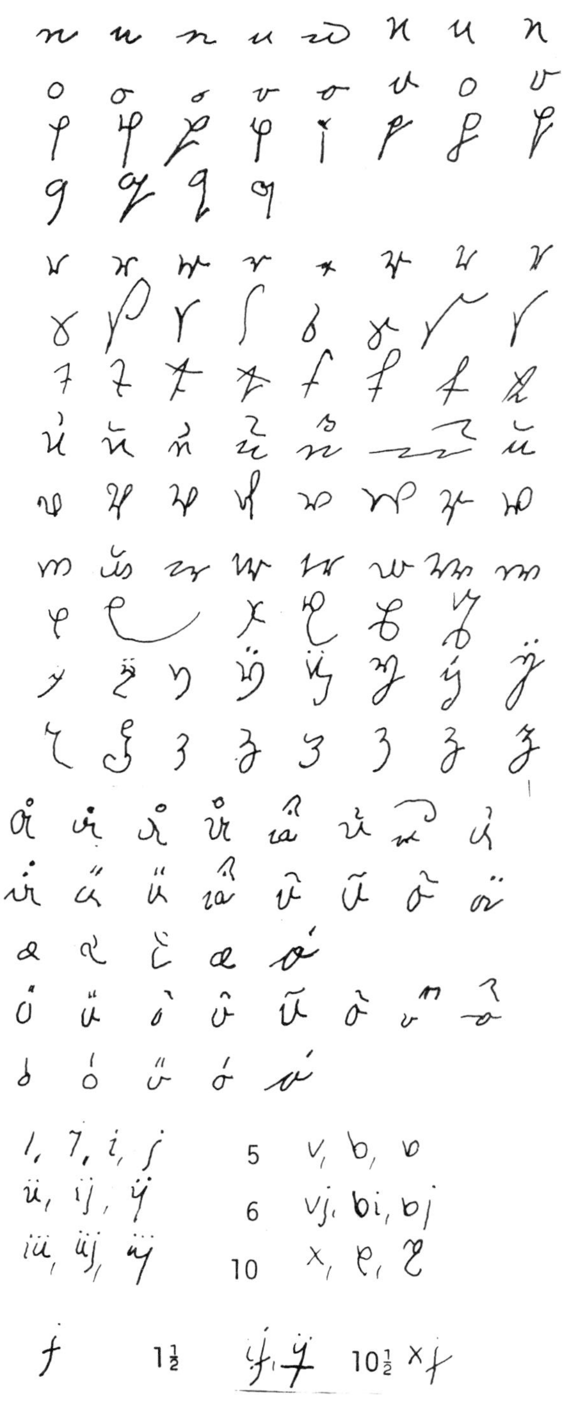

Some Reading Hints

Even if the text looks difficult and you say to yourself, that you will never be able to read it, you will be — and much faster than you think! Look at it for a few moments and you will see some system—the "hay stack" of letters and lines takes on character — you will recognize the same letter in several places, you will recognize the same word or maybe words in several places. If the text is completely strange to you, look for some of the more distinct letters like S, H, P or K and build your words from them. Look for the same words and letters in another place — higher up or lower down on the same page, or turn the page. It may look a little different — just enough for you to read it!

The words

It will not take long for you to read whole words and names just by a glance. If, however, you are able to read a full word or name like Kierstin, be sure to check the spelling carefully, as there may be a little variance from what you are used to. It may be spelled Kjerstina.

For your convenience and practise a few words are listed below, that were lifted from the original records.

Anders Esbjörn Kersti Trulls

Anna wid

Annicka Gustaf Kjerstin

Halfward Lars barn

Bengta Hindrich Marit födt

Brita

Isac Nils hustru

Carl

Cissa Jäppe

Dafwid Jon

Erick Karin

Erich Karin

Oluf

Pär

Päder

Sara

Sören

dödfödt

Änkan Karin

drängen Jonas

pigan Gunnila

hust. Anna

The Paragraphs

Having mastered the words (or even without mastering all of them) we are ready to go on to a whole paragraph. We have chosen a few lines from an incomplete birth record from Southern Sweden, written in 1733. It is a very good example of a very beautiful handwriting, which shows how common it was to abbreviate words. How to abbreviate was left to the individual writer, and he did so well that we are left to our imagination many times to figure out what he meant. However, knowing that inconsistency is the only consistent thing in genealogical research, we find by reading a few more lines, that the recorder very often wrote a word in full one time and abbreviated it the next, so he left the solution for us many times.

A(nn)o 1733

In the year 1733

som blef kallad Elina: Susc(eptix): war
who was called Elina. Carrying child was
hust(ru): Arna Jöns Pärs i Norra Uller(up):
wife Arna of Jöns Pärsson at Norra Ullerup.
Test(ati): hust(ru): Ingeborg Jöns Anders i Bon-
Witnesses: wife Ingeborg of Jöns Andersson at Bon-
derup, dräng(en) Pär Jönsson i N(orra): Uller(up):,

derup, farmhand Pär Jönsson at Norra Ullerup,
dräng(en). Ola Anderss(on): af Wisma(r)löf. etc.:
farmhand Ola Andersson from Wismarlöf, etc.
October(is): d(en) 14: Anders Pehrssons Son i Önneslöf, no-
October 14th, Anders Pehrsson's son at Önneslöf, call-
mine Pär: Susc(epta): war barnets faster
ed Pär. Carrying child was the child's father's sister

Ao 1733.

från Gjenarp: Test(ati): Hans Pärsson,
from Genarp. Witnesses: Hans Pärsson,
Ola Lind, dräng(en) Lars Månsson, Lars
Ola Lind, the farmhand Lars Månsson, Lars
Larssons hustru i Onneslöf, etc:
Larsson's wife at Onneslöf, etc.

Chapter 8

The Swedish Mission Records of The Church of Jesus Christ of Latter-Day Saints

The message of the Church of Jesus Christ of Latter-day Saints was first heard in Sweden in 1850. A few years later the first branch of the Church was organized at the Skönabäck estate in the parish of Slimminge in Malmöhus county. Other branches followed within days in and around Malmö city. On June 25, 1854, the first district of the Church was founded in Sweden, called Skåne Conference, which today is Malmö District. From then on the Church spread rapidly into all Sweden and districts (conferences) were organized in Stockholm in 1854, Göteborg 1857, Norrköping 1858 and Sundsvall 1859. The borders and the numbers of the districts have changed from time to time. Denmark, Norway and Sweden were all included in the Scandinavian Mission with headquarters in Copenhagen until 1905, when Sweden was made a separate mission with mission office in Stockholm.

Records of Members

Records of members were kept surprisingly well from the very beginning, and they are a great source of information for many people of Swedish descent in the Church. Even though the records were not standardized in the early days, nevertheless they contain in most cases similar information, showing guidance from the headquarters about record keeping. In them you will find the name of the member, his birthdate and place, parents' name, when, where, and by whom baptized and special remarks, moving, emigration, ordination etc.

Just as we find two languages, separately or mixed, in the Swedish parish registers, Swedish and Latin, the latter being the language of the clergy, even so we find in the branch records two languages, Swedish and Danish. Because the headquarters of the mission were located in Copenhagen and nearly all literature was printed in Danish during the first 25 years, a heavy mixture of Danish expressions were found in the Swedish "Mormon language" in the early days. It is well to keep this in mind in translating some of the entries by the help of a Swedish dictionary, as some words will not be found there, but will be found in a Danish dictionary. Some words, however, will not be found at all in any of the mentioned dictionaries, as they are a mixture of Swedish and Danish with their own interpretation peculiar to Mormon understanding. A few of the words and expressions found in these records are:

Gren — branch	Välsignelse — blessing
Conference — district	Wällsingelse — blessing
Äldste — elder	Uteluckt — excommunicated
Präst — priest	Uteslättat — excommunicated
Lärare — teacher	Konfirmerat — confirmed
Diakon — deacon	Doppare — baptizer
Ordinerad — ordained	Döpt — baptized
Borthflytat till andra grenar	moved to other branches
Utelukt vid råd den 29/1 1871	excommunicated by council 29 Jan 1871
Flyttat til Norge	moved to Norway

Names of Branches

Below you will find a list of all the branches of the Church in Sweden, and the earliest and latest dates of entries up to 1940. Some branches have been revived after 1940 but are not included in this table.

The record of members of the branches are found on microfilm at all of the Genealogical Society libraries, the originals being preserved in the Historical Department of the Church in Salt Lake City.

County	Branch	Period
Blekinge	Karlskrona	1871-1900
Gotland	Gotland sometimes called Visby	1858-1929
Gävleborg	Gävle	1855-present
Göteborgs och Bohus	Göteborg	1855-present
	Strömstad	1862-1869
Halland	Halmstad	1853-present
Jämtland	Ragunda	1857-1860
	Östersund	1861-1877
Jönköping	Jönköping	1872-present
Kalmar	Kalmar	1853-1864
	Västervik	1853-1912

County	Branch	Period
Kopparberg	Borlänge	1878-1923
	Solvarbo	1864-1914
Kristianstad	Hässleholm	1863-1874
	Kristianstad	1854-present
	Nä(f)vlinge	1854-1876
	Riseberga	1854-1894
	Vittskövle	1883-1889
Kronoberg	Växjö	1859-1870
Malmöhus	Gårdstånga	1861-1892
	Hälsingborg	1853-present
	Hörby	1857-1895
	Lund	1852-1899
	Lyngby	1854-1856
	Malmö	1852-present
	Sallerup	1857-1866
	Skönabäck	1853-1857
	Svedala	1854-1857
	Trelleborg	1856-1873
	Vallby (Valby)	1853-1863
	Viggarum	1853-1874
	Ystad	1857-1906
Norrbotten	Luleå	1880-1891
Skaraborg	Hjo	1853-1872
	Medelplana	1855-1863
	Skara	1854-1895
	Skövde	1854-1911
	Västergötland	1864-1866
Stockholm city	Stockholm	1854-present
Stockholm	Högmarsö	1916-present
Södermanland	Eskilstuna	1862-present
	Sventorp	1860-1862
	Vingåker	1879-present
Uppsala	Morgongåva	1855-1929
	Uppsala	1865-present
Värmland	Karlstad	1856-1876
Västernorrland	Härnösand	1859-present
	Sundsvall	1857-present
Västmanland	Sala	1855-1914
	Västerås	1866-present
Älvsborg	Frändefors	1862-1870
	Mellerud	1864-1878
	Råstock	1858-1866

County	Branch	Period
	Trollhättan	1861-1900
	Ulricehamn	1857-1884
	Vänersborg	1862-1868
	Västergötland	1864-1866
	Ärtemark	1864-1874
Örebro	Ljungstorp	1855-1860
	Nora	1856-1870
	Orebro	1855-present
Östergötland	Kvillinge or Quillinge	1858-1861
	Linköping	1857-1863
	Motala	1855-1863
	Norrköping	1855-present
	Risinge	1857-1859
	Vadstena	1860-1863

Swedish Members in Denmark

If you have reason to believe that somebody joined the Church in Southern Sweden, especially in the province of Skåne, and you cannot find his name on any of the listed records of members above, you ought to check the records of Copenhagen and surrounding branches also. It was customary for young people to cross the Öresund between Malmö and Copenhagen or Hälsingborg and Helsingör (Elsinore) to find work. Some of these Swedish people joined the Church in Denmark and some of them never returned to Sweden to live.

Emigration Records

From the very beginning the Saints (as the members were and are called) longed for their Zion in the midst of the Rocky Mountains, and already in the fall of 1852 the first emigrants left their native country on the long, adventurous journey to the unknown land "far in the West".

Most of the members joined the Church organized emigration, and most of the records of these undertakings from Sweden are preserved in the following records and registers:

A. **Emigration records of the Swedish mission 1905-1932** which give the name, age, place of departure and destination (sometimes even the street address), name of ship, etc. for every emigrant. These are among the most complete emigration records of the Church, at least for our purpose.

B. **Emigration records of the Scandinavian mission 1853-1920** (Sweden was part of that mission only until 1905). They contain all or part of the following information: name of conference (district), of ship and individual, age, sex, residence, place of birth (in most cases only **Sweden**), occupation and sailing date.

C. **Emigration records of the British mission 1849-1885, 1899-1925,** containing a register of emigrants from the Swedish mission at least up to 1913.

D. **Emigration records of the European mission 1849-1825.** Most Church sponsored emigration from Scandinavia went by way of Liverpool, where the Church maintained an office from which the emigration from all of Europe was supervised and coordinated, and a record was kept of all emigrants. Content: see under B above.

E. **Utah Immigration Card Index** contains the names of the Saints traveling overland to Utah 1847-1868. Content: name of head of household, first names of the rest of the family members, age, date of arrival in Salt Lake City, name of company and ship, etc.

Above mentioned emigration records are available on microfilm at all the Genealogical Society libraries. The originals are on file with the Historical Department of the Church in Salt Lake City, Utah.

Miscellaneous records

Some people did not go by Church sponsored emigration and thus there would be no record of their undertaking in the official files of the Church. This does not mean that we are to give up hope of finding them. They may have left Sweden on their own but joined the organized companies either in Hull, Liverpool or at the outfitting stations in the U.S.A. Look in those records!

Additional information, official and unofficial, may be had from some sources listed below, which list does not pretend to be complete, but rather suggests only a start in gathering clues and bits of information.

Record	Content	Where obtained
Diaries and journals Old letters	Day-by-day records of events, names and dates and places of family members	Historical Dept. Genealogical Society Daughters of Utah Pioneers Family archives
Family records Family bibles Private temple records	"	Family archives
Ward records of Church wards	Vital statistics	Historical Dept. Genealogical Society
Official temple records	Ordinance data Birth dates and relationships	Genealogical Society Respective temples
Patriarchal blessings	Names and birth of person and name of parents	Historical Dept. Family archives
Priesthood biographical records	Name and birth of person and name of parents	Genealogical Society
U.S. land settlement records	Homestead applications Name of parents, residence in Sweden, name of ship, citizenship application	Genealogical Society
Newspaper obituaries	Data about deceased	Genealogical Society
Swedish newspapers in Utah, Korresponden-ten, Utah-posten	Data about Swedish emigrants from everything to nothing	Genealogical Society on microfilm
Nordstjärnan Skandinaviens Stjerne	Monthly mission magazine articles and list of emigrants, dates of emigration, etc.	Genealogical Society Historical Dept.

Chapter 9

Emigration Records

The letter from Minnesota read: "All I know about my grandfather Nels Lindberg is that he was about six years of age when he came to this country with his parents. It must have been between 1885 and 1890. He always talked about Dallene. His mother died soon after they came over here. And I think the grave marker says Chersta on it. Can you help me find my relatives in Sweden. I would like to visit them."

This is a prototype of the kind of scant information many people have of their forebears, who took the big step across the ocean. It is, however, in most cases more than enough to establish contact across the great waters. The problem will most likely lend itself to several solutions, but the easiest will probably be by help of the emigration records. There are several kinds of them, and we will discuss the more common ones before we return to our problem. They are:

1) (Annual) extracts of parish registers
2) Police records
3) Bröderna (Brothers) Larsson's emigration papers.
4) Passport journals
5) U.S. shipping lists
6) Emigration archives

(Annual) Extracts of Parish Registers

From 1865 on the parish minister in every parish in Sweden made an extract annually of the people in his parish, who left for or had arrived from foreign countries during that year. The practice started in 1850 but did not become regular until 1865. These extracts were sent to the Central Bureau of Statistics in Stockholm, where they are still kept, and are registered according to the county and year. Thus all extracts from one county for one calendar year are put together and easy to find. These extracts are available for the years 1850-1940 on microfilm at the Genealogical Society libraries. There they are found in the **Sweden-General** file under the subtitle of **Emigration** and are listed according to years and county.

A look at these records will disclose that they were written on printed forms, alike for the whole country and for the whole period. This makes them very easy for us to understand even though we know no Swedish.

The annual extract from each parish consists of two or more pages. On the first page we will always find **the name of the parish** and some statistical information about the population in the parish, but all that we usually are interested in on that first page is the name of the parish, as it is not found on the other page. The name is found on the top line written in by hand. The sample below is divided into two lines but is actually only one.

Summarisk redogörelse för folkmängden i Furuby Annex - församling af

1 Folkmängden, enligt nästlidna Års redogörelse, den 31 December 1874
2 " " som från årets början intill mantalsskrifningen den 12 novemb. 1874
3 " " " " " " " " " "

Konga Prosteri, Kronobergs Län under år 1874

	Mankön.	Qvinkön.	Af båda könen tillsammans.
	660	716	1376
ökats med födde	15	20	35
" " inflyttade	37	55	92

It reads:

A summary information of the population of FURUBY ANNEX-parish of KONGA rural deanery, the county of KRONOBERG, for the year 1874. (Summarisk redogörelse för folkmängden i FURUBY ANNEX församling af KONGA Prosteri, KRONOBERGS Län under år 1874.

The second page (and additional pages if needed) has a paragraph which looks like the one on the next page, which reads: Register of those emigrating from the parish to foreign lands during the year. Note. Below is accounted for every emigrant (also for children under age). If no emigration has taken place, a special note should be made of it. (Förteckning å de från församlingen till främmande länder under året utflyttade. Obs. Härnedan redogöres för hvarje emigrant (således t.ex. äfven för minderåriga barn). Har ingen emigration ägt rum, göres härom uttrycklig anteckning.)

Förteckning å de från församlingen till främmande land under året utflyttade.

Obs. Härnedan redogöres för hvarje emigrant (således t. ex. äfven för minderåriga barn). Har ingen emigration ägt rum, göres härom uttrycklig anteckning.

Ogift. m.	Ogift. q.	Gift. m.	Gift. q.	Namn.	Yrke.	Födelseår.	Det land, dit utflyttningen uppgifvits skola ske.
	1			Johansdtr, Eva Christina, [illegible]	Piga	1859	Norra Amerika
			1	Johannesdtr, Ingrid, Enka, [illegible]	Undantags[illegible]	1826	"
1				Jonasson, Carl Magnus, D:o	Timmerm. Son	1862	"
	1			Jonasdtr, [illegible], D:o	" dotter	1850	"
	1			Jonasdtr, Stina Lisa, D:o	" "	1855	"
1				Jonasson, Sven Gustaf, D:o	" Son	1857	"
	1			[illegible], Gustafva Charlotta D:o	" dotter	1854	"

R. K. utdraget intygas [illegible]
R. Andersson
Pastor

The headings of the different columns are as follows:

Unmarried (Ogift) Married (gift) Male (m(anlig) Female (q(vinlig)

Year of birth (Födelseår) Name (Namn) Trade (Yrke)

The country to which moving according to statement. (Det land, dit utflyttningen uppgifvits skola ske)

We note that usually only the birth year is given and not the full birth date. Also, in the column for trade we very often find the relationship given.

The signature of the "kyrkoherde" or "pastor' is attached. These are the Swedish equivalents of parish minister.

The heading for the people moving into the parish would read something like this in a literal translation: Register of those into the parish from foreign countries arriving. (Förteckning å de till församlingen från främmande land under året inflyttade).

These records are the most centralized and complete emigration records, covering the whole country for every year and being catalogued by county and year. There is, however, no index of names of persons, so the only way to search them is to start with the first parish in "your" county and then continue on from parish to parish, until some lead shows up or until the last parish is searched.

Comparisons between these emigration records and other primary sources have shown that for various reasons about ten percent of those emigrating, legally or illegally, are not included Thus we should not be too dismayed if we cannot find "our" emigrant in these extracts. Let us just go on and check the clerical survey records and other emigrant records and we may hopefully find him. After all, the world's best and complete emigration records are still found in Sweden.

The Police Records

When a ship with emigrants left port, the ship master supplied the police authorities with a list of the emigrants on board. These records are preserved from the three major ports, Stockholm, Göteborg and Malmö. They usually give information about the name and sailing date of the ship and about each emigrant's name, birthplace, age, and destination.

The Police Records of Göteborg are being indexed at the time of printing. It will be several years before they are completed.

The **Stockholm Emigration Register** covers the years 1869-1904 and are preserved in the Stockholm city archive among the records of the Police authorities (Poliskammaren) with the catalogue number D.VII. They are not available at the Genealogical Society libraries as they have not been microfilmed.

The **Göteborg** records are kept in the Göteborg provincial archives, but they are part of the archives of the Police authorities (Göteborgs stads poliskammare). They cover the period 1869-1920 and are available on microfilm at the Genealogical Society libraries. They are not indexed but are kept in chronological order. Thus, in order to use them you have to know the approximate year of emigration. It is by far the largest collection of its kind in Sweden. Göteborg was the main port of departure for the million and a quarter emigrants from Sweden to the U.S.A. It is estimated that it will take 5 men 10 years to index them, showing the size of the collection.

In the Malmö city archive are stored the Police Chamber Register of emigrant contracts for the years 1874-1939. They are alphabetically indexed for the years 1874-1886. The index has specifications about the name, age, profession and home parish of the emigrant and his destination in the U.S.A. The 1874-1886 index is available at the Genealogical Society libraries on microfilm.

These police records do not take the place of the annual extracts, but only supplement them as do the other sources about emigration, which we will mention next.

The Larsson Brothers emigration papers

A few years ago a large collection of papers etc. was discovered having to do with the activities of one of the largest emigration agencies in Sweden, The Larsson Brothers, who operated in Central and Southern Sweden with main offices in Malmö and Göteborg, enticing people to emigrate to the United States. The papers cover a 40-year period from 1873 to 1913 and contain letters, letter copy books, letters from emigrants and immigrants, satisfied and dissatisfied, ticket stubs for steamers and railroads in England and the United States, etc. The collection is not indexed as to names, but classified as to items — ticket stubs, letters, etc. It is kept at the Göteborg's provincial archive and is microfilmed (165 rolls) and available at the Genealogical Society libraries.

It is different and valuable in that it gives places of destination in the United States for the individual emigrants, but it is slow in using when searching for an individual as there is no index, but the reward is great when something is found.

Passport Journals (Passjournaler)

These records, mostly from the 1800's, consist of a daily journal in chronological order over issued passports or permissions to leave the country or area. They give the name, home parish and destination of the applicant and date of permission granted. The offices were scattered across the nation. — Åmål in Dalsland, Linköping in Östergötland, Sölvesborg in Blekinge, etc. The original records which are few and incomplete are kept at the respective provincial archive and some are available on microfilm at the Genealogical Society libraries. They are catalogued under the name of the city in which the office was located.

Some of the more common ones, with the years for available records are:

Askersund	1818-1860
Borås	1815-1855
Hedemora	1797-1805
	1812-1824
	1833-1860
Kristinehamn	1812-1838
Lindesberg	1803-1877
Mariefred	1819-1824
Marstrand	1811-1812
	1817-1826
Nora	1813-1822
Västervik	1747-1858
Västerås	1737-1748
Åmål	1812-1863
	1877-1879
Östhammar	1812-1827
	1834-1859

A different set of passport journals for the years 1735-1851 are found in the Royal Swedish War Archives.

A person who wanted to travel abroad had to pay a special passport fee, which was submitted to the Naval Ministry. It was used among others for the pensioning of Swedish Navy personnel. The journal submitted with the fees contained the names, social status and residence parish of the traveler.

These passport journals have not been microfilmed as of 1971.

U. S. Shipping lists

In 1820 a law was enacted in the United States that specified that all ships arriving at American ports had to submit a list of their passengers. These lists contain the name of the vessel and and its master, the ports of embarkation and entry, the date of entry, the name of each passenger, his age, sex, occupation, country of origin and destination in the United States.

The originals kept in the National Archives in Washington, D. C. are:

Baltimore	1820-1891
Boston	1820-1874, 1883-1891
Mobile	1829-1886, very incomplete
New Bedford	1823-1899, very incomplete
New Orleans	1820-1902
New York	1820-1897
Philadelphia	1820-1899

For more recent arrivals the records are kept by respective port authorities. However, all of the shipping lists are available on microfilm for the researcher from respective caretakers and also from the Genealogical Society libraries.

These lists should be used in correlation with the Swedish emigration records listed above, and you will thereby find the destination of the emigrant in the United States, which most Swedish records do not give. It may be well to remember that most Swedish emigrants came by way of the East coast, and thus the lists of those ports ought to be searched first. Most of them are indexed in one way or another.

NOTE: Even though the shipping lists are very accurate as a whole, sometimes Sweden is mixed up with Switzerland as point or origin, so be on guard. Also, the spelling of names may not be exactly the Swedish way, as stated in Chapters 3 and 4.

Emigration Archives

In Sweden are being established emigration archives on a provincial basis. The movement is privately sponsored but supported by some government funds. The most prominent ones are found in the cities of Växjö in Småland and Karlstad in Värmland. The Emigrant Institute or House of Emigrants in Växjö is a combined archive and museum, telling the story of the Swedish emigration to the U.S.A. It houses emigrant journals and excerpts from the leading Swedish rural daily newspapers concerning emigration and emigrants. Within its walls are also found the largest collection of microfilmed Swedish-American church archives, containing minutes, membership, birth, confirmation, marriage and death records of hundreds of Swedish speaking congregations in the states of Illinois, Minnesota and Wisconsin. Other states will follow. It is the center of academic research in the field of Swedish-American emigrations.

The Karlstad emigrant archive contains an index of nearly all of the 100,000 known emigrants from the province of Värmland to the U.S.A., not only their names but often also their destiny in the great land on the other side of the ocean.

It would be well to mention that there are two main institutions in the United States whose great interest is to preserve the heritage of the Swedish people in this country. They are The Swedish Pioneer Historical Society with headquarters at 3225 Foster Avenue, Chicago, Illinois, and the Augustana College at Rock Island, Illinois.

The Use of the Emigration Records

Returning to the problem raised by the Minnesota letter at the beginning of this chapter, we find the following facts stated in the letter:

1) child Nils born in Sweden around 1880
2) family probably came from the landskap Dalarna (Dallene) as he always talked of it (just as a "Texan" would do of his Texas)
3) mother's name probably Kerstin or similar
4) father's last name may be Lindberg (could be taken in this country)
5) there were at least three people in the family when emigrating, father, mother and Nils.

It seems that the best approach would be to use the annual extracts of the emigration records from Kopparberg county (Dalarna) starting with the middle year 1888 and going through all parishes, looking for a family group where the father's last name may be Lindberg (or any patronymic name) with a wife Kerstin or similar and a young son Nils of about 6. All entries answering this or similar descriptions should be extracted for later evaluation. The years 1887, 1889, 1886, 1890 and 1885 ought next to be searched in that order. If only one entry answering the description is found we have probably found our family—we will have to correlate the information gained with the United States shipping lists to see if the family intended to go to Minnesota.

If no entry is found we have to search a few more years before 1885 and after 1890. If more than one entry is found, we will have to evaluate the most likely one and check it first against the shipping lists. Also, the letter writer should be asked a lot of questions about the family. Usually some bits of information may be had—an old letter with post mark, a picture, a ticket, naturalization papers, etc., to establish the identity of the emigrant. Once the emigrant is established in the emigration records, then it is time to turn to the parish registers, but not until then.

Statistics on Emigration and Immigration

It may be of interest to show how many people left Sweden for the golden shores of their new land in the West. The total population of Sweden was, on an average, less than five million at the time of the great exodus, 1850-1925.

Table 1

Län COUNTY	*1851-1860*	*1861-1870*	*1871-1880*	*1881-1890*	*1891-1900*	*1901-1910*	*1911-1920*	*1921-1925*
Stockholms stad . .	661	2 354	2 923	13 739	12 433	11 751	5 244	2 908
Stockholms län . .	41	234	602	2 814	1 973	2 533	1 432	966
Uppsala län . . .	4	207	612	2 280	1 153	1 356	441	292
Södermanlands län .	14	559	1 123	4 250	2 522	2 579	829	526
Östergötlands län .	1 929	9 219	10 039	23 731	11 171	10 087	2 922	1 579
Jönköpings län . .	2 349	11 514	8 584	23 136	11 837	10 525	3 827	2 751
Kronobergs län . .	1 381	5 552	6 525	17 404	9 840	8 777	3 744	2 221
Kalmar län . . .	501	8 219	6 990	22 900	15 426	15 255	6 350	4 020
Gotlands län . . .	50	613	1 354	4 484	2 702	2 146	705	269
Blekinge län . . .	1 026	1 460	2 447	7 953	7 122	6 897	3 490	2 277
Kristianstads län . .	1 729	6 334	7 428	18 345	10 776	8 476	3 553	2 029
Malmöhus län . .	284	2 981	6 691	21 974	11 287	11 844	5 179	2 534
Hallands län . . .	357	2 021	5 538	16 429	11 247	10 706	4 801	2 491
Göteb. o. Bohus län .	463	1 190	2 798	11 679	10 711	12 014	5 292	3 767
Älvsborgs län . . .	1 310	6 247	6 515	27 866	16 185	15 421	5 956	3 436
Skaraborgs län . .	673	5 352	5 854	21 926	11 532	9 465	2 746	1 315
Värmlands län . .	161	7 126	7 666	28 084	15 746	18 786	6 821	4 963
Örebro län	377	3 433	4 702	13 982	6 966	7 206	1 837	1 864
Västmanlands län .	72	897	1 685	4 562	2 175	2 273	742	961
Kopparbergs län . .	118	4 756	4 708	12 105	5 346	9 819	3 100	3 850
Gävleborgs län . .	1 190	5 476	2 574	9 835	5 843	11 140	3 401	2 346
Västernorrlands län .	75	1 181	1 498	5 484	8 912	10 983	3 446	2 518
Jämtlands län . . .	93	1 138	886	4 567	3 990	6 938	1 727	1 308
Västerbottens län .	—	393	383	2 044	1 976	5 092	1 767	1 008
Norrbottens län . .	2	278	1 054	2 712	1 653	7 180	2 185	2 307
Total .	14 860	88 734	101 179	324 285	200 524	219 249	81 537	54 506

The emigration to the United States from each county in Sweden between 1851 and 1925 for each 10-year period.

Table 2

Number of Swedish born people living in the States having more than 5,000 of them in 1890, according to the United States Census of that year. Included are also some Intermountain states with less than 5,000.

1. Minnesota	165,000	6. Michigan	41,000
2. Illinois	138,000	7. Wisconsin	34,000
3. Iowa	54,000	8. Kansas	33,000
4. Nebraska	49,000	9. Pennsylvania	28,000
5. New York	44,000	10. Massachusetts	26,000
(271,000 in 1930)		11. California	17,000

12. Connecticut	14,000	19. New Jersey	7,000
13. Washington	14,000	20. Oregon	6,000
14. Colorado	14,000	21. Ohio	6,000
15. Utah	13,000	22. Texas	5,000
16. Missourri	10,000	23. Idaho	2,700
17. North Dakota	9,000	24. Wyoming	2,100
18. Indiana	8,000	25. Nevada	500

Table 3

Total number of Swedish born people in the United States.

Year	Total Number	% of total population
1890	776,000	1,23
1910	1,364,000	1.48
1930	1,563,000	1.27
1960	1,047,000	0.58

Chapter 10

The Parish Registers

The Church law of 1686 made it mandatory for the minister of each of the 2,500 parishes in Sweden to keep a record of each person living within the parish and of all the ordinances he performed in his office as a minister. He should under certain headings keep a record of "all bridal couples with their and their parents' names and from where they came and what testimony they have about themselves". He should also record "all children, legitimite and illegitimite, with their parents, their sponsors, their names, birth- and christening date and the place where born".

A record should also be kept about the deceased in the parish in the same general manner, also about those moving into or out of the parish. Besides that, a record should also be kept about the clerical examination that took place once a year of every member of the parish. We will discuss this particular point and custom in our next chapter.

Those of us who think that this law makes it possible for us to study the records in every parish down to 1686, and those of us who think that there are no parish registers before that year, are all mistaken. Some records were destroyed by accident or carelessness or made useless by moisture etc. Sometimes the wars made it impossible to keep the records up to date. The minister in Ystad records in 1710 "that during these difficult and troublesome times with wars and pestilences everything could not be recorded."

Sometimes the records were kept by somewhat careless record keepers. The following note is found in the Härlunda parish registers of 1701: "If I remember correctly, my lord and minister married Ingemar from Illhafwan and the servant maid Brita Nilsdotter of Harahult." Thanks to such a conscientious parish clerk for recording this marriage, which otherwise would have been left unrecorded!

To our great joy we find that some parishes have records for periods of nearly one hundred years before the official decree about record keeping came. As a general rule we may say that there are good records from 1750 and on, and most of the things we may find of complete families before that time would be considered a bonus—however, we may find a lot of bonus and incomplete families before that time.

The records prior to the last century are kept at the respective provincial archive and from about 1870 to our day they are kept in each parish. All the parish records that are found in the provincial archives have been microfilmed and are available at the Genealogical Society libraries.

The minister kept the following records:

1) födelselängd	birth record
2) doplängd	christening record
3) konfirmationslängd	confirmation record
4) lysningslängd	bann record
5) vigsellängd	marriage record
6) dödslängd	death record
7) begravningslängd	burial record
8) inflyttningslängd	moving in record
9) utflyttningslängd	moving out record
10) utflyttningsbetyg	moving out certificates
11) räkenskapslängd	account book
12) husförhörslängd	clerical survey record

The above mentioned records are the practical records for research in our area, even though there may be a few more special records here and there, as the minutes of the parish councils, but if we know how to use the above mentioned records we do very well.

NOTE: The word used for record above is LÄNGD, however, in some places in Sweden the words BOK or RULLA may be used to signify the same record.

Birth and Christening Records (Födelse och Doplängd)

In the early days of record keeping very often only a christening record was kept, and no mentioning was made of the birth date. Also the entry may be very simple and many times not extensive enough to identify the person for a certainty. Below follow some actual samples from a parish in Småland for the year 1681:

D oca: 20: Trinit: christnades Isaks barn i Löfhult Kirstin bd. Dominica 20 post Trinitatis christnades Isaks barn i Löfhult Kirstin benämnd, which in translation would read: The 20th Sunday after Trinity the child of Isak in Löfhult was christened, called

Kirstin. Yes, all would be well if there only lived one Isak at Löfhult, but if there were two or more, what then? Only additional research in other records could tell us which one was the father of our Kirstin.

Doca: 1. post Festum Circumc: Christnades Leutnantens barn i Nääs Carl b., which in the language of our day would read:
The first Sunday after the Feast of the Circumcision was christened the child of the lieutenant at Nääs, named Carl.

A record from the city of Stockholm more than half a century earlier is much more complete as we read:
4 Maij 1615. Christnade h(err) Peer Jörgenn Skräddares barnn och stodho Fadder Hanns Bruun Smed, v(nge) Frantz skräddares Mesterswenn Böriel, Anthonius Skräddares hustru och Efwert Steenhuggares Hustru.
In translation this would be:
4 May 1615. Mr. Per christened Jörgen Tailor's child and stood (were) sponsors Hans Brun Smith, young Frantz Tailor's Master Apprentice Böriel, Anthonius Tailor's wife and Evert Stonecutter's wife.
But what about the mother of the child! Would we not love to know her name?

Later on we find both birth and christening dates as shown on the entry on top of page 78.

Transliterated and translated it reads:

Dec. 26. Nils Nilssons ock hustru Anna Jonsdotters barn i Högsjön födt, döpt den 28 dito Kallades Brita. Faddr. Inspectoren Jonas Engren wid Enboga, Trägårdsmästaren Olof Malmberg wid Björkwiks Säteri uti Ostergötland, hustru Charlotta Johanna Blomberg uti Malma, hustru Anna Maria Andersdotter	Nils Nilsson's and wife Anna Jonsdotter's child at Högsjön born, christened on the 28 ditto. Named Brita. Sponsors: The Inspector Jonas Engren at Enboga, Gardener (master) Olof Malmberg at the Manor of Björkvik in Östergötland, the wife Charlotta Johanna Blomberg at Malma, the wife Anna Maria Andersdotter.

Dec. 26

Nils Nilsson och hustru Anna Jonsdotters barn i Högsjön född, döpt den 28 dito Kallades **Brita**. Faddrar Inspectoren Jonas Engren vid Enbågen, Ernegårds Mästaren Olof Malmberg vid Björkeriks Patroni uti Östergötland. Hustru Charlotta Johanna Blomberg uti Malma, Hustru Anna Maria Nennarsdotter

Many birth records were organized into columns, the order of which you will have to figure out yourself many times, as it does not say, but the entry below will give you some idea:

		1815.				
	Dödfödd gosse oäkta.	Junii	9.	2.	qv: Christina Andersdotter på Häljesta ägor 34.	
51.	Pehr.	—	10.	11.	Olof Ersson i Norr Sylta, Hustr: Greta Olsdotter. 32	Hans Olss: N: Sylta, Dr: And Hanss: item: Hustr. Brita Ersd: Karstta Pig: Eva Maja i Sylta.

Column 1. 51 - this is the number of the child born in the parish that year. The next birth would be given the number of 52 etc.

Column 2. Dödfödd gosse oäkta — this is the column for the name of the child. On this entry we find that the child was stillborn, was a boy and was born out of wedlock as an illegitimite child. Pehr — here we find the name of the child of the second entry.

Column 3. 1815 Junii — the year and month of the entries.

Column 4. 9 and 10 — these dates are the birth dates of the respective children.

Column 5. 11 — this is the christening date. There would be none for the top entry, as the child was stillborn.

Column 6. 9/7 — this is the date of the mother entering church for the first time after the birth of her child to receive absolution. (9/7 = 9 July).

Column 7. The parents—gp: (gårdspigan) Christina Andersdotter på Häljesta ägor. 34, meaning the maid Christina Andersdotter living on the land of the manor Häljesta, age 34.

The second entry in this column reads: Olof Ersson i Norr Sylta, Hustr: Greta Olsdotter. 32.

It means: Olof Ersson (Eriksson) at the village of Norr Sylta and his wife Greta Olsdotter (Olofsdotter). She is 32 years old.

Column 8. The sponsors and witnesses — Hans Olss: (on) i N:(orra) Sylta, dr(ängen) And:(ers) Hanss:(on) ib(ide)m: Hust:(ru) Brita Ersd(otter) i) Ransta. Pig:(an) Eva Maja i Sylta.

As can be seen from above samples, all or part of the following information may be found in a birth record:

1) name of child
2) sex of child
3) birth date of child
4) christening date of child
5) live or still birth
6) if child lived beyond infancy
7) birth place of child
8) name of parents
9) residence of parents
10) age of mother (sometimes within a five or ten year period 35-40 or 20-30)
11) name of susceptrix
12) name of witnesses
13) residence of witnesses
14) relationship of witnesses to parents or child

Some customs at birth

In nearly all cases the christening took place only the day or a few days after the birth. This is contrary to the customs in most countries, where the christening came months after the birth.

When it was feared that a child would die before the minister would be able to perform the baptism, any person present could perform an emergency baptism (nöddop), and the child would thus avoid the awful fate of hell for the eternities, according to the doctrine of the Lutheran Church. This emergency baptism was most often performed by the father or the midwife. It was reported to the minister as soon as possible, and he confirmed it and sometimes made a note of it in the birth record.

About a month after the birth of the child the mother was brought or taken to the church and introduced anew to the congregation, signifying a cleansing sacrifice after the birth, which was considered unclean. (Leviticus 12) This practice is very rare today. The date for this event is often found in the birth record, sometimes only signified by the date, sometimes with the words kyrkotagen or kyrkogång, and sometimes with abbreviations for one of these words like ktg, kkg, kgg, etc.

Attending the christening were usually two godparents—a godmother (gudmor) and a godfather—and some witnesses (faddrar or vittnen). The godmother carried the child at the christening ceremony. The godparents were a second set of parents, so to speak, for the child. If something would happen to its real parents, that they could not take care of their child, the godparents would take their place. That is why we seldom see the grandparents of the child as godparents—they were one generation too old—but rather the aunts and uncles as they would be about the same age as the real parents.

In Southern Sweden, especially in Skåne, we find that older people carried the child at the christening. It was customary in that province that if the first child to a couple was a boy, the father's mother would carry the child at the christening, and if it was a girl the mother's mother would have the honor. What a blessing to the genealogical researcher these customs turn out to be. However, do not accept them until you have proven that it is so in your case, or you may work on the wrong lines before long.

We must realize that the custom of having godparents and witnesses at the christening meant much in former days within the family, and very often these honored people were all related—directly or as in-laws. This would be especially true, if the godparents and witnesses would live in another parish than the parents. In your research it is a good idea to check the birth records of the children of the godparents and witnesses, as you may find new clues to relationship etc.*

Confirmation Records

Some ministers kept a record of the boys and girls that were confirmed in his parish at the age of 15 or thereabout. It usually contains the name, age and residence of the one confirmed, and that is all. It appears very irregularly and is very incomplete and seldom used for research due to its scant information—only when no other records are available to identify a person with certainty. This record may also be called katekismilängd.

Marriage Records

This record usually does not contain too much information. We may expect to find the names of the bride and groom, their respective residences, once in a while the names of their parents and the bride's sponsor (giftoman), who very often was the father, the brother or even the mother or other close relative of hers. We may also find an entry about the size of the morning gift (morgongåva) and of the dates of the banns (lysningsdagarna).

Some Customs at Marriage

Before a marriage could be consummated a declaration of intention of marriage or bann (lysning) had to be read in the church or published in the papers. This was to be done three weeks in a row, and after that the couple was free to marry, if no objections had been raised against it.

The marriage usually took place in the home parish of the bride, and thus we ought to look for the marriage entry of a couple in her home parish.

It was customary, and for some time the law, that the husband present his wife with a gift, morning gift, morgongåva, at their marriage, which was hers to keep forever, and could not legally be shared with the children as other parts of the estate at husband's death. We could consider it some kind of life insurance or pension for the widow. Very often it was a sum of money but was also made in kind—a pair of "red spotted oxen", a horse and a saddle, etc. A notation of the amount of this gift is often found in the marriage record, but very often it only states **morgongåva enligt lag**—morning gift according to law. Very often

*For additional samples of birth records see THUS THEY WROTE, pp 67, 73, 77.

you find the word morgongåva abbreviated as mg, morg or similar.

If any of the marriage partners had been married earlier, there would be a court settlement of the earlier marriage in behalf of the children for their share of the first estate. A reference to this court settlement is often made in the marriage record, but you have to go into the court records to find the conditions of the settlement.

Divorces were very, very rare, especially among the people living in the country, until one hundred years ago. Special care should be taken to prove a suspected divorce from the records.

Death and Burial Records (Dödslängd, Begravningslängd)

The death and burial records are very often uneven as far as content goes, but usually contain the following information: name of the deceased person, his age and residence within the parish and the cause of death. The information about age is not too dependable and may be off several years. Below you will find a death entry from Kopparberg county on a printed form with ten columns, which reads across two pages:

År 1856.

N:o	Aflednas Namn och hemvist	Födelse År, Dag och Ort.	Gift eller Ogift.	Barn
1.	Enklingen f.d. Landbonden Per Nilsson Granberg i Hessten.	Född 1787 28/5 i Hessten Föräldrar Afs. Soldaten Nils [illegible]	Gift 1810 med [illegible] +1850 8/4 [illegible]	[illegible] Barn efterlefva 1 Son og 1 Dotter

The columns are transliterated and translated below and on the next page as follows:

Column 1: (Number) 1—first entry of the year.

Column 2: Aflednas Namn och hemvist—Name and residence of the deceased. Enklingen f(öre) d(etta) Landbonden Per Nilsson Granberg i Hessten.
The widower, the former farmer Per Nilsson Granberg at Hessten.

Column 3: Födelse År, Dag och Ort—Birth, Year, Day and Place Född. 1787 28/5 i Hessten Föräldrar Afs (kedade) Soldaten Nils

Born 1787 28/5 at Hessten. Parents the Discharged Ersson Kalk och H(ustr)u Stina Larsd(otte)r ib(ide)m Soldier Nils Ersson Kalk and Wife Stina Larsdotter at the same place,

Column 4: Gift eller Ogift—Married or Unmarried
Gift. 1810 med Carin Sundström från Hedsunda +(dog) 1850 8/7. se Liket No 19. s(amma) å(r)
Married. 1810 to Carin Sundström from Hedsunda died 1850 8 July
See Corps number 19 that same year (in this death record) (1856)

Column 5: Barn—Children
Af 4 Barn efterlefva 1 Son och 1 Dotter—
Of 4 Children survive 1 Son and 1 Daughter—

Upförande	Sjukdom	Döds- Dag och Ort	Ålder	Begrafnings- Dag
Föröfrigt klanderfritt men ej på Tiotal år begått H. H. Nattvard.	ålderdoms-krämpor —	Den 13 Januari. i Getmossen.	68 år 7 mån. 15 dagar	Den 19: Januari e. m.

Column 6 Upförande—Behavior
Föröfrigt klanderfritt men ej på Tiotal år begått H (errens)
With (one) exception irreproachable but not for about ten years partaken of the Lord's
H(eliga) Nattvard.
Holy Supper.

Column 7: Sjukdom—Decease
ålderdomskrämpor
infirmities of old age

Column 8: Döds — Dag och Ort — Death Date and Place
Den 13 Januari. i Getmossen
The January 13 at Getmossen

Column 9: Ålder — Age
68 år 7 mån(ader). 15 dagar
68 years 7 months 15 days

Column 10: Begrafnings—Dag— Burial Date
Den 19 January 19 p.m. e(fter) m(iddagen).
The 19th of January in the afternoon.

*For additional sample of death and burial records see THUS THEY WROTE, p. 75.

Special Obituaries (Personaliebok)

From Västmanland, Kopparberg and sometimes Södermanland counties we find some special death records mostly in the eighteenth century. They are the Personalieböcker, which give the life story of the deceased person. They are ideal records to use, even though once in a while they may contain irregular information, and thus will have to be checked out against the available primary sources, mostly birth and marriage records.*

Moving Records (Inflyttningslängd and Utflyttningslängd)

With the beginning of the nineteenth century we find many moving in and moving out records of the parishes preserved, while before that time they are very scarce. It is a simple list in chronological order giving the names of the persons moving in or out of the parish and the places wherefrom and whereto they are moving. As the moving in and moving out records usually are kept together, we have to be careful in using them, to be sure that we are reading the right list. Below you will find a sample of headings for respective columuns.

Inflyttade år 1851 Utflyttade

Moved in year 1851 Moved out

The six columns read in order:

Column 1: Month
Column 2: Date
Column 3: Numerical order of persons moving out
Column 4: Name of persons moving out

*For samples of special obituaries see THUS THEY WROTE, pp. 69, 71.

Column 5: Residence in parish when moving out
Column 6: Name of new parish

In transliteration it reads: (only columns 4-6)

Hustr(u) Mina Holgertz och 4 D(öttrar) Plåttorp Tuna
Enkan Brita Ericsd(otter) med 3 S(öner) 3 D(öttrar) Ulfveda Hjorttred
Skräddaren Carl Pet(er) Berg Figeholm Westervik (Västervik)
Pig(an) Christina Larsd(otte)r Hamnö Vesterum
Pig(an) Lovisa Larsd(otte)r Marsö ib(ide)m
Dr(ängen) Håkan Håkansson Baggstorp Döderhult
Torp(aren) Nils Olsson med H(ustru) 1 S(on) 1 D(otter) Mörtsjölund Döderhult*

When a person moved from one parish to another he was given a certificate of moving (flyttningsattest). This he presented at the new parish when moving in. Sometimes these certificates were printed, sometimes just made up by the parish parson. It was also called by the Swedish term Flyttningsbetyg. Below we show a sample of one from Småland around 1800.

N:o Pigan Stina Sunesdotter
År född år 1775 uti Odelöf
Kom år ifrån
Och flyttar nu til Grenna församling
Läser uti Bok väl
utan til: Doct. Luth. Catech., Ahn Symb. och H. Tafl., Doct. Sveb. Förkl.
Och förstår
Bevistat Cat. Förhör ordenteligen
Den H. Natty. 25/9
År til lefvernet
Ägtenskap ledig
Attest. af Odelöf d. 3 Nov 1796

*For additional sample of moving record see THUS THEY WROTE, p. 79.

From it we find the person's name, her birth place and date and the parish into which she moved. We also find a lot of interesting information about the person herself, that she reads well in books, that she knows her catechism well, that she attended the house examinations (clerical surveys) and partook of the holy sacrament and was free to marry. And at the bottom we find the place in the new parish whereto she moved.

The certificate of moving is thus to be found in the new parish and not in the old one. They give a lot of information about the person, as a rule. However, they are slow to search, as they are not indexed and usually not kept in very good chronological order.

These moving records have all been filmed in Sweden and are available on microfilm at the Genealogical Society libraries. The inflyttnings— and utflyttningslängderna are called member ship records, while the flyttningsattester are called membership certificates.

Parish Accounts (Räkenskapslängder)

The parish accounts may be of interest to the genealogical researcher, when no other records are available. They usually go far back in time, and some special accounts contain information about those who paid for the opening of a grave, indicating a death, or who paid the bride's money or gave a special donation at a christening. These people were usually very close relatives and thus these accounts may supplement some missing parish registers.*

Parish Records After 1860

The parish registers after 1860 are kept in each parish, while a copy or extract of them have been made annually and sent to the Central Bureau of Statistics in Stockholm where they are kept. They are of interest to us mainly because they have been microfilmed and are available at the Genealogical Society libraries up to the year 1897. They contain the extracts of the birth, marriage and death records in all Sweden. They are catalogued by year and county. They are not indexed but the parishes appear in the order of the list appearing in the beginning of each county record of each year. The order by the way, is very similar year after year. At the top of page 87 is part of the list of Södermanland county.

The records are divided into three parts for each county and year, first all the births, then all the marriages and last all the deaths within the county.

---

*For a sample of parish accounts see THUS THEY WROTE. p. 38.

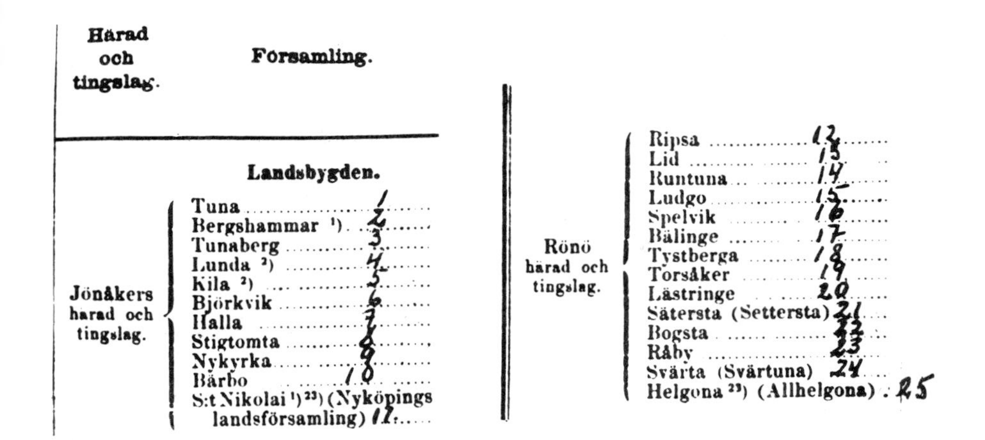

Härad och tingslag.	Församling.
	Landsbygden.
Jönåkers härad och tingslag.	Tuna 1
	Bergshammar [1] 2
	Tunaberg 3
	Lunda [2] 4
	Kila [2] 5
	Björkvik 6
	Halla 7
	Stigtomta 8
	Nykyrka 9
	Bärbo 10
	S:t Nikolai [1] [23] (Nyköpings landsförsamling) 11
Rönö härad och tingslag.	Ripsa 12
	Lid 13
	Runtuna 14
	Ludgo 15
	Spelvik 16
	Bälinge 17
	Tystberga 18
	Torsåker 19
	Lästringe 20
	Sätersta (Settersta) 21
	Bogsta 22
	Råby 23
	Svärta (Svärtuna) 24
	Helgona [23] (Allhelgona) . 25

They are standardized for the whole country with a heading, several columns and 10 entries per page. The top heading reads the same for all three records, only the words Födelsebok, (Birth record; Vigselbok (Marriage record) and Dödsbok (Death record) are changed. The heading reads something like this from 1880:

Utdrag ur	års Födelsebok för	församling i	
Extract of	year's Birth record of	parish in	
Prosteri	Stift,	Län	blad.
District	of Diocese	County	pages.

The dotted lines indicate the words written in by hand giving year, name of parish, name of district (several parishes), name of diocese, name of county and how many pages of this record for the parish.

Sometimes there appears after the name of the child a figure written within parenthesis — (3) or (3dje) — which indicates that it is the third child for this couple. This figure is not absolutely dependable, especially if there are many children in the family, or if a baby died within a few hours of birth.

These extracts of parish registers have been microfilmed for the years 1860-1897 and are available at the Genealogical Society libraries.

The Law of Secrecy

Under the Swedish law of secrecy no parish register is "public" until it is at least 70 years old. The ministers and court officials will, however, give information for any legitimate reason from the records under their jurisdiction, which are still under the 70-year rule.

Chapter 11

The Clerical Survey Records

According to the church law of 1686 regulating the order within the parish, ministers should "keep certain rolls of all their listeners, house to house, farm to farm, and know their progress and knowledge of the assigned sections of the catechism, and diligently admonish children, farm helpers and servant maids to read in book and with their own eyes see what God bids and commands in his Holy Word." The Swedish word for this was husförhörsrulla, which is translated into clerical survey record or house examination roll. Some of the records go back to about 1700, while most of them are at least half a century younger and in part of Skåne only available from about 1820 and on.

At the examination the minister checked on his parishioners' ability to read from a book. He divided them into three groups according to their degree of knowledge of the Christian faith:

1) those who had learned only the main parts of Luther's catechism

2) those who additionally knew the explanation given in the Catechism of the Decalogue, the Creed, the Lord's prayer, baptism and communion

3) those who "understand", that is, have caught the meaning of the text they learned by heart, and are able to answer questions on these subjects in their own words, and also knew the household tables of the Catechism and the scriptures referred to in the Catechism.

The examination took place once a year and an entry thereof was made annually, something like an annual census record. The same record was however, used for a number of years, often about five, with erasures and additions as needed. Also, the minister very often entered other happenings in between the examinations, which makes the record a continuous census record. While a regular census record is closed the moment the last entry is made, which is within seconds of the first one for a person, the clerical survey record gives a continuous story and not only a fleeting glimpse of the family.

There were no set rules how the clerical survey record would look and no printed forms were issued for the whole country. However, some dioceses had their own forms printed and thus we will find many different kinds of records, but they contain about the same information. In the 1700's they contained as a rule less information, also less correct, while in the 1800's we find both more, and more correct, information. About 100 years ago the forms were made more universal for the whole country and more easily read.

The word "husförhörslängd" has been translated differently by different organizations and individuals into English. We find both the expression house examination roll used and clerical survey record. This latter expression is used by the Genealogical Society libraries. The reason for the several translations is probably that these records are only found in Sweden, Finland and on Iceland, and thus there is no precedent to follow from any English speaking country in naming the record.

The Content of the Clerical Survey Record

Let us take a look at a couple of clerical survey records. The first one is from 1840 and shows what information can be had. The second one is nearly one hundred years older and the third one from about 1805.

120

Boningsställe.	Personerne.	Födelse- År.	Månad och Dag.	Ålder. 1840	Kan läsa i Bok.	Luth. Catechesen.	Svenskt Förkl.	Begreppet.	Förändringar. ankom från	afflyttat till
Backa										

The headings read:

Column 1: Boningsställe — Residence
Column 2: Personerne — Persons
Column 3: Födelse — Birth
left: År — Year
right: Månad och Dag — Month and Day
Column 4: Ålder — Age
Column 5: Kan läsa i Bok — Can read in Book
Column 6: Luth. Cateches — Knowledge of Luther's Catechism
Column 7: Svebilii Förkl. — The explanations to Luther's Catechism by Bishop Svebelius
Column 8: **Begreppet** — Understanding the Catechism
Column 9: Förändringar — Changes
left: ankom från — arrived from
right: Afflyttat till — moved to

Let us now transliterate line by line and make some comments at the same time:
120 — refers to page number
Backa — is the name of the village or farm in the parish
Undantag Åbo Per Larsson 1785 19/11 55 död 1845
Pensioner Farmer 19 Nov died
H. Anna Stina Johansdotter 1785 16/12 55 död 46
Wife 16 Dec died 1846
Son Barn Lars 1814 17/12 26 b b b se nedan
Son Child see below

The word child is crossed out and Son entered

The three b's are grades in respective subjects — corresponds to present day C's.

See below — indicates that the same person is entered anew on the same page — usually as a married person, or if grown children as servants.

Dess hustru Maria Pehrsdotter skrifven i Gräsryd 1839
(Its) his wife recorded in Gräsryd in the year 1839

The ringed tragic note reads as follows:
Död i barnsbörd dagen efter bröllopet
Gift till Gräsryd 39 82, which all means:
Died in child birth the day after the marriage
Married to the village or farm of Gräsryd in 1839, which is found on page 82 in this record.

Barn Carl 1839 23/1 1

Carl is the son of Lars and his deceased wife Maria

Britta Stina 1813 27/8 c c c
Johannes 1818 3/5 22 c b c

Britta Stina and Johannes may be the children of Per Larsson but the record does not state this information. Only a check of the birth record will tell who their parents are.

Åbo Lars Pehrsson 1814 7/12 26 absens 48
Farmer

This is the son Lars mentioned above, where a line goes through his name, indicating that he is not living home any more — he may have moved or may have died. In this case there was a remark stating Se nedan — see below — and here he is with his new wife, named

H: Anna Britta Bengtsdr 1812 4/1 19 b b Björboås Lillegd 41
Hustru (wife) Jan 4 came from Björboås

In moving to this place — Backa —in 1841 we have a good clue to the year of the wedding — 1841. In the name Björboås Lillegård the last part of the name — Lillegård — indicates that she lived in this same parish, as it is very rare to find the name of a farm from another parish given as the residence, maybe a village would be named, or a big manor or estate, but very, very seldom the name of a farm.

Barn i första giftet — Carl 1839 29/1 absens 48
Child from the first marriage absent from the examination in the year 1848

Andra Giftet: Maria 1842 31/3
Anders 1844 26/2
Pehr 1846 22/7
August 1849 15/4
The second marriage

We notice that in recording dates the day comes first and then the month. It is not always that the children are separated into the different marriages, so we have to check out the birth record to be sure that the wife of the husband also is the mother of all the children and not only of a few of them, the others being born in an earlier marriage. If a child is a stepchild of the husband, this would be indicated, as nearly always the relationship is figured to the husband.

The second sample is also on a printed form. It was unusual to have printed forms this early, but some are found in the Central Sweden area.

The entry is from a large estate, while the previous one was from a small family farm. The people living on a large estate would of course be of a different make up, as there were many servants, gardeners, coachmen, valets, etc.

Malmö Roten. Trindby Säteri 1.	Ålder	Kan läsa i bok.	Kan Luth. Catechés.	Förstår sin Christend.	Biwistat Förhör uti 1764 F.	H.	Gått til Skr.	Biwistat Förhör uti 1765 F.	H.	Gått til Skr.	Biwistat Förhör uti 1766 F.	H.	Gått til Skr.
Herr Öfverstelieutenant [illegible] Wilh. Gerh. von Engelhardt	1694	///				[illegible]	2. 4. 9.			[illegible]			[illegible]
Fröken Brita Marg. von Engelh.	1720 15/8	///				[illegible]	2. 4. 9.			[illegible]			[illegible]
Fröken Sophia Wilhelmina	1724 30/11	///				[illegible]	2. 4. 9.			[illegible]			[illegible]
Fröken Anna Maria	1730 2/3	///				[illegible]	2. 4. 9.			[illegible]			[illegible]
Fröken Eleonora Charlotta	1733 24/5	///				[illegible]	2. 4. 9.			[illegible]			[illegible]
Herr [illegible] Mårt. Fred. v. Engelh.	1734 15/9	///					[illegible]			[illegible]			[illegible]
Trädgårdsmäst. Anders Hellström	1719.	///	/////	/		[illegible]	3. 9.			[illegible]			[illegible]
Hustru Brita [illegible]	1724.	//	/////	/		[illegible]	3. 9.			[illegible]			[illegible]
~~[illegible]~~	1752	//	/////		[illegible]		til [illegible]endorp 1764.						

Here we find six basic columns with printed headings. The additional column to the right are only repeat columns for later years.

Column 1: Roten — ward or district, an organizational division within the parish, especially in the country. The cities were divided into blocks (kvarter) and then into house numbers within the block. In the rural area the ward (rote) was used for practical purposes when the parish was so large, that it had to raise several soldiers, when the paupers were many and had to be divided up between each ward, etc. Sometimes we find the expression rotesoldat (soldier for a particular rote) or rotehjon (a person who was a ward or charge of the rote). The parish was usually divided into two to eight wards (rotar).

Column 2: Ålder — Age

Column 3: Kan läsa i bok — Can read in book

Column 4: Kan Luth. Cateches — Knows Luther's Catechism

Column 5: Förstår sin Christend(om): Understands his/her religion (Lutheranism).

Column 6: Biwistat (bevistat) förhör uti — attended examination in (year)

Column 7: K.(atekes) — dates for different examinations

Column 8: h.(ustaflan) — part of the religious instruction, consisting of prayers to be known by heart, etc.

Column 9: Gåt(t) til(l) Skr(ift) — attended communion on the dates listed below, usually about three or four in a year.

The transliteration of the text is as follows:

Malma Roten — Name of the rote within the parish

Sundby Säteri — Name of the big estate or manor

Herr Översten och Ridd(aren) — Sir Colonel and Knight. Herr is a titel used by those of higher social standing, nobility, etc. Riddare is a titel within the different social orders of the realm, usually bestowed by the King or the King in Council.

Vilh(elm) Gerh(ardt) von Engelhardt—

The use of the word von between Christian names and family name indicates in nearly all cases a noble birth — member of the nobility.

frök(en) Brita Marg(areta) von Engelh(ardt) — Miss — was used as a titel for an unmarried daughter of nobility or other higher social class.

frök. Sophia Vilhelmina

frök. Anna Maria

frök. Eleanora Charlotta

Herr Mårt(en) Fred(rik) v(on) Engelh(ardt)

Trägårdsmäst(aren) Anders — The gardener Anders

Hellström — last name of Anders

East estate had a gardener, who had been trained for that particular profession. He nearly always changed his name from his patronymic to a family name with two syllables. So did also the special trades men within the parish, the parish shoemaker (sockenskomakare), the parish saddler (socken-sadelmakare), the parish tailor (sockenskräddare) etc.

hust. Brita Eriksdot(te)r — wife Brita Eriksdotter of the gardener

Anders

We find that the wife was always mentioned by her maiden name all her life. The only exception would be wives of higher social standing—nobility, clergy, richer merchants, and higher government officials.

They would sometimes be recorded with their husband's last name.

Son Peter — the line through his name indicates that he is not living with the family. In this case we find that he moved "til Fräkentorp 1764", meaning "to the farm or village of Fräkentorp in 1764".

In this third and last sample of the clerical survey record we find references to five years of examinations recorded 1803-1807. They report the progress of each of the three sons about their knowledge of Luthers Catechism, etc. Again we have to find a key to the minister's abbreviations before we understand what each notation signifies.

Meaning of Markings

Many were the systems used in the clerical survey record to indicate prowess in reading, Catechism and various Christian virtues. Very often an explanation is found on the inside of the cover of the clerical survey record or roll as how to read these signs. In the Nederluleå rolls we found the following extensive rules.

1. For those reading the A,B,C—book

to know it well and

also by heart

"For those reading other books the mark may be added to by

several lines."

2. For those recorded in the Catechism columns, when they know the main section

According to Luther's Catechism fairly well

According to the same Catechism well and clear

According to Svebelius' explanation fairly well

According to the same explanation well

Understanding fairly well

Understanding well

Reading the language of the Holy Writ by heart, or possessing exceptional knowledge and proficiency

3. For those being graded about knowledge

Of poor memory and weak understanding

Negligent at the examinations

Forgotten what they learned

Received the first warning

Warned several times

Been in the stocks or fined

Shut off from communion

4. For those being graded about behavior

Notorious for misconduct

Warned before the parish elders

Secretly brought to church

Been fined

Lost Honor

Shut off from Communion

From the fellowship of the parish

The mark may be changed in any way on repentence.

In the Västra Torsås clerical survey records of 1848 the marks of the parishioners' knowledge were indicated in the following way:

Means weak knowledge

Fair or Passable

Justifiable

Good

Praisworthy (cum laude)

We may also find the following indications of knowledge

m — Mediocre

b — Good

o — Excellent

k — Can read by heart

f — Understands

v — Well

n — Fairly well

i — Poor

o — Nothing

The marks recorded give a very vivid picture of the life lived by the people and the strict discipline exercised by the parish ministers, which all made for an honest and Christian society far beyond the average.

Sometimes the markings would not suffice to convey a proper idea of a parishioner's knowledge. In such cases the minister would add his own comments as in the case of Karin Jönsdotter from Leksand, about whom it is recorded in stern hand "knows neither inside or outside" of Luther's catechism.

Clerical Survey Records Extracts

The clerical survey records have been filmed from all parishes in Sweden up to 1895 — the original records up to 1870 being kept at respective provincial archives with the exception of the exempt parishes, where the records still are kept with the parish, as are those for the years after 1870. The clerical survey records from beginning to 1895 are available at the libraries of the Genealogical Society and are listed under each parish just as the parish registers are.

Also available at the Genealogical Society libraries are the extracts of the clerical survey records for the years 1860, 1870, 1880 and 1890, with the originals being preserved at the Central Bureau of Statistics in Stockholm.

These extracts are made up of a list of every person in the parish at time of extracting and would be more like a census record, giving the name of the person, his birth parish and birth year and relationship within the family. The best use of these records would be as substitutes for missing original clerical survey records.

The call numbers at the Genealogical Society library for these records are found in a special reference book with an excellent index.

Research Technique

After having studied the parish registers and the clerical survey records we are ready to start our actual search in earnest. The first important step is to establish the identity of "our" person. Sometimes we have to start one generation closer to us to do this. We always start from a certain and secure point—let us not hang in the air, not knowing what to look for — go from certainty to certainty. Let us say, that grandfather (farfar) Johan August Johansson was born 11 May 1865 at Asarum in Blekinge county. We have established him for sure by finding his birth entry in the parish register extracts. There it says, that his parents were Johan Nilsson and "h.h." (Hans Hustru — his wife) Johanna Petersdotter living at the village of Brummeberg in Asarum parish. As we want to find the brothers and sisters of Johan

August and also where and when his parents were born, we turn to the 1865 clerical survey record of Asarum parish. Looking at the index which may be found in the beginning or the end of the record we find Brummeberg on page 86 (this is a hypothetical case, so do not try to look it up in the records), and there we find the whole family with the baby Johan August just being born and entered on the record.

We next extract all the information found on this page about the family. Next we search the clerical survey closer to our time (usually 1866-70) and extract all the information in it. We continue from clerical survey to clerical survey as long as there is any information to be had about this family. Eventually we will find that a line goes through the name of Johan Nilsson and/or his wife, indicating either that they moved or died. Thus we have the story from the clerical survey of Johan Nilsson and his family from 1865 till their departure later on.

Now is time to start at 1865 again but go backwards in time (1860-65) until the family shows up for the first time in the records. This may be when they started the family or when they moved into Asarum from another parish. We may find Johan or his wife Johanna living with their parents and thus we have another generation started. In any case, we have now followed Johan Nilsson from his first to his last entry in the Asarum parish. We have built the "family skeleton".

To dress the family skeleton we turn to the parish registers. We see if we can find Johan Nilsson in the birth record from the information given in the clerical survey. In most cases it is correct, but sometimes a mistake may appear. Then we have to double check that all things add up so that we get the correct second great grandfather (Johan Nilsson's father).

The same procedure is followed with every person. First search the clerical survey high and low, then go into the parish registers, moving records, etc., to find the person's birth, marriage and death dates. Check out every date that is given in the clerical survey with the parish registers and if the information disagrees accept the parish register as the correct one.

Again it is emphasized that we build the "family skeleton" with the clerical survey as much as possible and then clothe it with details from the parish registers etc. This system we continue as far back as records are available, alternating between clerical surveys and the parish registers. But we are first extracting all information possible for a whole generation from the clerical survey. Make that record your main record!

Name Changes

When you search the clerical survey be on the alert for changes of names. You may trail a young boy, who left home after his confirmation at age 15, to work for some farmer. As a rule he would change employment about once a year, spring and fall, and move. When he became of soldier or apprentice age he may change his last name. You can, however, still identify him in the clerical survey by his first name, his birthdate and place etc. Just do not trust anybody to stay with his patronymic son-name all his life! But how exciting to trail him and read between the lines, to fill in the missing pieces of the puzzle of life and family!

Some Farmer Definitions

The largest part of the population was made up of the farming class which was divided into several different groups or classes. We find the expressions **bonde, åbo, torpare, statare, inhyses, undantag, backstugusittare,** etc. in the clerical survey from the country. We will try to define them briefly for you.

Allmogeman, see Bergsman.

Arrendator, farm tenant, leasing the farm and paying the lease in cash.

Backstugusittare, owned only a small cottage and a very small plot of ground and made his living from temporary employment.

Bergsman, miner or manufacturer who owned part of the land belonging to the mine.

Besittningshemmansbo, see Åbo.

Bonde, usually free farmer who owned his own farm.

Hemmansägare, see Bonde

Inhyses(hjon), living with somebody to whom they were not related or employed by.

Statare, married worker, hired per year by large estate, paid in cash and in kind — house, fuel, grain, milk, potato patch, etc.

Torpare, the user of a very small farm, they were as a rule very poor. There were two types: "jordtorpare" (farming the soil) and "skogtorpare" (farming the forest). The owner of the farm allowed the use of the farm in return for so many days of labor a year.

Undantag, to live as a former owner on a farm with certain rights to sustenance for life from part of the yield of the farm (grain, potato, meat, butter, milk, fuel etc.).

Åbo, did not own his own farm but had constant right to the farm he tilled, which was inherited within his family according to certain rules — sons before daughters, older before younger, the widow first of all, etc.

Chapter 12

Census Records and Land Records

In the earliest clerical survey record of Börje parish in Uppsala county we find an entry of a family reading this way:

Enckjan Kjerstin Pehrsdotter
dotter Chjerstin Hansdotter
son Sven Hansson

We want to know the last name of the deceased husband of the "Enckja" (widow), his first name obliviously being Hans. No clerical survey record to look at — we could not establish him in the death record, as only the first names of the deceased persons were given and there were several Hans.

Where do we turn now?

Great grandmother Hanna Nilsdotter was born on the third of February 1855 in Andrarum parish in Kristianstad county. We want to know the names of her parents. It is easy. Just look them up in the birth record. Oh, just wait a second! There does not seem to be any. How come? Oh, I see, the church burned down in 1875 and with it all parish registers and clerical survey records.

So, what do we do now?

Census Records (Mantalslängd)

We turn to the census record, which is not a census record, however, in the regular meaning of the word, but rather a tax list or a verification over the taxed or assessed property. Any regular census records are not found in Sweden, as the population count was done by the parish ministers with the help of the clerical survey records.

It got its name from the word mantal, which in early days indicated the size of a farm big enough to sustain one family. Around the year 1630 it took on the meaning of a measure for the assessing of taxes, and thus a farm is measured as being ½ mantal, ¼ mantal etc.

The census record (mantalslängden) contains the names of the persons who were supposed to pay the so called mantalspengar, a tax to be paid by every person between 15 and 63 years of age. It was kept in two copies, one by the exchequer archives and one by the county commission archives (länsstyrelsens arkiv), the latter being kept at respective provincial archives. The latter has been microfilmed and is available at the Genealogical Society libraries up to the year 1860. It starts around 1630.

Theoretically all people in Sweden between 16 and 63 would be included in this record. However, this is not the case. The soliders were freed from this tax and only their wives are mentioned, very often only indicated by "soldier's wife" (soldathustrun) and no name. Also, the children and the servants, maid servants (pigor) and farm hands (drängar), are not mentioned by name but only checked off in a column. Thus, we do not get the full benefit from these records that we could have had, if they would have listed the names of all persons.

The columns listing the different people living on the farm are listed in different orders in different records, but they usually contain the following headings: Bönder or Männer (men), Hustrur (wives), Söner (sons), Döttrar (daughters), Mågar (sons-in-law), Sonhustrar, (daughters-in-law), Drängar (farm hands), Pigor (maid servants), Inhyseshjon (tenants) and Summa (total).

If someone is dropped in a roll it means that he either died, moved away or was more than 63 years old. There is no indication of what it is in the records. They were not kept annually but sometimes 5-10 years or more between. No age of the people mentioned is given in the records.

It should be noted that in the 1800's the records contain some additional information from certain areas of the country, especially Skåne, where we find the names of all the persons living on the farm listed, their birth date and relationship. This makes it a census record and an invaluable help when the clerical survey is missing. This helps us solve the problem mentioned above at the beginning of this chapter. We simply use this so called census record (mantalslängden), as we used the clerical survey record before.

How can we benefit from this record? Let us take the first problem at the beginning of this chapter. We were looking for the last name of the deceased husband. By going into the place where the family lived, we ought to find the name of the farmers there, and if he is the only Hans living there, he ought to be "our man". Careful searching has to be done and no hasty judgments, for as the Swedish saying goes, "all is not gold that glitters."

In searching these records you would do well to have studied the names of the farms and villages in the parish and surrounding areas before using the record. The records are not in the best of shape many times, and the old script may be difficult to read, but by knowing every farm by name, it is much easier to read the names of the farms and find the place. You will save yourself a lot of time and headache by knowing the geography of the area.

Similar records were also made for other tax purposes, duties on the grist mills, etc. They are all included in this census record or tax list, as it ought to be called. Very few notes of personal interest are included; however, we may find such pleasant notes as this one from Tuna parish in Örebro county for the year 1820: "Undertecknad dricker vin och Caffe" and about his wife it was stated: "dricker The, nyttjar sidenkläder," which all means, "The undersigned drinks wine and coffee, and she drinks tea and uses silk clothes." The curate (komminister) Gadd of Nöbbelöv parish in Skåne writes about himself, his wife and sister-in-law: "Use silk, coffee and whiskey and a pocket watch; the latter only by myself." Refinement comes in many clothes!

At the Genealogical Society libraries these records are very well indexed in special books, which give the call number of the film for every parish for all years up to 1860. Otherwise the records are catalogued by county and some of them have a geographical index.*

Land Records (Jordeboken)

The land record gives the story of the land, the farm, the estate, etc., more than they give information about people living there. They ought to be checked when no other or very scant information is available, however, the hopes should not be too high of finding something of real value very often for our purpose. They start about 1630. They have been microfilmed and are available at the Genealogical Society libraries for the years up to around 1750, but none after that year. They ought to be used in the same way as the census records mentioned earlier in this chapter.

*For samples of the census record see THUS THEY WROTE, pp. 85 and 87.

Chapter 13

Court Records

The lowest or originating court in Sweden is the district court (häradsrätt) in the county, while the cities had their own city court (rådhusrätt). The Swedish word for court may be rätt, ting or domstol. All three mean the same thing. The next higher court is the court of appeals (hovrätt) of which there are three in Sweden, each for a certain geographical area, which are of interest to the genealogical researcher. These three courts of appeals are Svea hovrätt, Göta hovrätt, and Hovrätten över Skåne och Blekinge.

Svea court of appeals (Svea hovrätt) was originally some kind of supreme court under the king, but that distinction was changed around 1600, when it became the appelate court for Eastern and Northern Sweden. Its seat is in Stockholm and its records are kept by the National archives (Riksarkivet).

Göta court of appeals (Göta hovrätt) was founded in 1634 with headquarters in Jönköping. It has jurisdiction over the district courts (häradsrätterna) and the city courts (rådhusrätterna, sometimes called rådstugurätterna) in Western and Southern Sweden. The archive is located in Jönköping.

In 1820 the provinces of Skåne and Blekinge were assigned a special court of appeals (Hovrätten över Skåne och Blekinge), which was located in the city of Kristianstad until 1917, when it moved to Malmö, where the records are located.

The records of the district and city courts are kept at the respective provincial archives, with the exception for the records of the last one hundred years, which are usually still in the safekeep of the individual courts.

The Probate Records (Bouppteckningar)

The most important court record for the genealogist is the probate record. Although many times there is no probate record, the regular court records may contain information of great value.

The probate record is really a list of inventory and is called bouppteckning in Swedish. At the death of a person a legal inventory and appraisal of the death estate was made, so that it could be properly divided between the heirs. This was done by court appointed appraisers (värderingsmän), who turned the list of inventory over to the court for probate, which took place at the next court session. There were held between two and four sessions a year — winter, spring, summer and fall — vintertinget, vårtinget, sommartinget and hösttinget.

All probating was done by the district or city court — häradstinget or rådhusrätten — unless the deceased person belonged to the nobility, who had the privilege to have the probate processed by the court of appeals between the years 1737-1916.

There are few probate records antedating 1750 and many after that time are incomplete or missing. The indexing is constantly going on at the different archives, but it may be said that not even half of the records are indexed. This, however, should not prevent us from using them as they are fairly easy to search even though it is time consuming. How dreary research will be when the time comes that it will be only a looking at indexes and nothing else!

The probate record is usually made up of two parts, the preamble and the list of inventory. To that may be added a closing statement with signatures of the heirs or just their initials — I P S for Jeppa Persson or A T D for Anna Trulsdotter. Sometimes the probate record is followed by the division and distribution of the property among the heirs (arvskifte).

The Content of the Probate Record

The preamble usually contains most of the genealogical information. We may find all or part or, sadly to say, sometimes none of the following information:

1) date of inventory
2) by whom performed
3) name of deceased
4) death date of deceased (usually follows a few lines below the date of the inventory)
5) residence of the deceased before death
6) names of the heirs
7) their age
8) their residence
9) their relationship to the deceased

10) names of daughters' husbands
11) date of probate (or name of ting—vårtinget etc.)
12) name of guardian of under age children or heirs
13) residence of guardian
14) relationship of guardian to his charges

The list of property is usually divided into subtitles as gold (guld), silver, pewter (tenn), cattle (kreatur), horses (hästar), books (böcker), clothing (klädespersedlar or kläder), linnen (linnetyg), debt (skulder), assets (tillgångar), etc.

The Use of the Probate Record

A careful researcher would always study the probate record in order to get a complete picture of the family, which parish registers and clerical survey records (husförhörslängden) sometimes would not give.

A "completed" research on a family showed that among their eleven children were five girls with the name of Ingrid. All of them had exact birth dates checked out in the birth record, and for the three oldest there were also death dates checked out in the death record. However, the researcher had not been able to find a death date in the death record for the fourth Ingrid and assumed that she died in infancy and had so indicated on the record of the family. The fifth Ingrid was born about eight years after her namesake. If the researcher had checked out the probate record he would have found the following entry in the preamble among the heirs:

" . . . dottern Ingrid, 21 år gammal och yngsta dottern Ingrid 13 år . . . "

No parents never wanted a mature daughter by the name of Ingrid more than these did, and so they took no chances after three of their daughters had died. They named two with the same name.

Never assume that a child died in infancy just because a younger child is christened with the same name. If you cannot find a death date for the older child do not assume that the child died in infancy.

It pays to study the lists of debts and assets (boets skulder och tillgångar) of the estate very carefully. It was common then as now to lend or borrow from relatives, and they may be mentioned by name and relationship.

The guardian was supposed to be the nearest relative on the paternal side of the family, but this rule was not followed too strictly, but should aways be taken into consideration in the research, especially if he lives in another parish than his charges.

Åhr 1801 then 12 Martii Blef uppå skedd anmodan Laga Bouptekning förrättad ...

Jacob Hansson ... Flemminge ... Karna Ols dotter ... Hans 23 ... Jöns 22 ... Elna 27 ... Anders Olsson ...

The transliteration of the text of the probate on the preceding page.

(Avsk) rift d 11 Junii
Åhr 1801 then 12te Martii, Blef
uppå skedd anmodan, Laga Bouppteckning förrättad
af Undertecknad Frälse Inspector, efter med dö-
den, den 31te December förledit År afledne Präste Bonden **Jacob Hansson** uppå första halfwa-
delen of Annexe Hemmanet No 13 i Slemminge,
hwilken efter sig lämnat dess hustru Karna Olsdotter jemte 3ne Barn: Imo Sonen Hans 23 år,
2do Sonen Jöns 22 år och 3tio dottren Elna. 27 år,
gift med Präste Bonden Anders Olsson uppå
andra halfwa delen uti Annexe Hemmanet No
13 i Slemminge.

Til wärderingsmän, infan sig uppå kallelse
Nämdemannen Lars Trullsson i Solberga och Frälse Hemmans Åboen Pehr Olsson i Stenberget; Sedan
nu Enkian blifwit åtwarnat att enligt Lagens
föreskrift all Qwarlåtenskapen redeligen upgifwa,
sådan som den samma wid dess afledne Mans
dödsfall befants; företogs med förrättningen
i den ordning som följer:

Contante Penningar	Specie		Transport	1	4	12.40
	RDr	s	r			
Rijksgälds Sedlar	12		2 djupa tallrikar		10	
Silfver			1 flat dito		6	
			1 Smör fat		12	
bägare		40	1 Skål		12	1.44

The Translation of the Text

Copy the eleventh of June
The year 1801 the 12th of March was
upon given request, legal inventory performed
by the undersigned Frälse Inspector, after with
death, on the 31st of December last year deceased
Priest Farmer (leasing the farm belonging to the parish) Jacob
Hansson on the first half
part of the Annex farm with number 13 in Slemminge
(Slimminge in Malmöhus county)
who left behind (its) his wife Karna. Oldsdotter and 3 children:
1st the son Hans, 23 years of age, 2nd the son Jöns, 22, and 3rd the
daughter Elna, 27, married to the Priest Farmer Anders Olsson on
the other half part of Annex farm number

13 at Slemminge.

As appraisers appeared after summon (call)
the Juryman Lars Trullsson at Solberga and the Fräl-
se-Farmer Pehr Olsson at Stenberget; After
now the widow been warned to, according to the Law's
stature and rule, all the estate and property correctly state,
as it at her deceased husband's
death was; was started the function
in the order that follows:

Cash	Specie (money used)	Transport
	Riksdaler, Skilling, runstycken (see next page)	
Riksgäld bills		2 deep plates (soup plates)
Silver		1 flat dito (regular plate)
		1 butter dish
tumbler		1 bowl

The translation is of course literal to give the readers who do not understand any Swedish a chance to get some idea of the words that may be used in a probate records and what they mean.*

The Monetary System

The present monetary system in Sweden with krona and öre (100 öre to one krona) did not begin until 1873. Before that time the money units were riksdaler, skilling and runstycke or öre The riksdaler was divided into 48 skilling, and a skilling consisted of 12 runstycken.

There were different kinds of riksdaler with different values for different periods—riksdaler speci, riksdaler riksgäld, riksdaler banco, etc.

The currency picture is quite confusing through the ages in Sweden, and without a special study in the subject it is difficult to make out. The practical approach for the researcher is to compare the value of the whole estate with some tangible and easy to understand property like pigs, sheep, oxen, horses and cows. That will give us some idea of the value of the estate — grandpa was worth 6 oxen . . .

The Distribution of the Death Estate

Sometimes we find, as mentioned earlier in this chapter, the record of the distribution of the property. This arvskifte may read something like this for the surviving 4 sons and 2 daughters:

*For additional samples of probate records see THUS THEY WROTE, pp. 95 and 97.

Tvåhundra sextio riksdaler Banko fördelas lagligen i tio lika lotter och får varje 26 riksdaler, varav

Imo Sonen åboen Lars Nilsson i Sverresjö tager 2ne lotter med	52	D
2do Sonen Husmannen Lars Nilsson i Östra Wemmenhög taker 2ne lotter med	52	D
3tio Sonen Drängen Per Larsson i Lilla Biddinge Do Do	52	D
4to Åboen Anders Larsson ibm: Dito Dito	52	D
5to Dottren Anna gift med åboen Nils Larsson i Lindby tager en lott med	26	D
6to Dito Else gift med åboen Jeppa Persson i Westra Torp tager en lott med	26	D

We will leave the translation of this to the individual reader, and only mention here, that the sons inherited twice of what the daughters got.

Probate Records Available at the Genealogical Society Libraries

Nearly all of the probate records from their beginning to about 1860 have been filmed and are available at the Genealogical Society libraries. The indexing of probate records is continually going on at the provincial archives in Sweden, and if an index is not found at the Genealogical Society it may be well to write to the proper provincial archive and ask if an index is available for the district or city, that you are doing research in. A list by county and district of all the probate indexes available, the years covered, and the call numbers of the films is found in Appendix B on page 129. This list also indicates the year of the earliest probate record in every district and city of Sweden.

Other Court Records

Among the court records are found many that may be of great interest to the genealogical researcher. This is especially true for the wills (testamente), deeds of property (lagfart), guardian minutes (förmyndarskapsprotokoll), and mortgage transactions (lånehandlingar). Most of these records have been microfilmed and are available at the Genealogical Society libraries. The indexes are usually found within the record itself, if there are any. They may contain a wealth of information, as in the case of the widow, Kiersti Nilsdotter, who petitioned the Luggude district court in 1769 to be released from her duty as guardian for her son, Nils Gussarsson, in the presence of her stepson, Matts Gussarsson, of Fjärestad. Ola Gussarsson was named as the new guardian for brother Nils, and he would also occupy the farm left after their deceased father, Gussar Mattsson, of Fjärestad.*

Duplicate Court Records

The lower courts had to make an extract or copy of all proceedings at the court sessions and submit it to the court of appeals under which it sorted. Thus we have an original and a copy of the court records (probate not included). We may find things in one record that may not be in the other. It is best to search the original, even though the copy as a rule is easier to read. Sometimes the original record is lost and the copy preserved. If there are no original court records for the time and place you are interested in, it may be well to see if any copies are extant.**

---

*I am indebted to Roy A. Spjut of the Genealogical Society of Salt Lake City, Utah, for bringing this case to my attention.
**For additional interesting samples of court records see THUS THEY WROTE, pp. 109, 111, 113, 115, 117, 119.

Chapter 14

Military Records

Much of the history of Sweden before 1814 (the last time Sweden fought a war) is a history of war, of fighting against Russia, Prussia, Denmark, Poland, etc. to keep the borders intact and at times to expand them. It seems incredible that such a small population as the Swedish, only a million or two, could support the efficient war machine required for the many battles. It did, however, and the success must partly be ascribed to its organization. The Swedish people were a people of soldiers. Toward the end of the seventeenth century the idea had developed that weapons furnished by the crown should be found in every house with people who knew how to use them.

The provinces were given the responsibility to raise, maintain and support a standing army. The province was as a rule contracted by the crown to raise or furnish one regiment of either foot or horse soldiers. The navy units were smaller but furnished in a similar fashion. They were mostly company-sized and usually drawn from the coastal provinces and named after them, as Blekinge första båtsmanskompani (Blekinge first allotment seaman company). A complete list of army units and the years of their available records is found in Appendix A, on page 124.

The soldier was tied to the land. This was done by dividing each parish into wards or files **(rote)**, consisting of one or several farms, which had to furnish one equipped soldier, and in return nobody living within the ward boundaries was drafted. The ward or file paid the soldier usually by furnishing him with a croft **(torp, soldattorp, båtsmanstorp, ryttartorp)** and a few acres of tillable land and meadow, on which he lived and made a (poor) living while not on active duty. If the croft came without land, the "ward-farmers" were to furnish him something like two barrels of grain, two loads of hay and one load of straw a year, a load being what one horse could pull. When not busy in warfare or with his own croft, the soldier helped the farmers in his ward. In the eighteenth and nineteenth centuries these sturdy soldiers made a great contribution, in breaking new land on the outskirts of the villages.

The soldier did not have to be born within his ward or parish. In fact, the farmers had a right to force "loose people, idlers and vagrants, who do no lawful work" into the service. This accounts for the following note in a muster roll of 1684: "The vagrant Göran Pålsson Kil became a soldier" (**Lösdrivare Göran Pålsson Kil blir knekt).** However, we often find that sons of soldiers stayed with the profession of their fathers. A notation in the same muster roll states about a young soldier boy: "The father Johan Andersson Gammal, discharged, is old, having served for 24 years, turns over the ward to his son Anders for a small hire."

The Regiment

The regiment was commanded by a colonel and consisted of about 1000-1200 men, divided into companies, each of about 100 men. As a rule the first couple of companies were called by the titles of their commanders, being lieutenant colonel, first major and second major. The balance of the companies were usually called by the name of the area, district, or large parish in which its soldiers lived. Sometimes the first company was given the honorary title of life company (livkompani) to protect with its own life the lives of others, the King for example.

Uppland's regiment of 1739 may represent the naming of the regimental companies. Their names in order:

Livkompaniet	(Life or Body guard company)
Överstelöjnantens kompani	(The lieutenant colonel's company)
Majorens kompani	(The Major's company)
Siggetuna kompani	(Named after the geographical area in which the soldiers of the company were located)
Rasbo kompani	
Bälings kompani	
Hundra härads kompani	"
Lagunda kompani	"

The company was divided into corporalship of about 25 men, each commanded by a corporal.

Each ward was assigned to a certain regiment and company and kept the same number for its soldier through the years. With that number followed very often a certain name for the soldier, so that the one from Ekeby ward was named Ek, when he took over as the soldier there. When he was discharged, another man was appointed, taking the same name of Ek. Sometimes the first name of both of these soldiers could be the same. Thus we have to be careful in our search and not assume that soldier number 119 Lars Ek at Ekeby ward in 1790 would be the same 119 Lars Ek, that was there 15 years earlier. The muster rolls should be checked to make sure.

Records

The records kept of the soldiers are not very rich in content for the genealogical researcher. They should not be used until other records with more information have been found wanting. They are more valuable as a source of biographical information about a particular person, but not about his family or even his own vital data.

The main record is the general muster roll, which was kept by respective regiments about every 3 to 10 years. The Royal War Archives in Stockholm keeps all of the military records with the exception of one copy of the general muster roll, which is divided into areas corresponding to the jurisdiction of each provincial archive and is kept at the respective provincial archive. This means that we may be able to find a general muster both in Stockholm at the Royal War Archives and at the provincial archive.*

Some of these regimental records go back to 1620, but most of them start about 1680. They usually contain valuable information about the officers, but the lower the ranks of the soldiers the less information, as a rule. About the common soldier we most often find the following information:

1) number
2) name
3) origin (province, not parish)
4) age
5) years of service
6) height (feet and inches)
7) married or not
8) whom he replaced
9) date of discharge
10) if slain on the battle field

A soldier had to be replaced by the ward within three months in case he died or was discharged. If he was slain on the battle field he had to be replaced within a year but before the end of the month of March.

The information about a soldier's age may not be too accurate for several reasons. The roll was made out in several copies as mentioned earlier and the risk of copying errors was always pre-

*For samples of military rolls see THUS THEY WROTE, pp. 89, 91, 93.

sent; sometimes the recorder took the age in the previous roll and transferred it to the new one, forgetting to add the customary three years between musters; the soldier himself may not have known how old he was; or he may have wanted to stay in the service as long as possible and was cheating on his age.

If he happened to be a cavalryman we often find more information about his horse than about himself — black with white hair in the forehead, 15 years old, height, etc. Exciting for the family history, but of little help in finding his parentage!

How to Find Your Soldier in the Muster Roll

As many provinces had several regiments at the same time it is time consuming to search for our man, especially when we know that there were about 1,000 to 1200 men in each regiment. The book **Statistiskt Sammandrag af Svenska Indelningsverket** (Statistical Digest of the Swedish Army System) gives the names of each ward— rotehåll, rusthåll, and båtsmanshåll — having an alphabetical index of each of these. This makes it fairly easy to find what company and regiment a certain farm was assigned. Not all farms participated in this system. This book is out of print but available on microfilm at the Genealogical Society library with the call number 084652.

Enlisted Regiments

If a soldier cannot be found in any of the regiments of his province—infantry, cavalry or navy--he may have joined one of the enlisted regiments.

These were located in the cities — mainly Stockholm — the enlisted man was a full time soldier, not bound to the land or ward.

Additional Military Records

The Royal War Archives houses, among others, the accounts that every regiment sent annually to the crown or department of defense. The word account ought not to scare us off in using them. They contain much more than figures. In them may be found the salaries of all officers, high and low, at the regiment, their advancement, discharge and sometimes death dates. Included would also be a land record of all land and homes, houses and crofts under the regiment. Receipts of salaries would also be found, and in time of war, which was often, the wife signed the receipt of her warring husband. At last may be included a roll of every soldier with careful notes about death dates and places of those slain.

The Army Pension records 1757-1880 with an index and the Army Veteran's Register (Vadstena Krigsmanshus) 1639-1865 also contain valuable genealogical information. The Navy Pension rolls contain information about both officers and common navy men 1642-1937. They are very bulky, not registered, and very slow to use.

Also available and arranged in alphabetical order is an excellent biographical collection of notes, newspaper clippings, obituaries, etc., of army officers and civilian personnel in the army 1656-1955.

The Navy Pension Fund received certain income from passenger fees. The person applying for a passport had to pay a special fee, which was recorded together with the name of the person. This record is fairly complete and it is a simple matter to check those who went abroad 1790-1850.

All muster rolls and the additional records mentioned in this chapter are microfilmed and available at the Genealogical Society.

The Soldier Names

For many researchers the custom of soldiers taking or being assigned a new name, when entering the service, is most frustrating. The patronymic name was very rarely kept after 1750 and seldom before that time. However, upon leaving the service a man may or may not keep his soldier name. His children, as a rule, took the patronymic name, so that the son of Erik Asp called himself by the surname of Eriksson (Ersson).

If a soldier switched from one ward to another or from the army to the navy, he also exchanged his former soldier name for a new one. All this means that when searching the military records, you have to go slowly and prove every step.

Military Definitions

We will end this chapter with some typical Swedish military definitions.

avsked — discharged

båtsman — allotment seaman, sailor, marine, infantryman on ship.

dragon—dragoon—infantryman on horseback—fought on foot as a rule — differed in name and uniform only from the light cavalryman.

förare — noncommissioned staff officer of lower rank.

förstärkningskarl or förstärkningsman — conscript reserve soldier.

gardist — soldier at one of the King's Guards.
gratial — pension to a soldier from the army through Vadstena Krigsmanshus.
gratialist — soldier receiving "gratial" pension.
grenadjär, grenadier — elite infantryman, combined into grenadier regiments.
husar, hussar — light cavalryman.
karabinjär — marksman on horseback and later part of the heavy cavalry.
kavallerist — cavalry man
korpralskap — corporalship, squad of about 25 men commanded by a corporal.
livgardist — soldier at the King's Guard — the King himself commander-in-chief of all regiments and companies having the word **liv** as the first part of the name.
major — major.
männing — a special regiment in time of war — made up from the regular wards with 3-männingsregiment, which meant that every three wards together had to furnish one soldier (beyond the regular soldier). There were also 4-männings and 5-männingsregiment, where every four or five wards had to furnish an extra soldier.
mönsterrulla — muster roll.
regementsräkenskaper — regimental accounts.
reservkarl — reserve soldier.
rote — ward or fine, subdivision of parish.
rusthåll — ward or fine for the purpose of raising and supporting one soldier.
rusthållare — farmer who was a member of the ward raising the cavalry soldier.
ryttare — cavalryman.
ryttartorp — cavalry soldier's croft.
ryttmästare — captain in the cavalry.
soldattorp — soldier's croft
vargeringsman — reserve soldier.
värvad — enlisted.
överste — colonel.
överstelöjtnant — lieutenant-colonel.

Chapter 15

Genealogical Associations, Magazines And Printed Books

There are two outstanding associations interested in genealogical research in Sweden. They are The Genealogical Association (Genealogiska Föreningen) and The Family History Association (Personhistoriska Samfundet).

The Genealogical Association (Genealogiska Föreningen).

This organization was founded in 1933 and has as its objective "the promotion of Swedish genealogical research and the creating of interest for the same." Its headquarters are located in the former National Archives in Stockholm, with the address: Genealogiska Föreningen, Arkivgatan 3, S-111 28 Stockholm, Sweden. It has local organizations in the cities of Göteborg and Malmö. Total membership runs about 2,000, scattered in all of Sweden. A list of the names and addresses of all the association members was published in its quarterly magazine, "Släkt och Hävd" (Family and Origin) Volume 2-3, 1970.

The magazine was started in 1934 under the name of "Genealogiska Föreningens Medlemsblad", but in 1950 the name was changed to the present title. Every volume contains a list of additions to the association archive, many of them being more or less elaborate family genealogies and histories just published.

The association has a large index of family names (Släktnamnsregistret), and a geographical index (Geografiska registret) divided into provinces (landskap), cities (städer), districts (härader, tingslag or skeppslag), which refers to literature about the families in the area. This geographical index is still small and very incomplete.

The call numbers to the index of family names (Släktnamnsregistret) on microfilm at the Genealogical Society libraries are as follows:

Aab-Botzaeus	383557
Bouch-Ehrström	383558
Eich-Gröönfelt	383559

Guagnius-Jörstad	383560
Kaagh-Lundsten	383561
Lundsten-Pötter	383562
Quaase-Smitt	383563
Smitt-Uttini	383564
Vacano-Öttingen	383565

The call number to the geographical index is 383566.

An index of authors of genealogical literature is also listed under the call number 383565.

The Family History Association (Personhistoriska Samfundet).

As the name indicates, this organization is more interested in the history of the individual person or family, while The Genealogical Association puts the stress more on the genealogical facts of a person or family. The headquarters are located in the National Archives. Research results are published in the association quarterly, called "Personhistorisk Tidskrift", published since 1898. The general index of this publication contains more than 40,000 names. It is available on microfilm at the Genealogical Society libraries with call numbers:

Aaby-Benedictus	254961
Bengt-Erik	254962
Erikska-Ingolphus	254963
Ingrid-Mikkola	254964
Miley-Sköring	254965
Sladerbach-Öström	254966

Printed books

1. **Family Histories** are constantly being written, rewritten and printed. The Swedish Genealogical Association probably owns the largest collection found. In the Genealogical Society library in Salt Lake City are found printed histories of the following Swedish families:

Afzelius	Armfelt	Berggren	Bonnier
Ahnfelt	Aschan	Bergh	Bowallius
Albin	Aspegren	Berg Von Linde	Bratt
Alm	Asplund		Bröms
Almen	Bagge	Bernadotte	Bursie
Aminoff	Barnekow	Billman	Bågenholm
Anjou	Beckman	Bjuggren	Cederberg
Apell	Belfrage	Blomgren	Chace
Arfwedson	Bergengren	Bohnsack	Christiernsson

Clauson
Colliander
Dahlerus
Dahlström
Danckwardt
Danielsson
Dedering
Durling
Edgren
Edh
Esseen
Fahlander
Falk
Falkenberg
Falkman
Franzen
Frestare
Frick
Fries
Fryckbom
Fröding
Fågelberg
Geijer
Gellerstedt
Grau
Grotenfelt
Gustafsson
Göhle
Hamilton
Hammar
Hammarskjöld
Hedberg
Hedborg
Heijkenskjöld
Heraeus
Hermelin
Heurlin
Hillgren
Hjorth
Hoberg
Hoving
Hummel

Hünner
Kempe
Kexsund
Kindgren
Kjellberg
Klemming
Klint
Kyronius
Lagerberg
Lagerborg
Lagerheim
Landby
Laurin
Leberg
Leijonmarck
Lewenhaupt
Lindblad
Lindh
Linton
Livijn
Löfgren
Lundberg
Lundskog
Lundström
Lyth
Malmsten
Melin
Mellgren
Mendling
Meurling
Moberg
Munthe
Möller
Mörner
Nobel
Nordenfeldt
Nordenskjöld
Nordwall
Noreen
Norman
Norraeus
Nycander

Palme
Pauli
Poignant
Ponten
Qvist
Rehbinder
Rhen
Richert
Roempke
Rosell
Rosenhoff
Rothlöben
Runeberg
Ruths
Sandegren
Santesson
Sasse
Schalander
Schiultz
Schough
Schram
Schulman
Settergren
Silfverstolpe
Skjelderup
Skragge
Sonden
Stark
Strindberg
Sundblad
Sundström
Svedbom
Söderbaum
Söderhielm
Söderström
Taube
Thyselius
Toren
Tranchell
Tybeck
Törncrantz

Uggla
Unander
Unger
Vahlenberg
Vasa
Von Braun
Von Essen
Von Konow
Von Königsmarck
Von Lost
Von Platen
Von Post
Von Schulmann
Von Segebaden
Von Sydow
Von Warnstedt
Wachtmeister
Waern
Wallin
Wallwik
Warnstedt
Weidenhielm
Weidman
Weman
Wendt
Wennström
Wernsted
Westmüller
Westerlund
Westman
Wichman
Wilskman
Wulff
Zielfelt
Ziervogel
Zingmark
Åkerhielm
Åmark
Östrand

2. The histories of the ministers are written in each diocese (stift) in The Shepherd Memorials (Herdaminne), giving a short history of each minister serving within the diocese from before the Lutheran reformation in the beginning of the 1500's up to recent days. Available at the Genealogical Society are the following Memorials, indicating number of volumes and indexes available:

Name of Book	Index	No. of Vols.
1) Göteborg Stifts Herdaminne	Index	1
2) Göteborgs Stift 1885-1949	Index	1
3) Hernösands Stifts Herdaminne	Index (Vol. 4)	4
4) Karlstads Stifts Herdaminne 2&3	Index in each	3
5) Linköpings Stifts Herdaminne	No Index	4
6) Lunds Stifts Herdaminne	No Index Register of Parishes, arranged according to Parish	9
7) Skara Stifts Herdaminne	Index (Vol. II)	Volume I (Book) Volume II (Film)
	Supplement for subsequent years (1871-1903)	
8) Strengnäs Stifts Herdaminne	Index (Vol. 4)	4
9) Upsala Ärkestifts Herdaminne	Index (Vol. 4)	4
10) Visby Stifts Herdaminne	Index	1
11) Västerås Herdaminne	Vol. I Part I with Index	
12) Växjö Stifts Herdaminne	Index (Vol. 8)	8

3. The biographical encyclopedias deal mainly with the more prominent families within Sweden from way back until or up to our day. We will list the more common ones with the warning, that the information contained in them may be neither correct nor complete. However, as a guide in our research they fill a very useful and timesaving purpose. They are:

O. C. Ahlström, Norrländska släkter, Ostersund, 1890.
J. G. Anrep, Svenska Adelns Ättartaflor, Stockholm, 1958.
G. M. Elgenstierna, Den introducerade svenska adelns ättartavlor, Stockholm, 1935.
K. A. Leijonhufvud, Ny Svensk släktbok, Stockholm, 1901.

E.G. Swartz, Genealogia Gothica, Stockholm, 1930
Biographiskt Lexicon, Upsala, 1835
Svenska Släktkalendern, Stockholm, 1895.
Svenskt Biografiskt Lexikon, Stockholm, 1918

To this collection of biographical works may also be added the Palmsköld library of Swedish families 1130-1712, listed with the following call numbers at the Genealogical Society libraries:

A—Bere	277693
Bern—Bli	277694
Blo-Bü	277695
C—Cyg	277696
D—Em	277697
En—Gode	277698
Godi—Hår	277699
Hård—Ju	277700
K—Leh	277701
Lej—Mel	277702
Mem—Oxenstierna	277703
Pa—Reuterk	277704
Reuterk—Sch	277705
Sch—Stierne	277706
Stiernh—Ty	277707
U—Ö	277708
A—W	277709

Among the reference books we suggest the following two:

J.A. Almquist, Swedish genealogical literature, Stockholm, 1905, which is a catalogue of authors and their works, covering more than 3,000 families by surnames.

S.O. Brenner, Personhistoriska källor för Skåne, Halland och Blekinge, Malmö, 1967, giving a list of all genealogical sources for the three provinces mentioned in the title.

4. History of counties and provinces are found in a lot of printed books, periodicals, county histories, directories, and cultural magazines etc. These are all of great help in learning the history of the area in which we do research. They are somewhat time consuming in using, but the information found is usually of great use and interest to our research, giving hints and clues of geographical names, movements of people, the beginning of factories, mills etc.

We should take time to thumb and browse through these records. Information in the printed volumes should not be accepted as correct, when it comes to birth dates, etc. Let the printed material be guide posts along the trail, but use the original records as the final answer, so that you may feel fully satisfied that you have as correct information as it is possible to find.

APPENDIX A

List of Swedish And Finnish Army Units

Abbreviations: Art. Artillery Drag. Dragoon Ing. Engineers Kungl. Royal
Bat. Battlion Inf. Infantry Kav. Cavalry Mar. Navy or Marin Sj. Hospital

Branch	Name	Available Records
Kav.	Adelsfanorna	1684-1743
Inf.	Adlercreutzska inf. reg.	1804-1806
Inf.	Adlerfelts inf. reg.	1721-1736
Inf.	Andra gardesregementet	1792
Inf.	Andra livgardet	1812-1874
Inf.	Andra livgrenadjärregementet	1817-1883
Mar.	Armens flotta	1766-1817
Art.	Artilleriregementet	1681-1794
Inf.	Bergsregementet	1716-1720
Inf.	Björnbergs inf. reg. (Karl)	1763-1770
Inf.	Björneborgs läns inf. reg.	1712-1804
Kav.	Blåa husarregementet	1761-1764
Inf.	Blåa regementet	1698-1701
Inf.	Blixens inf. reg.	1767-1777
Drag.	Bohusläns dragonregemente	1737-1789
Drag.	Bohusläns dragonbataljon	1689-1720
Inf.	Bohusläns regemente	1680-1884
Inf.	Bousquests inf. reg.	1737-1744
Inf.	Bremiska inf. reg.	1709
Inf.	Cajana jägarbataljon	1740-1800
Kav.	Cederströms husarregemente	1816-1822
Inf.	Cronhielms inf. reg.	1757-1759
Inf.	Cronhielms inf. reg.	1763
Inf.	Cronhiorts inf. reg.	1750-1754
Inf.	Dalregementet	1691-1884
Inf.	Dankwardts inf. reg.	1797
Inf.	De la Gardies livländska inf. reg.	1700-1706
Inf.	Disciplinkompaniet	1873-1887
Inf.	Dohnas inf. reg.	1728-1737
Kav.	Drabanter (Kungl. Majestäts)	1686-1697
Inf.	Drottningens livregemente till fot	1722-1814
Inf.	Drottningens livregemente till fot	1689-1694
Kav.	Drottningens livregemente till häst	1693-1699
Drag.	Dückers preussiska dragoner	1705
Inf.	Elbingska inf. reg.	1704-1711
Inf.	Engelbrechtens inf. reg.	1797-1814
Kav.	Estniska lantdragonerna	1701
Inf.	Fabritius sammanslagna bataljon	1759
Art.	Finska artilleriregementet	1795-1810
Inf.	Finska gardesregementet	1803-1808
Drag.	Finska lantdragonerna	1712-1721
Drag.	Finska lätta dragonkåren	1771
Inf.	Flemings inf. reg. (Fredrik)	1778-1788
Ing.	Fortifikationsstaten	1735-1841
Inf.	Franska frikåren	1762
Inf.	Fredrik Adolfs inf. reg. (Prins)	1763-1770
Inf.	Fyrverkarkåren	1849-1872
Inf.	Första livgardet	1792
Inf.	Första livgrenadjärregementet	1818-1884
Inf.	De la Gardies livländska inf. reg.	1700-1706
Inf.	Garnisonsregementet i Göteborg	1724-1744
Inf.	Garnisonsregementet i Stralsund	1691-1702
Inf.	Garnisonsregementet i Stade	1695
Inf.	Garnisonsregementet i Wismar	1687-1710

Branch	Name	Available Records
Sj.	Garnisonssjukhuset	1813-1887
Inf.	Gotländska beväringen	1811-1883
Kav.	Gula husarregementet	1762-1764
Inf.	Gustafs inf. reg. (Prins)	1749
Inf.	Guvernörsregementet i Wismar	1691-1702
Inf.	Gyllengranats inf. reg.	1773
Inf.	Gyllenströms finska inf. bat.	1712
Art.	Göta artilleriregemente	1795-1884
Inf.	Göta gardesregemente	1794-1804
Inf.	Göta livgarde	1894
Inf.	Halländska regementet till fot	1712-1719
Inf.	Hamiltons inf. reg. (Axel Hugo)	1760
Inf.	Hamiltons inf. reg. (Gustav David)	1742-1757
Inf.	Hessensteins inf. reg.	1748-1769
Inf.	Hintzensterns inf. bat.	1790-1791
Inf.	Horns inf. reg. (Bengt)	1732-1735
Inf.	Horns inf. reg. (Ture Sigismund)	1724
Kav.	Horns husarregemente	1799-1801
Kav.	Husarregementet Konung Karl XV	1861-1881
Inf.	Hälsinge regemente	1684-1884
Inf.	Hälsinge, Gästriklands och Jämtlands tre, fyr-och femmänningsbataljon till fot	1711-1717
Inf.	Infanteribataljonen i Stade	1695
Ing.	Ingeniörkåren	1859-1881
Drag.	Ingermanländska dragonerna	1712
Kav.	Jägarkåren till häst	1759-1762
Kav.	Jämtlands dragonregemente	1686-1787
Inf.	Jägerhorns inf. reg.	1801-1805
Inf.	Jämtlands fältjägarregemente	1820-1885
Kav.	Jämtlands hästjägarkår	1836-1886
Inf.	Jämtlands regemente	1789-1817
Inf.	Jönköpings regemente	1686-1885
Inf.	Kajana jägarbataljon	1740-1800
Inf.	Kalmar regemente	1683-1886
Drag.	Karelska dragonregementet	1685-1806
Inf.	Karelska jägarkåren	1789-1806
Inf.	Karls livregemente till fot (Prins)	1683-1696
Inf.	Karl XII:s grenadjärbataljon	1719
Inf.	Klingstedts sammansatta inf. reg. i Wismar	1713
Inf.	Koloni eller Blå regementet	1695-1698
Inf.	Konungens Eget värvade reg.	1773-1829
Kav.	Konung Karl XV:s husarregemente	1861-1881
Kav.	Konungens värvade husarregemente	1860
Inf.	Kronobergs regemente	1686-1886
Kav.	Kronprinsens husarregemente	1828-1885
Inf.	Kronprinsens inf. reg.	1753-1770
Kav.	Kungliga Majestätets drabanter	1686-1697
Inf.	Köhlers jägarkompani	1762
Inf.	Landskrona garnisonskompani	1831-1858
Inf.	Lantingshausens inf. reg.	1749
Inf.	Lewenhaupts inf. reg.	1688
Inf.	Liewens livländska inf. reg.	1709
Drag.	Livdragonregementet	1700-1785
Inf.	Livgarde (Göta)	1894
Inf.	Livgardet (Andra)	1812-1874
Inf.	Livgardet (Första)	1792
Inf.	Livgardet till fot	1686-1791
Kav.	Livgardet till häst	1808-1885
Inf.	Livgrenadjärregementet	1793-1815
Inf.	Livgrenadjärregementet (Andra)	1817-1883
Inf.	Livgrenadjärregementet (Första)	1818-1884

Branch	Name	Available Records
Kav.	Livhusarregementet	1793-1795
Kav.	Livländska dragonregementet	1703-1707
Kav.	Livregementsbrigadens Cuirassierer	1795-1814
Kav.	Livregementsbrigadens lätta dragonkår	1795-1804
Inf.	Livregementsbrigadens lätta inf. bat.	1793-1806
Inf.	Livregementsbrigadens värvade lätta inf. bat.	1793-1801
Kav.	Livregementets dragoner	1816-1886
Inf.	Livregementets grenadjärer	1818-1882
Kav.	Livregementets husarer	1807-1885
Kav.	Livregementets kyrassiärer	1795-1814
Inf.	Livregemente till fot (Drottningens Ulrika Eleonora)	1722-1814
Inf.	Livregemente till fot (Drottningens Ulrika Eleonora)	1689-1694
Inf.	Livregemente till fot (Prins Karls)	1683-1696
Inf.	Livregemente till fot (Svenska värvade)	1706-1710
Inf.	Livregemente till fot (Tyska)	1690-1699
Inf.	Livregemente till fot (Änkedrottningens Hedvig Eleonora i Pommern)	1687-1710
Inf.	Livregemente till fot (Änkedrottningens Lovisa Ulrika)	1773-1805
Kav.	Livregemente till häst (Drottningens)	1693-1699
Kav.	Livregemente till häst (Riksänkedrottningens)	1689-1715
Kav.	Livregementet till häst	1683-1791
Kav.	Lätta dragonkåren	1774-1791
Kav.	Lätta dragonregementet	1798-1806
Inf.	Löwenfels inf. reg.	1759-1763
Inf.	Malmö garnisonsregemente	1695-1703
Inf.	Marinregementet	1874
Inf.	Mellins estniska inf. reg.	1706-1709
Inf.	Meyerfeldtska friskyttekåren	1789-1791
Kav.	Mörners husarregemente	1768-1797
Kav.	Mörners husarregemente	1803-1814
Inf.	Nerkes regemente	1819-1884
Inf.	Nerke-Värmlands regemente	1684-1811
Inf.	Nerke-Värmlands tremänningsregemente till fot	1713-1719
Inf.	Norra skånska inf. reg.	1818-1883
Kav.	Norra skånska kavalleriregementet	1791-1809
Inf.	Norrbottens inf. reg.	1843-1886
Inf.	Nylands inf. reg.	1689-1804
Inf.	Nylands jägarbataljon	1795-1806
Drag.	Nylands lätta dragonkår	1795-1806
Drag.	Nylands och Tavastehus dragonregemente	1735-1789
Kav.	Nylands och Tavastehus fördubblingskav.	1678
Kav.	Nylands och Tavastehus läns kavalleriregemente	1712-1721
Drag.	Pommerska dragonerna	1703-1708
Inf.	Pommerska inf. reg.	1691-1710
Inf.	Pommerska invalidkåren	1792-1806
Kav.	Pommerska kavalleriregementet	1694-1702
Inf.	Pommerska legionens inf. kår	1813
Kav.	Pommerska legionens kavallerikår	1813-1814
Inf.	Pontoniärbataljonen	1869-1881
Inf.	Posses inf. reg. (Karl)	1721-1726
Inf.	Posses inf. reg. (Mauritz)	1750-1759
Inf.	Psilanderhielms inf. reg.	1781-1795
Kav.	Putbus husarregemente	1761-1764
Inf.	Regiment du Roi	1809
Inf.	Regiment Royal Suedois	1814-1815
Inf.	Rigiska garnisonsregementet	1696-1701
Inf.	Rigiska guvernementsinfanteriet	1696-1701
Kav.	Riksänkedrottningens livregemente till häst	1689-1715
Inf.	Ruthensparres inf. reg.	1744-1748
Inf.	Sachsiska inf. reg.	1707-1721
Inf.	Saltzas inf. reg.	1776-1784

Branch	Name	Available Records
Inf.	Saltzas inf. reg.	1773
Inf.	Sandelska jägarkåren	1789-1790
Inf.	Savolaks fotjägarregemente	1771-1806
Inf.	Savolaks inf. reg.	1769
Inf.	Savolaks lätta inf. reg.	1775-1804
Inf.	Savolaks och Nyslotts läns inf. reg.	1712-1721
Inf.	Schwartzers jägarkompani	1761
Inf.	Schwengelns livländska inf. reg.	1704
Inf.	Schwerins inf. reg.	1725-1729
Drag.	Schwerins dragonregemente	1711
Inf.	Schwerins inf. reg.	1740-1754
Inf.	Skaraborgs frikår	1789-1789
Inf.	Skaraborgs regemente	1687-1885
Inf.	Skyttes inf. reg.	1775-1776
Kav.	Skånska dragonregementet	1823-1883
Kav.	Skånska husarregementet	1807-1885
Kav.	Skånska husarskyttekåren	1760-1761
Kav.	Skånska karabinjärregementet	1806-1820
Kav.	Skånska ståndsdragonerna	1716-1721
Kav.	Skånska tremänningskavallerireg.	1710-1720
Kav.	Smålands dragonregemente	1804-1821
Inf.	Smålands femmänningsregemente till fot	1710-1719
Inf.	Smålands grenadjärbataljon	1824-1883
Kav.	Smålands husarregemente	1824-1884
Kav.	Smålands kavalleriregemente	1692-1798
Inf.	Smålands tremänningsregemente till fot	1719
Inf.	Smålands tre och femmänningsregemente till fot	1720-1722
Inf.	Spens inf. reg.	1750-1763
Inf.	Sprengtportens inf. reg.	1767-1795
Inf.	Stackelbergs livländska inf. reg.	1704
Inf.	Stackelbergs inf. reg.	1789-1799
Inf.	Stedingks inf. reg.	1790-1801
Kav.	Stockholms stads borgerskap till häst	1740-1800
Inf.	Storamiralens regemente	1790
Inf.	Stralsundska garnisonsregementet	1721
Art.	Svea artilleriregemente	1795-1885
Inf.	Svea livgarde	1794-1874
Inf.	Svenska gardesregementet	1806-1807
Inf.	Svenska grenadjärbataljonen	1760
Inf.	Svenska värvade livregementet till fot	1706-1710
Inf.	Södermanlands regemente	1686-1883
Inf.	Södra skånska inf. reg.	1818-1885
Kav.	Södra skånska kavalleriregementet	1710-1803
Kav.	Taubes dragonregemente	1704-1705
Inf.	Tavastehus inf. reg.	1712-1805
Kav.	Tyska dragonregementet	1716-1721
Inf.	Tyska grenadjärbataljonen	1806
Inf.	Tyska grenadjärbataljonen (Andra)	1761
Inf.	Tyska grenadjärbataljonen (Första)	1761
Inf.	Tyska livregementet till fot	1690-1699
Inf.	Uleåborgs lätta inf. reg.	1790
Inf.	Upplands femmänningsregemete till fot	1713-1719
Inf.	Upplands regemente	1684-1881
Kav.	Upplands ståndsdragoner	1704-1721
Inf.	Upplands tremänningsregemente till fot	1719
Kav.	Upplands tremänningskavalleriregemente	1715-1719
Kav.	Upplands tre-och femmänningskavalleriregemente	1710-1721
Inf.	Wachtmeisters inf. reg.	1786-1788
Art.	Wendes artilleriregemente	1795-1886
Inf.	Viborgs /Kymmenegårds/ läns inf. reg.	1716-1789
Inf.	Willebrands inf. reg.	1739

Branch	Name	Available Records
Kav.	Wrangels husarregemente	1762-1764
Inf.	Värmlands fältjägarkår	1790-1883
Inf.	Värmlands regemente	1819-1884
Inf.	Västgöta-Dals regemente	1683-1882
Drag.	Västgöta dragonregemente	1802-1805
Inf.	Västgöta fry-och femmänningsregemente till fot	1712-1719
Kav.	Västgöta kavalleriregemente	1685-1798
Inf.	Västgöta regemente	1817-1879
Kav.	Västgöta ståndsdragoner	1709-1716
Inf.	Västgöta tremänningsregemente till fot	1713-1721
Kav.	Västgöta tre-och femmänningskavallerireg.	1708-1721
Inf.	Västerbottens regemente	1689-1886
Inf.	Västmanlands regemente	1684-1885
Inf.	Västra skånska regementet till fot	1713-1721
Kav.	Zelowske kosackkåren	1790
Inf.	Åbo inf. reg.	1690-1804
Kav.	Åbo och Björneborgs kav. reg.	1712-1721
Inf.	Älvsborgs regemente	1683-1881
Inf.	Änkedrottningens livregemente i Pommern	1687-1710
Inf.	Änkedrottningens livregemente till fot	1773-1805
Kav.	Öselska lantdragonerna	1703-1704
Inf.	Österbottens regemente	1698-1802
Kav.	Östgöta kavalleriregemente	1684-1791
Inf.	Östgöta och Södermanlands tremänningsregemente till fot	1715-1721
Inf.	Östgöta regemente till fot	1684-1790
Inf.	Östra skånska regementet till fot	1713-1721

APPENDIX B

Swedish Probate Records With Indexes

District or City	Probate Years	Record Index G.S. Call No.	Earliest available record
BLEKINGE COUNTY			
Bräkne			1738
Karlshamn			1683
Karlskrona			1765
Lister	1725-1850	555247	1725
Medelstad			1699
Sölvesborg			1773
Östra			1737
GOTLAND COUNTY			
Gotlands Norra	1644-1800	133352	1644
	1644-1800	133353	
	1644-1800	133354	
	1651-1851	133355	
Gotlands Södra			1737
	1737-1828	133298	
	1829-1839	133299	
	1838-1849	133300	
	1849-1874	133301	
	1850-1907	133302	
Visby	1657-1788	383455	1718
GÄVLEBORG COUNTY			
Gästrikland	(Abe-Jan) 1710-1851	383456	1710
	(Jan-Olo) 1710-1851	383457	
	(Olo-Öve) 1710-1851	383458	
Gävle			1655
Alfta			1758
Arbrå			1757
Bergsjö			1738
Bollnäs			1763
Delsbo			1752
Enånger			1748
Forsa			1736
Hamrånge			1853
Hanebo			1759
Hedesunda	1851-1861	383459	1851
Hille			1853
Hudiksvall			1709
Järvsö	1762-1849	383460	1762
Ljusdal	1758-1780	383461	1758
Norrala	1718-1876	383462	1718
Ockelbo			1853
Ovansjö			1853
Söderhamn	1718-1839	383455	1718
Torsåker			1853
Valbo			1853
Årsunda			1853
Österfärnebo	1851-1861	383459	1851
GÖTEBORG OCH BOHUS COUNTY			
Askim	1713-1887	131325	1713
Bullaren			1824
Göteborg	1698-1856	216192	1696

District or City	Probate Years	Record Index G.S. Call No.	Earliest available record
GÖTEBORG OCH BOHUS COUNTY (CONTINUED)			
Inlands Fräkne	1743-1899	131706	1790
Inlands Norde	1746-1900	131576	1764
Inlands Södre	1704-1900	131452	1704
Inlands Torpe	1719-1900	131648	1786
Kungälv			1617
Kville			1752
Lane			1801
Marstrand			1769
Norrviken	1720-1840	132091	1692
Orust och Tjörn	1737-1842	132258	1700
Sunnerviken	1738-1833	132638	1738
Sävedal	1727-1887	132423	1727
Tanum			1824
Uddevalla			1724
Vette			1825
Västra Hising	1723-1887	132866	1723
östra Hising	1713-1823	131325	1713
	1824-1887	132866	
HALLAND COUNTY			
Fauräs			1721
Fjäre			1703
Halmstad			1689
Himle			1719
Hök	1686-1850	483572	1686
Tönnersjö			1679
Viske			1742
Årstad			1707
JÄMTLAND COUNTY			
Jämtland	1786-1797	134523	
Berg	1741-1841	134524	1741
Brunflo	1741-1839	134524	1741
Hallen	1741-1849	134524	1830
Hammerdal	1741-1910	134524	1759
Hede	1741-1841	134524	1757
Lit	1741-1912	134525	1741
Offerdal	1740-1878	134525	1740
Oviken	1736-1839	134525	1736
Ragunda	1741-1839	134524	1741
Revsund	1741-1839	134524	1741
Rödön	1741-1912	134525	1741
Sunne	1748-1849	134525	1768
Sveg	1741-1841	134524	1743
Undersåker	1741-1829	134525	1741
JÖNKÖPING COUNTY			
Gränna	1739-1904	254926	1739
Jönköping			1755
Mo	1736-1810	254915	1736
Norra Vedbo	1690-1820	254915	1690
Södra Vedbo	1820-1849	254915	1820
Tveta	1737-1820	254915	1711
Vista	1749-1820	254915	1749
Västbo	1740-1820	254916	1740
Västra	1738-1820	254917	1738
östbo	1758-1786	254918	1835
östra	1744-1820	254918	1772

District or City	Probate Record Index Years	G.S. Call No.	Earliest available record
KALMAR COUNTY			
Aspeland	1699-1829	254919	1699
Handbörd	1703-1829	254919	1703
Kalmar	1643-1832	254927	1643
Norra Möre	1706-1820	254920	1706
Sevede	1693-1822	254921	1693
Stranda	1712-1829	254922	1712
Södra Möre	1767-1820	254921	1767
Tjust	1685-1800	254922	1685
	1800-1875	276822	
Tunalän	1699-1821	254923	1699
Vimmerby	1767-1852	254928	1759
Västervik	1672-1860	254929	1672
Ölands Norra Mot	1739-1820	254924	1739
Ölands Södra Mot	1730-1820	254924	1730
KOPPARBERG COUNTY			
North and Central	1783-1801	140325	1783
Gagnef parish		140326	1795
Leksand, Ål, Bjursås parishes		140327	1786
Rättvik, Ore parishes			1784
Falun	1727-1841	383451	1727
Floda			1657
Folkare			1735
Gagnef			1818
Grangärde			1622
Hedemora			1726
Husby			1736
Kopparberg och Aspeboda			1790
Leksand			1818
Malung			1734
Norrbärke			1719
Nås			1808
Rättvik			1818
Rättvik parish			1695
Stora Skedvi			1799
Stora Tuna			1816
Sundborn			1780
Svärdsjö			1781
Säter city	1666-1830	383452	1666
Säter district			1733
Söderbärke			1691
Torsång			1781
Vika			1781
KRISTIANSTAD COUNTY			
Albo	1711-1850	271182	1711
Bjäre			1677
Gärd	1708-1850	271183	1716
Ingelstad	1700-1840	271182	1700
Järrestad	1707-1839	271182	1707
Kristianstad			1642
Norra Åsbo			1677
Simrishamn			1643
Södra Åsbo			1657
Villand	1712-1840	271183	1712
Västra Göinge	1680-1810	143131	1690
	1811-1850	143161	
Ängelholm			1709
Östra Göinge	1706-1840	271183	1706

District or City		Probate Years	Record Index G.S. Call No.	Earliest available record
KRONOBERG COUNTY				
Allbo		1739-1821	143516	1739
Kinnevald		1752-1829	143731	1739
Konga	(A-H)	1777-1821	143904	1710
	(H-P)	1777-1821	143905	
	(P-Ö)	1777-1821	143906	
Norrvidinge		1759-1829	144058	1759
Sunnerbo		1800-1831	144350	1758
Uppvidinge		1800-1827	144556	1756
Växjö		1725-1857	144715	1725
MALMÖHUS COUNTY				
Bara		1664-1841	145063	1664
Falsterbo				1707
Frosta		1677-1841	271185	1709
Färs		1698-1842	271185	1698
Harjager		1688-1839	145697	1688
Herrestad		1759-1839	271185	1763
Hälsingborg				1661
Landskrona				1619
Ljunits		1754-1839	271185	1772
Luggude		1677-1850	483573	1677
Lund				1660
Malmö		1546-1960	146482	1546
Onsjö				1705
Oxie		1811-1850	146840	1690
Rönneberg				1677
Skanör				1707
Skytts		1677-1850	147308	1677
Torna		1678-1840	147582	1678
Vemmenhög		1681-1840	271185	1681
Ystad				1611
NORRBOTTEN COUNTY				
Arjeplog		1721-1876	383491	1821
Arvidsjaur		1743-1876	383492	1793
Enonteki		1806-1869	383493	1806
Gällivare		1753-1849	383494	1810
Jokkmokk				1762
Jukkasjärvi		1784-1862	383495	1783
Karesuando, see Enonteki				
Karl Gustaf	(A-M)	1763-1862	383499	1763
	(N-ö)	1763-1862	383500	
Luleå		1731-1830	383496	1691
		1696-1893	383490	1698
Nederkalix		1710-1859	383497	1777
Nederluleå		1824-1840	383498	1731
Nedertorneå	(A-M)	1763-1862	383499	1763
	(N-ö)	1763-1862	383500	
Pajala		1814-1862	383501	1824
Piteå		1693-1851	383502	1777
		1689-1852	383503	1786
Råneå		1756-1858	383504	1775
Överkalix		1777-1864	383505	1777
Överluleå				1831
Övertorneå		1774-1860	383506	1692
SKARABORG COUNTY				
Barne		1749-1859	182478	1749
Binneberg		1737-1860	434329	1737

District or City		Probate Record Index Years	G.S. Call No.	Earliest available record
		SKARABORG COUNTY (CONTINUED)		
Dimbo		1743-1860	434330	1743
Falköping				1807
Gudhem		1737-1860	434331	1740
Hasslerör		1719-1870	434332	1719
Hova		1738-1840	185697	1738
Kinne		1740-1840	185770	1740
Kinnefjärding		1737-1842	185828	1737
Kåkind		1736-1860	555239	1736
Kålland		1736-1841	189561	1736
Laske		1732-1862	189632	1732
Leaby		1748-1834	434333	1748
Lidköping				1661
Mariestad				1751
Skara				1727
Skänings		1733-1860	190277	1738
Skövde				1711
Slättäng		1749-1838	434334	1749
Valla		1737-1860	217965	1737
Valle		1738-1860	555240	1738
Vilske		1727-1851	435142	1727
Viste		1737-1859	435143	1737
Åse		1737-1859	435143	1748
		STOCKHOLM COUNTY		
Bro och Vätö				1758
Danderyd				1762
Frösåker				1747
Frötuna och Länna				1759
Färentuna				1743
Lyhundra				1739
Långhundra				1767
Norrtälje		1740-1829	383441	1740
Närdinghundra				1759
Seminghundra				1769
Sigtuna		1711-1889	383442	1711
Sjuhundra				1743
Sollentuna				1750
Sotholm				1768
Stockholm City	(A-L)	1578-1700	078580	1598
	(M-Ö)	1578-1700	078581	
	(A-G)	1701-1750	078582	
	(H-M)	1701-1750	078583	
	(N-Ö)	1701-1750	078584	
	(A-H)	1751-1775	078585	
	(H-R)	1751-1775	078586	
	(S-Ö)	1751-1775	078587	
	(A-N)	1776-1800	078588	
	(H-Q)	1776-1800	078589	
	(R-Ö)	1776-1800	078590	
Svartlösa				1762
Södertälje		1710-1839	383443	1710
Vallentuna				1699
Vaxholm				1753
Väddö och Häverö				1749
Värmdö				1750
Åker				1769
Ärlinghundra				1741
Öknebo				1718

District or City		Probate Years	Record Index G.S. Call No.	Earliest available record
STOCKHOLM COUNTY (CONTINUED)				
Öregrund				1810
Östhammar		1667-1846	383444	1667
SÖDERMANLAND COUNTY				
Daga				1746
Eskilstuna		1669-1833	383446	1669
Hölebo				1737
Jönåker				1766
Oppunda				1785
Rönö				1653
Selebo				1750
Strängnäs		1809-1914	194823	1669
Torshälla				1639
Trosa				1738
Villåttinge				1765
Väster Rekarne				1738
Åker				1719
Öster Rekarne				1735
UPPSALA COUNTY				
Bro		1737-1903	434379	1737
Bälinge				1742
Enköping		1628-1859	383445	1628
Films och Dannemora		1722-1883	434373	1772
		1883-1903	434378	
Hagunda				1695
Håbo		1681-1903	434380	1681
Lagunda		1884-1903	434378	1733
Lövsta		1738-1883	434374	1738
		1884-1903	434378	
Norunda		1744-1883	434371	1744
		1884-1903	434378	
Oland		1701-1883	434372	1796
		1884-1903	434378	
Rasbo				1683
Tierp		1757-1883	434375	1757
		1884-1903	434378	
Trögd		1737-1903	434381	1737
Ulleråker				1744
		1632-1899	434156	
Uppsala		1702-1819	169117	1632
Vaksala				1677
Vendel		1736-1883	434376	1736
		1884-1903	434378	
Västland		1716-1883	434377	1770
		1884-1903	434378	
Åsunda		1723-1903	434382	1723
Älvkarleby		1716-1883	434377	1716
		1884-1903	434378	
VÄRMLAND COUNTY				
Filipstad				1761
Fryksdal		1737-1842	434335	1737
Färnebo				1698
Gillberg		1737-1859	555241	1737
Grums		1719-1860	434336	1719
Jösse		1737-1860	555242	1737
Karlstad		1737-1860	213552	1737
Kil	(A-P)	1737-1860	435145	1737
	(Q-Ö)	1737-1860	213683	1737

District or City		Probate Record Index Years	G.S. Call No.	Earliest available record
VÄRMLAND COUNTY (CONTINUED)				
Kristinehamn				1758
Nordmark				1750
Nyed				1737
Näs				1729
Visnum		1736-1860	555243	1736
Väse		1751-1860	555244	1751
Älvdal				1690
Ölme		1739-1876	555245	1739
VÄSTERBOTTEN COUNTY				
Burträsk		1768-1863	383479	1792
Bygdeå		1737-1859	383480	1737
Degerfors		1769-1857	383481	1816
Lycksele		1765-1865	383482	1769
Lövånger	(A-O)	1731-1853	383483	1731
	(P-Ö)	1731-1853	383484	
Nordmaling		1752-1859	383485	1752
Nysätra		1834-1864	383486	1828
Skellefteå		1763-1869	383487	1798
Umeå		1612-1849	383488	1737
Åsele		1780-1897	383489	1750
VÄSTERNORRLAND COUNTY				
Arnäs		1759-1858	383464	1759
		1867-1880		
Boteå		1740-1855	383465	1742
Gudmundrå		1737-1896	383466	1737
Härnösand		1709-1870	383463	1709
Indal		1784-1785	383467	
Ljustorp		1814-1876	383467	
Nora		1751-1903	383468	1718
Nordingrå		1772-1896	383469	1772
Nätra		1777-1853	383470	1777
Ramsele		1737-1879	383471	1737
Selånger		1773-1881	383472	1774
Själevad		1773-1855	383473	1774
Skön		1774-1894	383474	
Sollefteå		1753-1852	383475	1753
Säbrå		1719-1868	383476	1719
Torp		1776-1840	383477	1775
Tuna		1783-1849	383478	1781
VÄSTMANLAND COUNTY				
Gamla Norberg				1770
Köping				1680
Norrbo				1751
Sala		1797-1848	181174	1678
Siende				1699
Simtuna				1727
Skinnskatteberg				1759
Snevringe				1629
Torstuna				1736
Tuhundra				1707
Vagnsbro				1770
Våla				1746
Västerås	(A-K)	1630-1841	383449	1630
	(L-Ö)	1630-1841	383450	
Yttertjurbo				1744
Åkerbo				1670

District or City	Probate Record Index Years	G.S. Call No.	Earliest available record
VÄSTMANLAND COUNTY (CONTINUED)			
övertjurbo			1739
ÄLVSBORG COUNTY			
Ale	1733-1833	084899	1733
Alingsås			1744
Bjärke	1736-1829	084899	1725
Bollebygd	1742-1842	085041	1742
Borås	1789-1876	311366	1791
Flundre	1831-1860	085128	1831
Gäsene	1712-1843	085244	1712
Kind	1736-1840	085587	1736
Kulling	1710-1840	157486	1710
Mark	1736-1839	157738	1738
Nordal	1736-1840	157851	1736
Redväg	1722-1841	166396	1722
Sundal	1736-1840	166539	1736
Tössbo	1709-1850	166621	1709
Ulricehamn	1689-1863	435141	1689
Valbo	1736-1839	166726	1694
Vedbo	1737-1859	171729	1683
Veden	1737-1840	171819	1737
Väne	1720-1842	171954	1720
Vänersborg			1831
Vättle			1734
Åmål	1691-1769	259746	1681
	1719-1859	259752	
Ås	1688-1843	179873	1688
ÖREBRO COUNTY			
Asker			1804
Askersund	1778-1790	195808	1764
Edsberg			1773
Fellingsbro			1760
Glanshammar			1772
Grimsten			1740
Grythytte och Hällefors			1760
Hardemo			1738
Karlskoga			1718
Kumla			1741
Lekebergslagen			1806
Linde och Ramsberg			1755
Nora city			1733
Nora och Hjulsjö			1763
Nya Kopparberg			1788
Sköllersta			1739
Sundbo			1742
örebro city	1635-1830	383447	1700
örebro district			1776
ÖSTERGÖTLAND COUNTY			
Aska	1702-1849	254902	1702
Bankekind	1736-1826	254903	1736
Björkekind	1750-1855	254904	1750
Boberg	1729-1850	254905	1729
Bråbo	1795-1858	254905	1796
Dal	1719-1850	254906	1719
Gullberg	1737-1834	254906	1737
Göstring	1738-1824	254906	1738
Hammarkind	1760-1820	254907	1760
Hanekind	1734-1819	254907	1734

District or City	Probate Record Years	Index G.S. Call No.	Earliest available record
ÖSTERGÖTLAND COUNTY (CONTINUED)			
Hällestad	1739-1809	254908	1739
Kinda	1737-1820	254908	1737
Linköping	1622-1830	254925	1622
Lysing	1688-1858	254909	1688
Lösing	1759-1809	254910	1759
Memming	1738-1818	254910	1738
Norrköping	1709-1900	152686	1711
Risinge	1750-1818	254910	1750
Skänninge	1742-1850	276823	1676
	1851-1888	254925	
Skärkind	1738-1818	254910	1738
Stegeborg	1742-1810	254911	1755
Söderköping	1614-1850	276823	1614
	1851-1854	254925	
Tjällmo (see Hällestad)			
Vadstena			1651
Valkebo	1743-1831	254911	1743
Vifolka	1747-1843	254912	1748
Ydre	1748-1822	254912	1748
Åkerbo	1737-1818	254913	1737
Östkind	1755-1821	254913	1755

APPENDIX C

An Alphabetical Index Of All Parishes In Sweden

The index is made up according to the Swedish alphabet, the letters å, ä, and ö following z as the last three letters of the alphabet.

The six columns contain the following information:

Column 1 — the original name of the parish as it was before the administrative reorganization of 1952.
Column 2 — the new name after the reorganization of 1952.
Column 3 — the name of the district (härad, tingslag, or skeppslag) under which the court records with probate records may be found.
Column 4 — the name of the county in which the parish is located.
Column 5 — the earliest year from which any birth, marriage and death records are available (original or microfilm).
Column 6 — the earliest year from which any clerical survey record is available.

ABBREVIATIONS:

Stads — city parish
Lands — rural parish
Ble — Blekinge
Got — Gotland
Gäv — Gävleborg
GoB — Göteborg och Bohus
Hal — Halland
Jäm — Jämtland
Jön — Jönköping
Kal — Kalmar
Kop — Kopparberg
Kri — Kristianstad
Kro — Kronoberg
Mal — Malmöhus
Nbt — Norrbotten
Ska — Skaraborg
Sto — Stockholm
Söd — Södermanland
Upp — Uppsala
Vär — Värmland
Vbn — Västerbotten
Vno — Västernorrland
Vma — Västmanland
Älv — Älvsborg
öre — örebro
öst — östergötland

Name of Parish		Name of		Earliest year of	
Before 1952	After 1952	District	County	Parish register	Clerical survey record
Abild	Årstad	Årstad	Hal	1716	1777
Acklinga	Dimbo	Vartofta	Ska	1648	1800
Adelsö	Ekerö	Färentuna	Sto	1688	1727
Adelöv	Linderås	Norra Vedbo	Jön	1689	1789
Adolf Fredrik	Adolf Fredrik	Stockholm	Sto	1741	1693
Agnetorp	Hökensås	Vartofta	Ska	1648	1774
Agunnaryd	Ryssby	Sunnerbo	Kro	1612	1785
Akebäck	Romakloster	Norra	Got	—	1790
Ala	Romakloster	Norra	Got	1853	1760

Name of Parish Before 1952	After 1952	Name of District	County	Earliest year of Parish register	Clerical survey record
Alanäs	Ström	Hammerdal	Jäm	1810	1809
Alboga	Gäsene	Gäsene	Älv	1688	1808
Alböke	Köpingsvik	Slättbo	Kal	1652	1790
Ale-Skövde	Lödöse	Ale	Älv	1688	1811
Alfshög	Vessigebro	Fauràs	Hal	1691	1784
Alfta	Alfta	Bollnäs	Gäv	1678	1678
Algutsboda	Algutsboda	Uppvidinge	Kro	1722	1757
Algutsrum	Torslunda	Algutsrum	Kal	1705	1767
Algutstorp	Vårgårda	Kulling	Älv	1748	1767
Alingsås					
Stads		Alingsås	Älv	1688	1742
Lands		Alingsås	Älv	1688	1732
Allerum	Ödåkra	Luggude	Mal	1690	1813
Allhelgona	Nyköping	Rönö	Söd	1735	1777
Allhelgona	Skänninge	Göstring	Öst	1842	1760
Allmänna barnbördshuset	Allmänna barnbördshuset	Stockholm	Sto	1847	—
Almby	Örebro	Örebro	Öre	1652	1765
Almesåkra	Malmbäck	Västra	Jön	1677	1714
Almundsryd	Almundsryd	Kinnevald	Kro	1721	1728
Almunge	Almunge	Närdingshundra	Sto	1580	1783
Alnö	Alnö	Skön	Vno	1721	1770
Alseda	Alseda	Östra	Jön	1681	1727
Alsen	Alsen	Jämtlands västra	Jäm	1689	1749
Alsike	Knivsta	Ärlinghundra	Sto	1635	1792
Alskog	Ljugarn	Södra	Got	1744	1745
Alster	Nyed	Väse	Vär	1688	1721
Altuna	Fjärdhundra	Simtuna	Vma	1714	1714
Alunda	Oland	Oland	Upp	1679	1752
Alva	Hemse	Södra	Got	1684	1744
Alvesta	Alvesta	Allbo	Kro	1726	1718
Ambjörnarp	Tranemo	Kind	Älv	1663	1793
Amnehärad	Amnehärad	Vadsbo	Ska	1683	1735
Amsberg	Stora Tuna	Falu södra	Kop	1726	1727
Anderslöv	Anderslöv	Skytt	Mal	1757	1813
Anderstorp	Anderstorp	Västbo	Jön	1688	1789
Andrarum	Brösarp	Albo	Kri	1690	1813
Aneboda	Lammhult	Norrvidinge	Kro	1688	1751
Anga	Romakloster	Norra	Got	1845	1760
Angarn	Össeby	Vallentuna	Sto	1721	1776
Angelstad	Annerstad	Sunnerbo	Kro	1708	1718
Angerdshestra	Norra Mo	Mo	Jön	1711	1779
Angered	Angered	Vättle	Älv	1753	1821
Annelöv	Dösjebro	Onsjö	Mal	1682	1805
Annefors	Bollnäs	Bollnäs	Gäv	1843	1843
Annerstad	Annerstad	Sunnerbo	Kro	1708	1718
Anundsjö	Anundsjö	Nätra	Vno	1688	1726
Appuna	Folkunga	Göstring	Öst	1700	1788
Arboga					
Stads	Arboga	Arboga	Vma	1670	1691
Lands	Medåker	Åkerbo	Vma	1659	1664
Arbrå	Arbrå	Arbrå och Järvsö	Gäv	1688	1747
Arby	Södermöre	Södra Möre	Kal	1701	1731
Ardre	Ljugarn	Norra	Got		1783
Aringsås					
Arjeplog	Arjeplog	Arjeplogs lappmark	Nbt	1717	1740
Arnäs	Arnäs	Själevads och Arnäs	Vno	1668	1749
Arnö	Södra Trögd	Trögd	Upp	1637	1752

Name of Parish Before 1952	Name of Parish After 1952	Name of District	County	Earliest year of Parish register	Earliest year of Clerical survey record
Arrie	Månstorp	Oxie	Mal	1688	1813
Arvidsjaur	Arvidsjaur	Arjeplogs lappmark	Nbt	1654	1744
Arvika					
Stads	Arvika	Arvika	Vär	1688	1826
Lands	Arvika	Jösse	Vär	1688	1760
Asa	Lammhult	Norrvidinge	Kro	1718	1718
Asarum	Asarum	Bräkne	Ble	1706	1794
Asby	Ydre	Ydre	Öst	1661	1781
Asige	Årstad	Årstad	Hal	1813	1785
Ask	Röstånga	Onsjö	Mal	1813	1811
Ask	Boberg	Aska	Öst	1699	1790
Askeby	Askeby	Bankekind	Öst	1700	1796
Asker	Asker	Asker	Öre	1666	1689
Askersund					
Stads		Askersund	Öre	1684	1752
Lands		Sundbo	Öre	1653	1789
Askeryd	Bredestad	Norra Vedbo	Jön	1671	1713
Askim	Askim	Askim	GoB	1737	1814
Asklanda	Vårgårda	Gäsene	Älv	1722	1823
Askome	Vessigebro	Årstad	Hal	1690	1767
Askum	Södra Sotenäs	Sotenäs	GoB	1821	1795
Asmundtorp	Rönneberga	Rönneberg	Mal	1736	1791
Aspeboda	Stora Kopparberg	Falu norra	Kop	1661	1706
Aspås	Rödön	Lit och Rödön	Jäm	1688	1707
Aspö	Tosterö	Selebo	Söd	1693	1702
Atlingbo	Stenkumla	Södra	Got	1714	1729
Attmar	Attmar	Medelpads västra	Vno	1694	1788
Augerum	Lyckeby	Östra	Ble	1695	1808
Ausås	Ausås	Södra Åsbo	Kri	1646	1786
Avesta	Avesta	Avesta	Kop	1760	1746
Axberg	Axberg	Örebro	Öre	1689	1707
Backa	Göteborg	Västra Hising	GoB		1861
Backaryd	Hallabro	Medelstad	Ble	1707	1813
Badelunda	Västerås	Siende	Vma	1684	1667
Baldringe	Herrestad	Herrestad	Mal	1758	1797
Balingsta	Södra Hagunda	Hagunda	Upp	1698	1715
Balkåkra	Ljunits	Ljunits	Mal	1688	1804
Baltak	Hökensås	Vartofta	Ska	1648	1804
Bankekind	Askeby	Bankekind	Öst	1688	1807
Bankeryd	Bankeryd	Tveta	Jön	1749	1731
Bara	Bara	Bara	Mal	1719	1784
Barkeryd	Forserum	Tveta	Jön	1680	1771
Barkåkra	Barkåkra	Bjäre	Kri	1736	1812
Barlingbo	Romakloser	Norra	Got	1717	1798
Barnarp	Tenhult	Tveta	Jön	1681	1721
Barne-Åsaka	Essunga	Barne	Ska	1689	1808
Barsebäck	Löddeköpinge	Harjager	Mal	1648	1787
Barva	Kafjärden	Österrekane	Söd	1756	1784
Beateberg	Moholm	Vadsbo	Ska	1688	1778
Bellö	Ingatorp	Södra Vedbo	Jön	1660	1787
Benestad	Tomelilla	Ingelstad	Kri	1686	1813
Berg	Berg	Berg	Jäm	1695	1695
Berg	Lammhult	Norrvidinge	Kro	1755	1779
Berg	Timmersdala	Vadsbo	Ska	1630	1765
Berg	Hallstahammar	Snevringe	Vma	1672	1665
Berga	Berga	Sunnerbo	Kro	1680	1762
Berga	Hasselrör	Vadsbo	Ska	1690	1766
Berghem	Västra Mark	Mark	Älv	1681	1730
Bergshammar	Jönåker	Jönåker	Söd	1680	1724

Name of Parish Before 1952	After 1952	Name of District	County	Earliest year of Parish register	Clerical survey record
Bergsjö	Bergsjö	Bergsjö och Forsa	Gäv	1682	1693
Bergstena	Vårgårda	Kulling	Älv	1705	1739
Bergum	Stora Lundby	Vättle	Älv	1741	1820
Bergunda	Bergunda	Kinnevald	Kro	1694	1744
Bettna	Bettna	Oppunda	Söd	1688	1765
Billeberga	Rönneberga	Rönneberg	Mal	1703	1814
Billinge	Röstånga	Onsjö	Mal	1646	1751
Billingsfors	Lelång	Vedbo	Älv	1738	1763
Bingsjö-Dådran	Rättvik	Rättvik	Kop		1837
Binneberg	Binneberg	Vadsbo	Ska	1688	1812
Biskopskulla	Lagunda	Lagunda	Upp	1690	1688
Bjurbäck	Mullsjö	Vartofta	Ska	1733	1784
Bjurholm	Bjurholm	Nordmaling och Bjurholm	Vbn	1809	1819
Bjursås	Bjursås	Leksand och Gagnef	Kop	1666	1710
Bjurtjärn	Ullvättern	Karlskoga	Vär	1688	1704
Bjurum	Gudhem	Gudhem	Ska	1711	1792
Bjuråker	Bjuråker	Delsbo	Gäv	1716	1697
Bjuv	Bjuv	Luggude	Mal	1710	1805
Bjälbo	Skänninge	Göstring	Öst	1645	1747
Bjällerup	Staffanstorp	Torna	Mal	1689	1792
Bjärby	Grästorp	Viste	Ska	1688	1767
Bjäresjö	Ljunits	Herrestad	Mal	1689	1799
Bjärka	Gudhem	Gudhem	Ska	1700	1779
Bjärshög	Bara	Bara	Mal	1687	1809
Bjärtrå	Bjärtrå	Ångermanland Södra	Vno	1695	1702
Björka	Sjöbo	Färs	Mal	1783	1808
Björke	Romakloster	Norra	Got	1797	1783
Björkeberg	Norra Valkebo	Gullberg	Öst	1685	1747
Björketorp	Björketorp	Bollebygd	Älv	1681	1794
Björklinge	Björklinge	Norunda	Upp	1670	1686
Björskog	Kung Karl	Åkerbo	Vma	1626	1643
Björksta	Kungsåra	Yttertjurbo	Vma	1688	1687
Björkvik	Björkvik	Jönåker	Söd	1686	1688
Björkäng, see Toreboda					
Björkö	Björkö	Östra	Jön	1680	1753
Björlanda	Torslanda	Västra Hising	GoB	1792	1786
Björna	Björna	Själevad och Arnås	Vno	1797	1797
Björnekulla	Åstorp	Södra Åsbo	Kri	1689	1812
Björnlunda	Daga	Daga	Söd	1682	1760
Björskog	Kung Karl	Åkerbo	Vma	1626	1643
Björsäter	Lugnås	Vadsbo	Ska	1688	1739
Björsäter	Björsäter	Bankekind	Öst	1603	1792
Blackstad	Locknevi	Södra Tjust	Kal	1715	1759
Blackstad	Bettna	Oppunda	Söd	1669	1735
Bladåker	Knutby	Närdinghundra	Sto	1736	1738
Blentarp	Blentarp	Torna	Mal	1693	1683
Blidsberg	Redväg	Redväg	Älv	1695	1779
Blidö	Blidö	Frötuna och Länna	Sto	1797	1807
Blomskog	Holmedal	Nordmark	Vär	1688	1771
Blädinge	Vislanda	Allbo	Kro	1688	1717
Bo	Sköllersta	Sköllersta	Öre	1736	1773
Boda	Boda	Rättvik	Kop	1742	1760
Boda	Brunskog	Jösse	Vär	1688	1734
Bodarp	Skegrie	Skytt	Mal	1688	1734
Bodsjö	Revsund	Brunflo och Näs	Jäm	1689	1697
Bodum	Fjällsjö	Fjällsjö	Vno	1826	1827
Boge	Slite	Norra	Got	1845	1788

Name of Parish Before 1952	After 1952	Name of District	County	Earliest year of Parish register	Clerical survey record
Bogen	Gunnarskog	Jösse	Vär	1850	1851
Boglösa	Södra Trögd	Trögd	Upp	1688	1750
Bogsta	Tystberga	Rönö	Söd	1673	1787
Bokenäs	Skaftö	Lane	GoB	1685	1766
Bollebygd	Bollebygd	Bollebygd	Älv	1682	1748
Bollerup	Glemmingebro	Ingelstad	Kri	1689	1813
Bollnäs	Bollnäs	Bollnäs	Gäv	1698	1738
Bolmsö	Unnaryd	Västbo	Jön	1688	1727
Bolshög	Tommarp	Järrestad	Kri	1717	1815
Bolstad	Bolstad	Sundal	Älv	1763	1729
Bolum	Gudhem	Valle	Ska	1703	1790
Bonderup	Dalby	Torna	Mal	1681	1799
Bondkyrka, see Heliga Trefaldighet					
Bondstorp	Vaggeryd	Östbo	Jön	1688	1788
Boo	Boo	Värmdö	Sto	1671	1772
Borg	Norrköping	Memming	Öst	1662	1696
Borgeby	Flädie	Torna	Mal	1724	1787
Borgholm	Borgholm	Borgholm	Kal	1826	1826
Borgsjö	Borgsjö	Medelpads Västra	Vno	1844	1844
Borgstena	Fristad	Veden	Älv	1655	1818
Borgunda	Stenstorp	Gudhem	Ska	1715	1775
Borgvattnet	Stugun	Ragunda	Jäm	1782	1805
Borgvik	Ed	Grums	Vär	1718	1737
Borlunda	Skarhult	Frosta	Mal	1687	1804
Borrby	Borrby	Ingelstad	Kri	1701	1813
Borrie	Herrestad	Herrestad	Mal	1717	1792
Borås	Borås	Borås	Älv	1642	1741
Bosarp	Bosarp	Onsjö	Mal	1647	1814
Bosebo	Gislaved	Västbo	Jön	1805	1717
Bosjökloster	Snogeröd	Frosta	Mal	1688	1811
Boteå	Boteå	Boteå	Vno	1756	1782
Botilsäter	Värmlandsnäs	Näs	Vär	1721	1764
Botkyrka	Botkyrka	Svartlösa	Sto	1664	1718
Bottna	Kville	Kville	GoB	1860	1860
Bottnaryd	Norra Mo	Mo	Jön	1711	1752
Brandstad	Vollsjö	Färs	Mal	1689	1802
Brandstorp	Fågelås	Vartofta	Ska	1680	1790
Brastad	Stångenäs	Stångenäs	GoB	1703	1804
Brattfors	Värmlandsberg	Färnebo	Vär	1737	1743
Breared	Simlångsdalen	Tönnersjö	Hal	1719	1805
Bred	Åsunda	Åsunda	Upp	1711	1735
Bredared	Sandhult	Veden	Älv	1688	1736
Bredaryd	Bredaryd	Norra Vedbo	Jön	1695	1757
Bredestad	Bredestad	Norra Vedbo	Jön	1695	1791
Bredsäter	Lugnås	Kinne	Ska	1688	1794
Bredsätra	Köpingsvik	Runsten	Kal	1693	1813
Brevik	Mölltorp	Vadsbo	Ska	1698	1791
Bringetofta	Norra Sandsjö	Västra	Jön	1706	1791
Brismene	Frökind	Frökind	Ska	1688	1777
Bro	Tingstäde	Norra	Got	1667	1764
Bro	Stångenäs	Stångenäs	GoB	1703	1793
Bro	Upplands-Bro	Bro	Upp	1669	1757
Bro	Värmlandsnäs	Näs	Vär	1689	1751
Bro	Kolsva	Åkerbo	Vma	1772	1725
Broby	Husaby	Kinnefjärding	Ska	1694	1690
Broddarp	Gäsene	Gäsene	Älv	1711	1802
Broddetorp	Gudhem	Gudhem	Ska	1703	1790
Bromma	Herrestad	Herrestad	Mal	1690	1810
Bromma	Bromma	Stockholm	Sto	1721	1779

Name of Parish Before 1952	After 1952	Name of District	County	Earliest year of Parish register	Clerical survey record
Brunflo	Brunflo	Brunflo och Näs	Jäm	1688	1741
Brunn	Ulricehamn	Redvägs	Älv	1807	1779
Brunnby	Brunnby	Luggude	Mal	1747	1813
Brunneby	Borensberg	Boberg	Öst	1674	1766
Brunnhem	Stenstorp	Gudhem	Ska	1673	1746
Brunskog	Brunskog	Jösse	Vär	1688	1760
Brågarp	Staffanstorp	Bara	Mal	1735	1825
Brålanda	Brålanda	Sundal	Älv	1727	1789
Brattensby	Herrljunga	Kulling	Älv	1748	1768
Bräcke	Bräcke	Brunflo och Näs	Jäm	1780	1807
Bräkne-Hoby	Bräkne-Hoby	Bräkne	Ble	1677	1749
Brämhult	Brämhult	Ås	Älv	1730	1745
Brännkyrka	Brännkyrka	Stockholm	Sto	1761	1772
Brönnestad	Sösdala	Västra Göinge	Kri	1647	1799
Brösarp	Brösarp	Albo	Kri	1701	1779
Bunge	Fårösund	Norra	Got	1871	1871
Bunkeflo	Bunkeflo	Oxie	Mal	1768	1789
Burlöv	Burlöv	Bara	Mal	1689	1805
Burs	Stånga	Södra	Got	1713	1720
Burträsk	Burträsk	Burträsk	Vbn	1740	1710
Burseryd	Burseryd	Västbo	Jön	1680	1717
Buttle	Romakloster	Norra	Got		1761
By	By	Folkare	Kop	1672	1672
By	Säffle	Näs	Vär	1689	1751
Byarum	Vaggeryd	Östbo	Jön	1698	1717
Bygdeå	Bygdeå	Nysätra	Vbn	1724	1746
Byske	Byske	Skelleftå	Vbn	1838	1846
Båraryd, see Gislaved					
Bårslöv	Vallåkra	Luggude	Mal	1830	1838
Båstad	Båstad köping	Bjäre	Kri		1870
Bäck	Töreboda	Vadsbo	Ska	1745	1806
Bäckaby	Bäckaby	Västra	Jön	1688	1688
Bäcke	Bäckefors	Vedbo	Älv	1688	1780
Bäckebo	Alsterbo	Norra Möre	Kal	1712	1758
Bäckseda	Vetlanda	Östra	Jön	1688	1749
Bäl	Tingstäde	Norra	Got	1704	1749
Bälaryd	Bredestad	N. Vedbo	Jön	1688	1789
Bälinge	Tystberga	Rönö	Söd	1688	1689
Bälinge	Bälinge	Bälinge	Upp	1683	1685
Bälinge	Alingsås	Kulling	Älv	1733	1723
Bällefors	Moholm	Vadsbo	Ska	1688	1777
Bärbo	Stigtomta	Jönåker	Söd	1651	1746
Bäreberg	Essunga	Viste	Ska	1836	1818
Bärfendal	Svarteborg	Sotenäs	GoB	1688	1812
Bäve	Uddevalla	Lane	GoB	1698	1813
Böda	Ölands-Åkerbo	Åkerbo	Kal	1688	1768
Böja	Timmersdala	Vadsbo	Ska	1630	1773
Böne	Redväg	Redväg	Älv	1721	1792
Börje	Bälinge	Ulleråker	Upp	1656	1726
Börringe	Anderslöv	Vemmenhög	Mal	1689	1813
Börrum	Stegeborg	Hammarkind	Öst	1754	1788
Börstig	Frökind	Frökind	Ska	1688	1777
Börstil	Östhammar	Frösåker	Sto	1702	1764
Bösarp	Gislöv	Skytt	Mal	1734	1804
Dagsberg	Västra Vikbolandet	Lösing	Öst	1695	1747
Dagstorp	Dösjebro	Harjager	Mal	1737	1737
Dagsås	Tvååker	Faurås	Hal	1828	1832
Dal	Ytterlännäs	Boteå	Vno	1688	1808

Name of Parish Before 1952	After 1952	Name of District	County	Earliest year of Parish register	Clerical survey record
Dala	Stenstorp	Gudhem	Ska	1688	1776
Dalarö	Österhaninge	Sotholm	Sto	1690	1688
Dalarö Skans	Österhaninge	Sotholm	Sto	1702	1825
Dalby	Dalby	Torna	Mal	1667	1799
Dalby	Södra Hagunda	Hagunda	Upp	1782	1696
Dalby	Finnskoga-Dalby	Älvdal	Vär	1694	1716
Dalhem	Dalhem	Norra	Got	1694	1750
Dalhem	Överum	Tjust	Kal	1687	1751
Dalköpinge	Gislöv	Skytt	Mal	1688	1805
Dals-Ed	Dals-Ed	Vedbo	Älv	1706	1789
Dalskog	Kroppefjäll	Nordal	Älv	1702	1688
Dalstorp	Dalstorp	Kind	Älv	1699	1745
Dalum	Redväg	Redväg	Älv	1695	1819
Danderyd	Danderyd	Danderyd	Sto	1703	1735
Danmark	Vaksala	Vaksala	Upp	1690	1704
Dannemora	Dannemora	Oland	Upp	1694	1686
Dannike	Länghem	Kind	Älv	1714	1812
Dannäs	Forsheda	Västbo	Jön	1679	1786
Danvik & Siklaö	Nacka	Svartlösa	Sto	1691	1703
Daretorp	Hökensås	Vartofta	Ska	1680	1790
Degeberga	Degeberga	Gärd	Kri	1688	1825
Degerfors	Degerfors	Degerfors	Vbn	1770	1794
Degerfors	Degerfors	Karlskoga	Öre		1883
Dalsbo	Delsbo	Delsbo	Gäv	1682	1673
Dillnäs	Daga	Daga	Söd	1691	1771
Dimbo	Dimbo	Vartofta	Ska	1658	1747
Dingtuna	Dingtuna	Tuhundra	Vma	1635	1685
Djurröld	Träne	Gärd	Kri	1692	1813
Djursdala	Södra Vi	Sevede	Kal	1693	1773
Djurö	Djurö	Värmdö	Sto	1679	1754
Dorotea	Dorotea	Vilhelmina	Vbn	1796	1798
Dragsmark	Skaftö	Lane	GoB	1685	1766
Drev	Braås	Uppvidinge	Kro	1690	1718
Drothem	Söderköping	Hammarkind	Öst	1666	1795
Drängsered	Torup	Årstad	Hal	1694	1755
Dunker	Malmköping	Villåttinge	Söd	1666	1736
Dylta Bruk	Axberg	Örebro	Öre	1711	1753
Dädesjö	Braås	Uppvidinge	Kro	1688	1717
Dänningelanda	Mellersta Kinnevald	Kinnevald	Kro	1732	1797
Döderhult	Döderhult	Stranda	Kal	1653	1766
Dörarp	Berga	Sunnerbo	Kro	1680	1827
Dörby	Dörby	Norra Möre	Kal	1713	1768
Ed	Upplands-Väsby	Sollentuna	Sto	1731	1692
Ed	Ed	Grums	Vär	1699	1777
Ed	Resele	Sollefteå	Vno	1688	1794
Eda	Eda	Jösse	Vär	1680	1696
Edebo	Häverö	Frösåker	Sto	1688	1727
Edestad	Listerby	Medelstad	Ble	1721	1801
Edsberg	Lekeberg	Edsberg	Öre	1745	1746
Edsbro	Knutby	Näringhundra	Sto	1740	1772
Edsele	Damsele	Ramsele och Resele	Vno	1818	1807
Edshult	Höreda	Södra Vedbo	Jön	1669	1789
Edsleskog	Tössbo	Tössbo	Älv	1686	1774
Edsvära	Kvänum	Skåning	Ska	1850	1737
Edåsa	Värsås	Gudhem	Ska	1654	1861
Eftra	Årstad	Årstad	Hal	1690	1790
Egby	Köpingsvik	Slättbo	Kal	1790	1808
Eggby	Valle	Valle	Ska	1688	1791
Eggvena	Herrljunga	Kulling	Älv	1718	1790

Name of Parish Before 1952	Name of Parish After 1952	Name of District	County	Earliest year of Parish register	Earliest year of Clerical survey record
Ek	Ullervad	Vadsbo	Ska	1691	1816
Ekby	Ullervad	Vadsbo	Ska	1688	1704
Eke	Havdhem	Södra	Got	1820	1796
Ekeberga	Ekeberga	Uppvidinge	Kro	1689	1772
Ekeby	Dalhem	Norra	Got		1799
(See also Barlingbo)					
Ekeby	Ekeby	Luggude	Mal	1690	1813
Ekeby	Oland	Oland	Upp	1743	1783
Ekeby	Eke och Gällersta	Sköllersta	Öre	1666	1739
Ekeby	Boxholm	Göstring	Öst	1760	1788
Ekebyborna	Boberg	Boberg	Öst	1634	1713
Eker	Örebro	Örebro	Öre	1692	1777
Ekerö	Ekerö	Färentuna	Sto	1685	1694
Ekeskog	Moholm	Vadsbo		1688	1777
Ekshärad	Ekshärad	Älvdal	Vär	1665	1720
Eksjö					
Stads		Eksjö	Jön	1633	1788
Lands		Södra Vedbo	Jön	1794	1788
Eksta	Klintehamn	Södra	Got	1754	1730
Eldsberga	Eldsberga	Tönnersjö	Hal	1765	1760
Eling	Vedum	Barne	Ska	1710	1818
Eljaröd	Brösarp	Albo	Kri	1722	1867
Elleholm	Mörrum	Lister	Ble	1696	1813
Emmislöv	Broby	Östra Göinge	Kri	1647	1813
Endre	Romakloster	Norra	Got	1721	1720
Enköping	Enköping	Enköping	Upp	1663	1743
Enköpings-Näs	Åsunda	Åsunda	Upp	1628	1690
Enslöv	Enslöv	Tönnersjö	Hal	1692	1785
Enviken	Enviken	Falu norra	Kop		1849
Enåker	Västerlövsta	Simtuna	Vma	1692	1696
Enånger	Enånger	Enånger	Gäv	1688	1712
Enåsa	Hasslerör	Vadsbo	Ska	1690	1778
Eriksberg	Gäsene	Gäsene	Älv	1711	1815
Erikstad	Bolstad	Sundal	Älv	1763	1761
Eringsboda	Tving	Medelstad	Ble	1843	1786
Erska	Bjärke	Bjärke	Älv	1688	1785
Ervalla	Axberg	Västra Fellingsbro	Öre	1672	1745
Esarp	Staffanstorp	Bara	Mal	1726	1813
Eskelhem	Stenkumla	Södra	Got	1730	1718
Eskiltorp	Vellinge	Oxie	Mal	1726	1831
Eskilstuna					
Stads		Eskilstuna	Söd	1666	1869
Fors		Västerrekarne	Söd	1835	1779
Fristaden		Eskilstuna	Söd		1779
Karl Gustafs Stad		Eskilstuna	Söd		1779
Kloster		Eskilstuna	Söd	1835	1779
Nya och Gamla Staden		Eskilstuna	Söd		1779
Eskilsäter	Värmlandsnäs	Näs	Vär	1688	1751
Essunga	Essunga	Barne	Ska	1689	1779
Esterna (now Fasterna)	Sjuhundra	Sjuhundra	Sto	1687	1697
Estuna	Lyhundra	Lyhundra	Sto	1688	1705
Etelhem	Ljugarn	Södra	Got	1855	1784
Everlöv	Blentarp	Torna	Mal	1768	1795
Everöd	Everöd	Gärd	Kri	1688	1791
Fagered	Ullared	Faurås	Hal	1685	1784
Fagerhult	Fagerhult	Handbörd	Kal	1634	1830
Falkenberg	Falkenberg	Falkenberg	Hal	1689	1755

Name of Parish Before 1952	After 1952	Name of District	County	Earliest year of Parish register	Clerical survey record
Falköping	Falköping	Falköping	Ska	1688	1796
Falköpings Östra	Vartofta	Vartofta	Ska	1726	1798
Falsterbo	Skanör med Falsterbo	Falsterbo	Mal	1685	1811
Falun	Falun	Falun	Kop	1694	1776
Fardhem	Hemse	Södra	Got		
Farhult	Jonstorp	Luggude	Mal	1689	1785
Faringe	Knutby	Näringhundra	Sto	1674	1731
Farstorp	Hästveda	Västra Göinge	Kri	1690	1813
Fasta (now Fasterna)	Sjuhundra	Sjuhundra	Sto	1745	1761
Fasterna	Sjuhundra	Sjuhundra	Sto	1807	1807
Felestad	Svalöv	Rönneberg	Mal	1749	1799
Fellingsbro	Fellingsbro	Fellingsbro	Öre	1641	1654
Femsjö	Hylte	Västbo	Jön	1688	1717
Fide	Hoburg	Södra	Got	1658	1805
Filipstad	Filipstad	Filipstad	Vär	1651	1743
Film	Dannemora	Oland	Upp	1679	1712
Finja	Tyringe	Västra Göinge	Kri	1690	1793
Finnekumla	Åsunden	Kind	Älv	1724	1811
Finnerödja	Tiveden	Vadsbo	Ska	1688	1793
Fiskebäckskil	Skaftö	Orusts-Västra	GoB	1711	1794
Fittja	Lagunda	Lagunda	Upp	1688	1786
Fivelstad	Aska	Aska	Öst	1700	1780
Fivlered	Redväg	Redväg	Älv	1721	1792
Fjelie	Flädie	Torna	Mal	1696	1805
Fjälkestad	Nosaby	Villand	Kri	1747	1797
Fjälkinge	Fjälkinge	Villand	Kri	1690	1783
Fjällbacka	Kville	Kville	GoB		1882
Fjällsjö	Fjällsjö	Fjällsjö	Vno	1684	1780
Fjärestad	Vallåkra	Luggude	Mal	1830	1791
Fjärås	Fjärås	Fjäre	Hal	1688	1755
Flackarp	Staffanstorp	Bara	Mal	1779	1768
Flakeberg	Grästorp	Viste	Ska	1688	1768
Flen	Flen	Villåttinge	Söd	1693	1707
Fleninge	Ödåkra	Luggude	Mal	1690	1813
Fleringe	Fårösund	Norra	Got		1871
Flisby	Solberga	Södra Vedbo	Jön	1635	1757
Fliseryd	Fliseryd	Handbörds	Kal	1712	1784
Flistad	Tidan	Vadsbo	Ska	1688	1746
Flistad	Vreta Kloster	Gullberg	Öst	1694	1809
Flo	Grästorp	Åse	Ska	1771	1781
Floby	Vilske	Vilske	Ska	1690	1795
Floda	Floda	Näs	Kop	1672	1663
Floda	Floda	Oppunda	Söd	1686	1749
Fläckebo	Väster Färnebo	Norrbo	Vma	1649	1677
Flädie	Flädie	Torna	Mal	1697	1805
Fogdö	Vårfruberga	Åker	Söd	1681	1688
Fole	Tingstäde	Norra	Got	1718	1757
Folkärna	Folkärna	Nås	Kop	1667	1673
Follingbo	Romakloster	Norra	Got	1684	1736
Fornåsa	Boberg	Boberg	Öst	1662	1782
Fors	Fors	Ragunda	Jäm	1689	1693
Fors	Eskilstuna	Västerrekarne	Söd	1835	1779
Fors	Flundre	Flundre	Älv	1688	1766
Forsa	Forsa	Bergsjö och Forsa	Gäs	1692	1700
Forsby	Värsås	Forsa Kåkind	Ska	1690	1770
Forserum	Forserum	Tveta	Jön	1687	1717
Forsheda	Forsheda	Västbo	Jön	1688	1757
Forshem	Kinnekulle	Kinne	Ska	1688	1772

Name of Parish		Name of		Earliest year of	
Before 1952	After 1952	District	County	Parish register	Clerical survey record
Forshälla	Forshälla	Inlands Fräkne	GoB	1688	1809
Forsmark	Östhammar	Frösåker	Sto	1677	1750
Forssa	Bettna	Villåttinge	Söd	1682	1747
Fosie	Malmö	Oxie	Mal	1688	1799
Foss	Munkedal	Tunge	GoB	1688	1799
Fotskäl	Västra Mark	Mark	Älv		1858
Fransk-Lutherska	Fransk-Lutherska	Stockholm	Sto	1690	—
Fredrika	Fredrika	Åsele	Vbn	1800	1800
Fredsberg	Töreboda	Vadsbo	Ska	1745	1813
Fresta	Upplands-Väsby	Vallentuna	Sto	1677	1713
Fridene	Fröjered	Vartofta	Ska	1727	1740
Fridlevstad	Fridlevstad	Medelstad	Ble	1660	1733
Friel	Tun	Åse	Ska	1672	1744
Friggeråker	Falköping	Gudhem	Ska	1688	1820
Frillestad	Mörarp	Luggude	Mal	1690	1813
Frillesås	Löftadalen	Fjäre	Hal	1689	1750
Frinnaryd	Bredestad	Norra Vedbo	Jön	1657	1790
Fristad	Fristad	Veden	Älv	1655	1775
Fristaden	Eskilstuna	Eskilstuna	Söd		1779
Fritsla	Fritsla	Mark	Älv	1681	1750
Frostviken	Frostviken	Hammerdal	Jäm	1842	1813
Fru Alstad	Alstad	Skytt	Mal	1688	1816
Frustuna	Gnesta	Daga	Söd	1688	1786
Fryele	Klevshult	Östbo	Jön	1688	1731
Frykerud	Frykerud	Kil	Vär	1672	1725
Fryksände	Fryksände	Fryksdal	Vär	1707	1698
Främmestad	Essunga	Vist	Ska	1657	1776
Frändefors	Frändefors	Sundal	Älv	1751	1778
Fränninge	Vollsjö	Färs	Mal	1730	1813
Fröderyd	Bäckaby	Västra	Jön	1688	1688
Frödinge	Sevede	Sevede	Kal	1670	1776
Fröjel	Klintehamn	Södra	Got	1681	1784
Fröjered	Fröjered	Vartofta	Ska	1727	1740
Frösthult	Fjärdhundra	Fjällsjö	Vma	1684	1687
Fröskog	Tössbo	Tössbo	Älv	1703	1795
Fröslunda	Lagunda	Lagunda	Upp	1688	1692
Fröstuna	Vallentuna	Seminghundra	Sto	1711	1711
Frösve	Binneberg	Konga	Ska	1688	1788
Frösö	Frösö	Sunne, Ovikens och Hallen	Jäm	1692	1693
Frötuna	Frötuna	Frötuna och Länna	Sto	1690	1696
Fuglie	Skegrie	Skytt	Mal	1756	1786
Fullestad	Vårgårda	Kulling	Älv	1705	1757
Fulltofta	Östra Frosta	Frosta	Mal	1621	1813
Fullösa	Kinnekulle	Kinne	Ska	1688	1772
Funbo	Vaksala	Rasbo	Upp	1680	1713
Furingstad	Västra Vikbolandet	Lösing	Öst	1677	1803
Furuby	Hovmantorp	Konga	Kro	1659	1756
Fuxerna					
Fyrunga	Kvänum	Skåning	Ska	1688	1793
Fågelfors	Högsby	Handbörd	Kal		1886
Fågeltofta	Brösarp	Albo	Kri	1709	1813
Fåglum	Essunga	Barne	Ska	1689	1808
Fårö	Fårösund	Norra	Got	1688	1756
Fägre	Moholm	Vadsbo	Ska	1695	1810
Fänneslunda	Hökerum	Ås	Älv	1740	1769
Färed	Hasslerör	Vadsbo	Ska	1690	1769
Färentuna	Färingsö	Färentuna	Sto	1687	1764
Färgaryd	Hylte	Västbo	Jön	1686	1757

Name of Parish Before 1952	After 1952	Name of District	County	Earliest year of Parish register	Clerical survey record
Färgelanda	Färgelanda	Valbo	Älv	1688	1737
Färila	Färila-Kårböle	Ljusdal	Gäv	1680	1721
Färingtofta	Riseberga	Norra Åsbo	Kri	1689	1806
Färlöv	Araslöv	östra Göinge	Kri	1690	1771
Färnebo	Värmlandsberg	Färnebo	Vär	1853	1718
Fässberg, see Mölndal					
Fölene	Herrljunga	Kulling	Älv	1718	1766
Föllinge	Föllinge	Lits och Rödö	Jäm	1736	1693
Föra	Köpingsvik	Åkerbo	Kal	1656	1737
Förkärla	Listerby	Medelstad	Ble	1713	1801
Förlanda	Fjärås	Fjäre	Hal	1732	1790
Förlösa	Läckeby	Norra Möre	Kal	1686	1786
Förslöv	Förslövsholm	Bjäre	Kri	1711	1784
Gagnef	Gagnef	Leksand och Gagnef	Kop	1673	1738
Galtström	Njurunda	Njurunda, Skön och Ljustorp	Vno	1679	1747
Gamla Uppsala	Uppsala	Vaksala	Upp	1681	1684
Gamleby	Gamleby	Södra Tjust	Kal	1694	1735
Gammalkil	Södra Valkebo	Valkebo	öst	1634	1756
Gammalstorp	Gammalstorp	Lister	Ble	1689	1766
Gammelgarn	Romakloster	Norra	Got		1783
Ganthem	Dalhem	Norra	Got	1727	1784
Garde	Ljugarn	Södra	Got	1732	1690
Garpenberg	Hedemora	Hedemora	Kop	1667	1678
Genarp	Genarp	Bara	Mal	1692	1772
Gerum	Hemse	Södra	Got	1845	1784
Gestad	Brålanda	Sundal	Älv	1763	1761
Gesäter	Dals-Ed	Vedbo	Älv	1707	1810
Getinge	Getinge	Halmstad	Hal	1820	1866
Gideå (see also Arnäs)	Gideå	Själevad och Arnäs	Vno	1807	1807
Gillberga	Västra Rekarne	Västerrekarne	Söd	1677	1749
Gillberga	Gillberga	Gillberg	Vär	1688	1733
Gillstad	örslösa	Kålland	Ska	1710	1752
Gingri	Fristad	Ås	Älv	1655	1797
Ginneröd	Ljungskile	Inlands Fräkne	GoB	1762	1813
Giresta	Lagunda	Lagunda	Upp	1680	1721
Gislaved	Gislaved	Västbo	Jön	1688	1717
Gislöv	Gislöv	Skytt	Mal	1756	1805
Gistad	Åkerbo	Skärkind	Öst	1631	1759
Gladhammar	Gladhammar	Södra Tjust	Kal	1633	1760
Gladsax	Simrishamn	Järrestad	Kri	1653	1800
Glanshammar	Glanshammar	Glanshammar	öre	1719	1719
Glava	Glava	Gillberg	Vär	1696	1779
Glemminge	Glemmingebro	Ingelstad	Kri	1756	1818
Glimåkra	Glimåkra	Östra Göinge	Kri	1693	1772
Glostorp	Oxie	Oxie	Mal	1688	1811
Glumslöv	Härslöv	Rönneberg	Mal	1690	1792
Glömminge	Torslunda	Algutsrum	Kal	1704	1770
Gnarp	Gnarp	Norra Hälsingland	Gäv	1677	1739
Gnosjö	Gnosjö	Västbo	Jön	1717	1759
Godegård	Godegård	Finspångalän	öst	1688	1740
Gothem	Dalhem	Norra	Got	1708	1733
Gottröra	Skepptuna	Långhundra	Sto	1699	1778
Granhult	Nottebäck	Uppvidinge	Kro	1696	1788
Grangärde	Grangärde	Västerbergslag	Kop	1628	1653
Graninge	Långsele	Sollefteå	Vno	1770	1805
Grava	Grava	Karlstad	Vär	1688	1751

Name of Parish Before 1952	After 1952	Name of District	County	Earliest year of Parish register	Clerical survey record
Grebo	Björsäter	Bankekind	Öst	1661	1795
Grevbäck	Hjo	Kåkind	Ska	1704	1804
Grevie	Förslövsholm	Bjäre	Kri	1711	1785
Grimeton	Himledalen	Himle	Hal	1695	1808
Grimmared	Kungsäter	Mark	Älv	1689	1798
Grinstad	Bolstad	Sundal	Älv	1763	1711
Grolanda	Vilske	Vilske	Ska	1695	1721
Grovare	Hökerum	Ås	Älv	1740	1769
Grude	Gäsene	Gäsene	Älv	1647	1780
Grums	Grums	Grums	Vär	1727	1750
Grundsund	Skaftö	Orust västra	GoB	1799	1820
Grundsunda	Grundsunda	Själevad och Arnäs	Vno	1721	1786
Gryt	Knislinge	Östra Göings	Kri	1647	1815
Gryt	Daga	Daga	Söd	1695	1700
Gryt	Gryt	Hammarkind	Öst	1635	1725
Gryta	Lagunda	Hagunda	Upp	1733	1747
Gryteryd	Burseryd	Västbo	Jön	1688	1717
Grythyttan	Grythyttan	Grythyttan och Hällefors	Öre	1699	1698
Grytnäs	Grytnäs	Folkare	Kop	1681	1723
Gråmanstorp	Klippan	Norra Åsbo	Kri	1782	1813
Gränna					
Stads		Gränna	Jön	1648	1688
Lands		Vista	Jön	1648	1688
Gräsgård	Ottenby	Gräsgård	Kal	1690	1788
Gräsmark	Gräsmark	Fryksdal	Vär	1688	1765
Gräsö	Öregrund	Frösåker	Sto	1689	1750
Gräve	Tysslinge	Örebro	Öre	1617	1708
Grödinge	Grödinge	Svartlösa	Sto	1666	1689
Grönahög	Åsunden	Kind	Älv	1724	1810
Grönby	Anderslöv	Vemmenhög	Mal	1689	1789
Grötlingbo	Havdhem	Södra	Got	1723	1805
Gualöv	Ivetofta	Villand	Kri	1696	1825
Gudhem	Gudhem	Gudhem	Ska	1721	1765
Gudmundrå	Kramfors	Ångermanlands södra	Vno	1686	1820
Gudmuntorp	Snogeröd	Frosta	Mal	1796	1813
Guldrupe	Romakloster	Norra	Got		1785
Gullabo (Before 1871 see Torsås)	Torsås	Södra Möre Skogsbygd	Kal		1871
Gullered	Redväg	Redväg	Älv	1692	1802
Gullholmen	Morlanda	Orusts västra	GoB	1799	1794
Gumlösa	Vinslöv	Västra Göinge	Kri	1649	1821
Gunnarp	Ätran	Fauräs	Hal	1688	1784
Gunnarsjö	Kungsäter	Mark	Älv	1689	1798
Gunnarskog	Gunnarskog	Jösse	Vär	1688	1781
Gunnarsnäs	Kroppefjäll	Nordal	Älv	1703	1778
Gunnilbo	Skinnskatteberg	Skinnskatteberg	Vma	1660	1688
Gustaf Adolf	Fjälkinge	Villand	Kri	1690	1813
Gustafs	Gustafs	Falu södra	Kop	1723	1677
Gustav, see Börringe					
Gustav Adolf	Habo	Vartofta	Ska	1704	1800
Gustav Adolf	Gustav Adolf	Älvdal	Vär	1789	1786
Gustavsberg, see Värmdö					
Gusum	Ringarum	Hammarkind	Öst	1722	1817
Gylle	Gislöv	Skytts	Mal	1689	1801
Gålsjö	Boteå	Boteå	Vno	1774	1814
Gårdby	Torslunda	Möckleby	Kal	1640	1846
Gårdeby	Aspveden	Skärkind	Öst	1665	1694

Name of Parish Before 1952	After 1952	Name of District	County	Earliest year of Parish register	Clerical survey record
Gårdsby	Rottne	Norrvidinge	Kro	1693	1783
Gårdstånga	Skarhult	Frosta	Mal	1689	1813
Gårdveda	Målilla	Aspeland	Kal	1632	1788
Gåsborn	Vämlandsberg	Färnebo	Vär	1695	1789
Gåsinge	Daga	Daga	Söd	1686	1790
Gällared	Ätran	Faurås	Hal	1732	1784
Gällaryd	Bor	Östbo	Jön	1725	1754
Gällersta	Ekeby och Gällersta	Sköllersta	Öre	1718	1718
Gällinge	Löftadalen	Fjäre	Hal	1689	1750
Gällivare	Gällivare	Gällivare lappmark	Nbt	1742	1758
Gällstad	Åsunden	Kind	Älv	1724	1812
Gärdhem	Södra Väne	Väne	Älv	1643	1813
Gärdserum	Uknadalen	Norra Tjust	Kal	1702	1805
Gärdslöv	Anderslöv	Vemmenhög	Mal	1749	1813
Gärdslösa	Gärdslösa	Runsten	Kal	1738	1770
Gässie	Vellinge	Oxie	Mal	1726	1830
Gävle	Gävle	Gävle	Gäv	1695	1783
Gödelöv	Genarp	Torna	Mal	1697	1796
Gödestad	Himledalen	Himle	Hal	1614	1777
Gökhem	Vilske	Vilske	Ska	1695	1788
Görslöv	Staffanstorp	Bara	Mal	1688	1813
Gösslunda	Norra Kålland	Kålland	Ska	1753	1786
Göteborg					
Amiralitet		Göteborg	GoB	1730	1789
Engelska		Göteborg	GoB	1774	1774
Fattighus		Göteborg	GoB	1763	1812
Gamlestad		Göteborg	GoB	—	1883
Garnison		Göteborg	GoB	1693	1869
Gustavi Domkyrko		Göteborg	GoB	1669	1861
Haga		Göteborg	GoB	—	1883
Hospital		Göteborg	GoB	1732	1820
Karl Johan		Göteborg	GoB	1730	1828
Kristine		Göteborg	GoB	1624	1824
Kristine		Göteborg	GoB	1781	—
Lundby		Göteborg	GoB	1693	1753
Marieberg		Göteborg	GoB	1730	1800
Masthugg		Göteborg	GoB	—	1883
Nya Varvet		Göteborg	GoB	1816	1826
Nya Älvsborg		Göteborg	GoB	1690	1847
Västra Hisingen		Göteborg	GoB	—	1844
Örgryte		Göteborg	GoB	1740	1773
Götene	Götene	Kinne	Ska	1807	1768
Göteryd	Göteryd	Sunnerbo	Kro	1688	1769
Göteve	Vilske	Vilske	Ska	1690	1816
Götlunda	Glanshammar	Glanshammar	Öre	1703	1740
Götlunda	Tidan	Vadsbo	Ska	1724	1775
Hablingbo	Hävdhem	Södra	Got	1689	1737
Habo	Habo	Vartofta	Ska	1675	1800
Hackstad	Norra Trögd	Trögd	Upp	1676	1738
Hackvad	Lekeberg	Grimsten	Öre	1696	1746
Hackås	Hackås	Revsunda, Brunflo och Näs	Jäm	1688	1781
Haga	Sigtuna	Ärlinghundra	Sto	1751	1754
Hagby	Södermöre	Södra Möre	Kal	1701	1755
Hagby	Södra Hagunda	Hagunda	Upp	1682	1767
Hagebyhöga	Aska	Aska	Öst	1700	1789
Hagelberg	Skultorp	Kåkind	Ska	1610	1770
Hagshult	Klevshult	Östbo	Jön	1688	1738
Hajom	Västra Mark	Mark	Älv	1681	1753

Name of Parish Before 1952	After 1952	Name of District	County	Earliest year of Parish register	Clerical survey record
Hakarp	Hakarp	Tveta	Jön	1680	1764
Hall	Lärbro	Norra	Got	—	1840
Halla	Romakloster	Norra	Got	1727	1784
Halla	Stigtomta	Jönåker	Söd	1702	1689
Hallaryd	Göteryd	Sunnerbo	Kro	1638	1718
Hallaröd	Norra Frosta	Onsjö	Mal	1647	1813
Hallen	Hallen	Sunne, Oviken och Hallen	Jäm	1693	1693
Hallingeberg	Hallingeberg	Tjust	Kal	1663	1730
Hallsberg	Hallsberg	Kumla	öre	1700	1702
Hallstahammar, see	Svedvi				
Halltorp	Södermöre	Södra Möre	Kal	1714	1763
Halmstad	Halmstad	Halmstad	Hal	1711	1812
Halmstad	Kåkeröd	Luggude	Mal	1646	1809
Halna	Undenäs	Vadsbo	Ska	1689	1782
Halvås	Ryda	Barne	Ska	1859	—
Hammar	Hammar	Sundbo	öre	1652	1791
Hammarby	Upplands-Väsby	Vallentuna	Sto	1677	1741
Hammarby	Kafjärden	österrekarne	Söd	1696	1788
Hammarlunda	Löberöd	Frosta	Mal	1815	1814
Hammarlöv	Skegrie	Skytt	Mal	1689	1816
Hammarö	Hammarö	Karlstad	Vär	1734	1758
Hammenhög	Hammenhög	Ingelstad	Kri	1692	1820
Hammerdal	Hammerdal	Hammerdal	Jäm	1687	1694
Hamneda	Hamneda	Sunnerbo	Kro	1671	1757
Hamra	Hoburg	Södra	Got	—	1783
Hamra	Los	Västra Hälsingland	Gäv	—	1712
Hamrånge	Hamrånge	Gästriklands östra	Gäv	1721	1723
Hanebo	Hanebo	Bollnäs	Gäv	1678	1748
Hangelösa	Husaby	Kinnefjärding	Ska	1694	1691
Hangvar	Lärbro	Norra	Got	1766	1807
Hanhals	Fjärås	Fjäre	Hal	1688	1772
Hannas	Hammenhög	Ingelstad	Kri	1692	1820
Hannäs	Uknadalen	Tjust	Kal	1695	1814
Haparanda	Haparanda	Haparanda	Nbt	1823	1836
Haraker	Skultuna	Norrbo	Vma	1667	1689
Harbo	östervåla	Våla	Vma	1680	1687
Hardeberga	Södra Sandby	Torna	Mal	1745	1759
Hardemo	Kumla	Hardemo	öre	1688	1707
Harestad	Hermansby	Inlands södra	GoB	1760	1809
Harg	östhammar	Frösåker	Sto	1719	1741
Harlösa	Löberöd	Frosta	Mal	1722	1814
Harmånger	Harmånger	Bergjö och Forsa	Gäv	1688	1755
Harplinge	Harplinge	Halmstad	Hal	1685	1814
Hastad	Folkunga	Göstring	öst	1646	1789
Hassela	Hassela	Bergsjö och Forsa	Gäv	1688	1689
Hassle	Hasslerör	Vadsbo	Ska	1690	1763
Hassle-Bösarp	Skurup	Vemmenhög	Mal	1711	1813
Hasslösa	Vinninga	Kinnefjärding	Ska	1647	1770
Hasslöv	Karup	Hök	Hal	1693	1766
Haurida	Hullaryd	Vedbo	Jön	1689	1808
Havdhem	Havdhem	Södra	Got	1675	1737
Haverö	Haverö	Medelpads västra	Vno	1660	1731
Hed	Skinnskatteberg	Skinnskatteberg	Vma	1683	1715
Heda	Alvastra	Lysing	öst	1667	1812
Hedared	Sandhult	Veden	Älv	1770	1815
Hede	Sörbygden	Sörbygden	GoB	1688	1803
Hede	Hede	Hede	Jäm	1777	1738

Name of Parish Before 1952	After 1952	Name of District	County	Earliest year of Parish register	Clerical survey record
Hedemora					
Stads		Hedemora	Kop	1660	1660
Lands		Hedemora	Kop	1660	1660
Hedeskoga	Herrestad	Herrestad	Mal	1679	1794
Hedesunda	Hedesunda	Gästriklands östra	Gäv	1688	1688
Hedvig, see Norrköping					
Hejde	Klintehamn	Södra	Got	1734	1785
Hejdeby	Romakloster	Norra	Got	1881	1792
Hejnum	Tingstäde	Norra	Got	1688	1690
Helgarö	Vårfruberga	Åker	Söd	1681	1725
Helgesta	Sparreholm	Villåttinge	Söd	1689	1758
Helgum	Helgum	Ramsele och Resele	Vno	1684	1786
Heliga Trefaldighet	Uppsala	Ulleråker	Upp	1608	1682
Hellvi	Lärbro	Norra	Got	1840	1768
Hemmesdynge	Klagstorp	Vemmenhög	Mal	1688	1811
Hemmesjö	östra Torsås	Konga	Kro	1693	1718
Hemse	Hemse	Södra	Got	1684	1796
Hemsjö	Hemsjö	Kulling	Älv	1688	1732
Hemsö	Säbrå	Ångermanlands södra	Vno		1847
Herrberga	Vifolka	Vifolka	öst	1683	1790
Herrestad	Skredsvik	Lane	GoB	1689	1756
Herrestad	Östgöta-Dal	Dal	öst	1633	1714
Herrljunga	Herrljunga	Kulling	Älv	1718	1790
Herråkra	Lenhovda	Uppvidinge	Kro	1720	1717
Hidinge	Lekeberg	Edsberg	öre	1725	1775
Hietaniemi	Hietaniemi	Torneå	Nbt	1721	1741
Hillared	Lysjö	Kind	Älv	1721	1837
Hille	Hille	Gästriklands östra	Gäv	1688	1749
Hilleshög	Färingsö	Färentuna	Sto	1688	1779
Himmeta	Medåker	Åkerbo	Vma	1718	1671
Hinneryd	Traryd	Sunnerbo	Kro	1712	1717
Hishult	Hishult	Hök	Hal	1682	1817
Hjo					
Stads		Hjo	Ska	1694	1789
Lands		Kåkind	Ska	1811	1788
Hjorted	Hjorted	Södra Tjust	Kal	1633	1774
Hjortsberga	Listerby	Medelstad	Ble	1721	1801
Hjortsberga	Hjortberga	Allbo	Kro	1793	1752
Hjulsjö	Noraskog	Nora och Hjulsjö	öre	1674	1766
Hjälmseryd	Hjälmseryd	Västra	Jön	1689	1717
Hjälsta	Lagunda	Lagunda	Upp	1749	1777
Hjälstad	Moholm	Vadsbo	Ska	1688	1764
Hjärnarp	Hjärnarp	Bjäre	Kri	1763	1818
Hjärsås	Hjärsås	Östra Göinge	Kri	1790	1861
Hjärtlanda	Sävsjö	Västra	Jön	1703	1753
Hjärtum	Inlands Torpe	Inlands Torpe	GoB	1686	1792
Hofterup	Löddeköpinge	Harjager	Mal	1716	1787
Hogdal	Vette	Vette	GoB	1708	1812
Hogrån	Stenkumla	Södra	Got	1782	1783
Hogstad	Folkunga	Göstring	öst	1645	1811
Hol	Vårgårda	Kulling	Älv	1700	1774
Holm	Kvibille	Halmstad	Hal	1687	1753
Holm	Lagunda	Lagunda	Upp	1672	1680
Holm	Indals-Liden	Indal	Vno	1748	1803
Holm	Mellerud	Nordal	Älv	1749	1726
Holmby	Skarhult	Frosta	Mal	1689	1813
Holmedal	Holmedal	Nordmark	Vär	1717	1754

Name of Parish Before 1952	After 1952	Name of District	County	Earliest year of Parish register	Clerical survey record
Holmestad	Götene	Kinne	Ska	1751	1757
Holmsund	Holmsund	Umeå	Vbn	—	1863
Holmön	Holmön	Umeå	Vbn	1820	1820
Holsljunga	Hogvad	Kind	Älv	1712	1812
Horla	Vårgårda	Kulling	Älv	1700	1775
Horn	Binneberg	Vadsbo	Ska	1688	1788
Horn	Södra Kinda	Kinda	Öst	1843	1805
Hornaryd	Braås	Uppvidinge	Kro	1707	1718
Hornborga	Gudhem	Gudhem	Ska	1703	1800
Horred	Horred	Mark	Älv	1685	1756
Hosjö	Vika	Falu norra	Kop	1725	1683
Hossmo	Dörby	Möre	Kal	1697	1771
Hotagen	Hotagen	Lits och Rödön	Jäm	1846	1801
Hov	Västra Bjäre	Bjäre	Kri	1744	1791
Hov	Gäsene	Gäsene	Älv	1706	1820
Hov	Folkunga	Göstring	Öst	1634	1788
Hova	Hova	Vadsbo	Ska	1688	1793
Hovby	Vinninga	Kinnefjärding	Ska	1699	1792
Hovmantorp	Hovmantorp	Konga	Kro	1688	1733
Hovsta	Axberg	Örebro	Öre	1680	1707
Huaröd	Degeberga	Gärd	Kri	1689	1802
Hubbo	Tillberga	Siende	Vma	1696	1750
Huddinge	Huddinge	Svartlösa	Sto	1668	1689
Huddunge	Västerlövsta	Våla	Vma	1688	1770
Hudene	Gäsene	Gäsene	Älv	1647	1758
Hudiksvall	Hudiksvall	Hudiksvall	Gäv	1716	1752
Huggenäs	Värmlandsnäs	Näs	Vär	1689	1775
Hulared	Dalstorp	Kind	Älv	1699	1748
Hult	Höreda	Vedbo	Jön	1669	1789
Hulterstad	Mörbylånga	Möckleby	Kal	1717	1749
Hultsjö	Hjälmseryd	Västra	Jön	1703	1717
Hulma	Redväg	Redväg	Älv	1695	1801
Hunnestad	Himledalen	Himle	Hal	1615	1777
Hurva	Snogeröd	Frosta	Mal	1796	1813
Husaby	Husaby	Kinnefjärding	Ska	1685	1749
Husby	Husby	Hedemora	Kop	1653	1670
Husby-Lyhundra	Sjuhundra	Lyhundra	Sto	1700	1755
Husby-Långhundra	Skepptuna	Långhundra	Sto	1717	1736
Husby-Oppunda	Bettna	Oppunda	Söd	1671	1689
Husby-Rekarne	Husby-Rekarne	Österrekarne	Söd	1670	1689
Husby-Sjutolft	Norra Trögd	Trögd	Upp	1688	1695
Husby-Ärlinghundra	Märsta	Ärlinghundra	Sto	1780	1716
Husie	Malmö	Oxie	Mal	1688	1815
Hyby	Bara	Bara	Mal	1689	1778
Hycklinge	Södra Kinda	Kinda	Öst	1845	1713
Hylletofta	Vrigstad	Västra	Jön	1705	1717
Hyllie	Malmö	Oxie	Mal	1689	1789
Hyltinge	Sparreholm	Villåttinge	Söd	1652	1758
Hyringa	Grästorp	Viste	Ska	1717	1725
Hyssna	Sätila	Mark	Älv	1681	1787
Håbo-Tibble	Upplands-Bro	Håbo	Upp	1705	1752
Håbol	Dals-Ed	Vedbo	Älv	1688	1786
Håby	Munkedal	Tunge	GoB	1688	1799
Håcksvik	Kindaholm	Kind	Älv	1704	1810
Håkantorp	Stenstorp	Gudhem	Ska	1688	1740
Hålanda	Skepplanda	Ale	Älv	1687	1811
Håle	Grästorp	Åse	Ska	1688	1766
Hållnäs	Hållnäs	Oland	Upp	1664	1755
Hålta	Kode	Inlands-Nordre	GoB	1659	1795

Name of Parish: Before 1952	Name of Parish: After 1952	Name of District	County	Earliest year of: Parish register	Earliest year of: Clerical survey record
Hånger	Forsheda	Östbo	Jön	1688	1717
Hångsdala	Dimbo	Vartofta	Ska	1702	1824
Håsjö	Kälarne	Ragunda	Jäm	1689	1815
Håslöv	Räng	Skytt	Mal	1688	1734
Håstad	Torn	Torna	Mal	1724	1812
Håtuna	Upplands-Bro	Håbo	Upp	1674	1732
Hägerstad	Norra Kinda	Kinda	Öst	1676	1713
Häggdånger	Säbrå	Ångermanlands Södra	Vno	1684	1750
Häggeby	Håbo	Håbo	Upp	1728	1703
Häggenås	Häggenås	Lits och Rödön	Jäm	1693	1804
Häggesled	Järpås	Kålland	Ska	1648	1688
Häggum	Skultorp	Valle	Ska	1696	1763
Häglinga	Sösdala	Västra Göinge	Kri	1806	1683
Hällaryd	Hällaryd	Bräkne	Ble	1647	1813
Hälleberga	Hälleberga	Uppvidinge	Kro	1751	1747
Hällefors	Hällefors	Grythytte och Hällefors	Öre	1676	1749
Hällesjö	Kälarne	Ragunda	Jäm	1689	1815
Hällestad	Dalby	Torna	Mal	1747	1799
Hällestad	Vilske	Vilske	Ska	1690	1816
Hällestad	Hällestad	Finspångalän	Öst	1636	1750
Hällstad	Hökerum	Ås	Älv	1701	1766
Hällum	Ryda	Barne	Ska	1667	1791
Hälsingborg					
Stads		Hälsingborg	Mal	1688	1712
Lands		Hälsingborg	Mal	1688	1712
Garnisons		Hälsingborg	Mal	1822	1820
Hälsingtuna	Hälsingtuna	Norra Hälsingland	Gäv	1688	1765
Händene	Ardala	Skåning	Ska	1680	1775
Härad	Vårfruberga	Åker	Söd	1669	1706
Häradshammar	Östra Vikbolandet	Östkind	Öst	1668	1773
Härja	Hökensås	Vartofta	Ska	1691	1774
Härjevad	Saleby	Skåning	Ska	1741	1735
Härkeberga	Norra Trögd	Trögd	Upp	1690	1720
Härlunda	Almundsryd	Allbo	Kro	1689	1717
Härlunda	Ardala	Allbo	Ska	1657	1709
Härlöv	Alvesta	Allbo	Kro	1688	1688
Härna	Hökerum	Ås	Älv	1709	1769
Härnevi	Fjärdhundra	Torstuna	Vma	1690	1691
Härnösand					
Stads		Härnösand	Vno	1721	1732
Hospitals		Härnösand	Vno	1865	1846
Härryda	Landvetter	Sävedal	GoB	1687	1771
Härslöv	Härslöv	Rönneberg	Mal	1721	1787
Hässjö	Hässjö	Njurunda Skön och Ljustorp	Vno	1688	1814
Hässleby	Mariannelund	Södra Vedbo	Jön	1724	1798
Hässlunda	Mörarp	Luggude	Mal	1743	1813
Hästveda	Hästveda	Östra Göinge	Kri	1690	1811
Häverö	Häverö	Väddö och Häverö	Sto	1688	1766
Hög	Forsa	Bergsjö och Forsa	Gäv	1729	1740
Hög	Löddeköpinge	Harjager	Mal	1685	1811
Höganäs (before 1854 see Väsby)	Höganäs	Luggude	Mal	1854	1854
Högbo	Sandviken	Gästriklands östra	Gäv	1778	1780
Högby	Ölands-Åkerbo	Åkerbo	Kal	1653	1785
Högby	Mjölby	Göstring	Öst	1645	1788
Högerud	Stavnäs	Gillberg	Vär	1689	1776

Name of Parish Before 1952	After 1952	Name of District	County	Earliest year of Parish register	Clerical survey record
Högestad	Herrestad	Herrestad	Mal	1758	1813
Högsby	Högsby	Handbörd	Kal	1635	1789
Högseröd	Löberöd	Frosta	Mal	1805	1825
Högsjö	Högsjö	Ångermanlands södra	Vno	1689	1764
Högsrum	Gärdslösa	Slättbo	Kal	1742	1834
Högstena	Stenstorp	Gudhem	Ska	1724	1776
Högsäter	Högsäter	Vadbo	Älv	1682	1747
Högås	Skredsvik	Lane	GoB	1689	1756
Höja	Ängelholm	Södra Åsby	Kri	1693	1813
Hökhuvud	Östhammar	Frösåker	Sto	1740	1745
Hököpinge	Vellinge	Oxie	Mal	1688	1813
Hölö	Hölö	Hölebo	Söd	1685	1762
Hömb	Dimbo	Vartofta	Ska	1680	1704
Höra	Järpås	Kålland	Ska	1648	1781
Hörby	Östra Fosta	Frosta	Mal	1688	1795
Höreda	Höreda	Södra Vedbo	Jön	1634	1762
Hörja	Tyringe	Västra Göinge	Kri	1690	1794
Hörnefors	Hörnefors	Nordmaling och Bjurholm	Vbn	1810	1842
Hörröd	Degeberga	Gärd	Kri	1687	1810
Hörsne	Dalhem	Norra	Got	1684	1743
Hörup	Löderup	Ingelstad	Kri	1684	1750
Hössna	Redväg	Redväg	Älv	1692	1790
Höör	Norra Frosta	Frosta	Mal	1795	1813
Idala	Löftadalen	Fjäre	Hal	1689	1750
Idenor	Hudiksvall	Bergsjö och Forsa	Gäv	1729	1752
Idre	Idre	Särna och Idre	Kop	1682	1797
Igelösa	Torn	Torna	Mal	1707	1803
Ignaberga	Stoby	Västra Göinge	Kri	1690	1822
Ilsbo	Harmånger	Bergsjö och Forsa	Gäv	1735	1764
Ilstorp	Sjöbo	Färs	Mal		1808
Indal	Indals-Liden	Indal	Vno	1662	1698
Ingarö	Gustavsberg	Värmdö	Sto	1810	1826
Ingatorp	Ingatorp	Södra Vedbo	Jön	1660	1793
Ingelstorp	Glemmingebro	Ingelstad	Kri	1678	1804
Irsta	Kungsåra	Siende	Vma	1621	1656
Istorp	Horred	Mark	Älv	1682	1752
Istrum	Valle	Valle	Ska	1688	1791
Ivetofta	Ivetofta	Villand	Kri	1732	1802
Ivö	Fjälkinge	Villand	Kri	1695	1786
Jakob	Jakob	Stockholm	Sto	1639	1672
Johannes	Johannes	Stockholm	Sto	1637	1672
Jokkmokk	Jokkmokk	Jokkmokks lappmark	Nbt	1701	1758
Jonsberg	Östra Vikbolandet	Östkind	Öst	1708	1765
Jonstorp	Jonstorp	Luggude	Mal	1689	1794
Jukkasjärvi	Kiruna	Jukkasjärvis lappmark	Nbt	1719	1765
Julita	Julita	Oppunda	Söd	1712	1783
Jumkil	Bälinge	Ulleråker	Upp	1691	1698
Jung	Kvänum	Skåning	Ska	1658	1793
Junsele	Junsele	Fjällsjö	Vno	1742	1777
Jäder	Kafjärden	Österrekarne	Söd	1664	1749
Jäla	Vilske	Vilske	Ska	1695	1724
Jällby	Gäsene	Gäsene	Älv	1707	1804
Jälluntofta	Unnaryd	Västbo	Jön	1682	1711
Jämjö	Jämjö	Östra	Ble	1682	1802
Jämshög	Jämshög	Lister	Ble	1726	1816
Järbo	Järbo	Gästriklands västra	Gäv		1866

Name of Parish Before 1952	Name of Parish After 1952	Name of District	County	Earliest year of Parish register	Earliest year of Clerical survey record
Järbo	Högsäter	Valbo	Älv	1656	1774
Järeda	Virserum	Aspeland	Kal	1713	1753
Järfälla	Järfälla	Sollentuna	Sto	1702	1710
Järlåsa	Norra Hagunda	Hagunda	Upp	1645	1696
Järn	Mellerud	Nordal	Älv	1702	1776
Järna	Järna	Nås	Kop	1671	1716
Järnboås	Noraskog	Nora och Hjulsjö	Öre	1689	1730
Järnskog	Järnskog	Nordmark	Vär	1664	1696
Järpås	Järpås	Kålland	Ska	1648	1688
Järrestad	Simrishamn	Järrestad	Kri	1689	1807
Järsnäs	Lekeryd	Tveta	Jön	1688	1753
Järstad	Skänninge	Göstring	Öst	1688	1694
Järstorp	Jönköping	Tveta	Jön	1669	1725
Järvsö	Järvsö	Västra Hälsingland	Gäv	1679	1692
Jät	Väckelsång	Kinnevald	Kro	1676	1718
Jättendal	Harmånger	Bergsjö och Forsa	Gäv	1688	1740
Jönköping					
Kristina		Jönköping	Jön	1680	1689
Ljungarum		Jönköping	Jön	1708	1720
Sofia		Jönköping	Jön	1726	1718
Jörlanda	Kode	Inlands Nordre	GoB	1659	1800
Jörn	Jörn	Skellefteå	Vbn	1849	1831
Kaga	Kärna	Hanekind	Öst	1694	1808
Kall	Kall	Undersåker och Offerdal	Jäm	1688	1695
Kalmar					
Stads		Kalmar	Kal	1710	1773
Lands		Kalmar	Kal	1701	1821
Slotts		Kalmar	Kal	1753	1806
Kalmar	Håbo	Håbo	Upp	1713	1751
Kalv	Kindaholm	Kind	Älv	1702	1775
Kalvsvik	Mellersta Kinnevald	Kinnevald	Kro	1683	1718
Karaby	Tun	Åse	Ska	1672	1744
Karbenning	Västerfärnebo	Vagnsbro	Vma	1690	1731
Kareby	Romelanda	Inlands-södra	GoB	1815	1815
Karesuando	Karesuando	Karesuando lappmark	Nbt	1814	1816
Karlanda	Holmedal	Nordmark	Vär	1694	1774
Karlberg	Solna	Danderyd	Sto	1792	1793
Karleby	Vartofta	Vartofta	Ska	1712	1756
Karl Gustaf	Karl Gustaf	Torneå	Nbt	1762	1784
Karl Gustafs stad	Eskilstuna	Eskilstuna	Söd	—	1779
Karl Gustav	Kungsäter	Mark	Älv	1689	1798
Karlsborg	Karlsborg	Vadsbo	Ska	1831	1827
Karlsdal	Karlskoga	Karlskoga	Öre	1785	1790
Karlshamn	Karlshamn	Karlshamn	Ble	1687	1794
Karlskoga	Karlskoga	Karlskoga	Öre	1680	1757
Karlskrona					
Stads		Karlskrona	Ble	1750	1810
Amiralitets		Karlskrona	Ble	1693	1811
Tyska		Karlskrona	Ble	1690	1806
Karlskyrka, see Kung Karl					
Karlslunda	Mortorp	Södra Möre	Kal	1851	1816
Karlstad					
Stads		Karlstad	Vär	1698	1721
Lands		Karlstad	Vär	1698	1721
Karlsten	Marstrand	Marstrand	GoB	1694	1835
Karlstorp	Alseda	Östra	Jön	1679	1728
Karlsvik	Mellersta Kinnevald	Kinnevald	Kro	1683	1718

Name of Parish Before 1952	After 1952	Name of District	County	Earliest year of Parish register	Clerical survey record
Kastlösa	Mörbylånga	Gräsgård	Kal	1628	1776
Katarina	Katarina	Stockholm	Sto	1665	1707
Katrineberg	Bollnäs	Bollnäs	Gäv	1843	1812
Katrineholm	Katrineholm	Katrineholm	Söd		1886
Katslösa	Rydsgård	Ljunit	Mal	1702	1776
Kattarp	Kattarp	Luggude	Mal	1687	1813
Kattnäs	Gnesta	Daga	Söd	1688	1786
Kestad	Kinnekulle	Kinne	Ska	1732	1740
Kiaby	Fjälkinge	Villand	Kri	1694	1799
Kil	Axberg	örebro	Öre	1666	1727
Kila	Jönåker	Jönåker	Söd	1670	1768
Kila	Gillberga	Näs	Vär	1640	1761
Kila	Tärna	Övertjurbo	Vma	1678	1663
Kilanda	Starrkärr	Ale	Älv	1697	1790
Kimstad	Norsholm	Memming	öst	1674	1806
Kinna	Kinna	Mark	Älv	1762	1798
Kinnared	Torup	Halmstad	Hal	1679	1840
Kinnarumma	Kinnarumma	Mark	Älv	1681	1758
Kinne-Kleva	Husaby	Husaby	Ska	1688	1747
Kinneved	Frökind	Frökind	Ska	1713	1792
Kinne-Vedum	Götene	Kinne	Ska		1781
Kisa	Västra Kinda	Kinda	öst	1633	1798
Kjula	Kafjärden	österrekarne	Söd	1696	1764
Klara	Klara	Stockholm	Sto	1680	1787
Klinte	Klintehamn	Södra	Got	1681	1784
Klippans köping	Klippan	Norra Åbo	Kri	1720	1813
Klockrike	Borensberg	Boberg	öst	1688	1760
Kloster	Eskilstuna	Eskilstuna	Söd	1835	1779
Kläckeberga	Dörby	Norra Möre	Kal	1713	1812
Klädesholmen	Tjörn	Tjörn	GoB	1795	1801
Klövedal	Tjörn	Tjörn	GoB	1688	1805
Klövsjö	Övre Ljungadalen	Berg	Jäm	1695	1827
Knislinge	Knislinge	Östra Göinge	Kri	1851	1861
Knista	Lekeberg	Edsberg	Öre	1725	1769
Knivsta	Knivsta	Arlinghundra	Sto	1747	1790
Knutby	Knutby	Näringhundra	Sto	1674	1731
Knäred	Knäred	Hök	Hal	1688	1808
Knästorp	Staffanstorp	Bara	Mal	1661	1791
Knätte	Redväg	Redväg	Älv	1721	1792
Kolbäck	Kolbäck	Snevringe	Vma	1688	1724
Konga	Röstånga	Onsjö	Mal	1813	1811
Konungsund	Västra Vikbolandet	Björkekind	Öst	1657	1790
Korpilombolo	Korpilombolo	Pajala och Korpilombolo	Nbt		1856
Korsberga	Korsberga	östra	Jön	1750	1717
Korsberga	Fröjered	Vartofta	Ska	1727	1740
Kristberg	Borensberg	Boberg	öst	1650	1762
Kristdala	Kristdala	Tunalän	Kal	1681	1785
Kristianopel	Kristianopel	Östra	Ble	1713	1789
Kristianstad					
Stads		Kristianstad	Kri	1646	1809
Garnisons		Kristianstad	Kri	1798	1811
Kristinehamn	Kristinehamn	Kristinehamn	Vär	1645	1730
Kristvalla	Madesjö	Norra Möre	Kal	1664	1787
Krogsered	Ätran	Årstad	Hal	1694	1775
Krokek	Kolmården	Lösing	Öst	1778	1791
Krokstad	Sörbygden	Sörbygden	GoB	1688	1803
Kropp	Mörarp	Luggude	Mal	1689	1810
Kroppa	Kroppa	Färnebo	Vär	1687	1738

Name of Parish Before 1952	After 1952	Name of District	County	Earliest year of Parish register	Clerical survey record
Kråkshult	Mariannelund	Östra	Jön	1714	1715
Kråksmåla	Alsterbo	Handbörd	Kal	1759	1830
Kräcklinge	Lekeberg	Edsberg	Öre	1709	1726
Kräklingbo	Romakloster	Norra	Got	1688	1760
Kuddby	Västra Vikbolandet	Björkekind	Öst	1639	1805
Kulla	Lagunda	Lagunda	Upp	1671	1695
Kullerstad	Skärblacka	Memming	Öst	1652	1793
Kullings-Skövde	Vårgårda	Kulling	Älv	1688	1768
Kulltorp	Gnosjö	Västbo	Jön	1716	1758
Kumla	Tärna	Övertjurbo	Vma	1654	1661
Kumla	Kumla	Kumla	Öre	1697	1723
Kumla	Folkunga	Lysing	Öst	1675	1714
Kung Karl	Kung Karl	Åkerbo	Vma	1684	1774
Kungsbacka	Kungsbacka	Kungsbacka	Hal	1688	1771
Kungs-Barkarö	Kung Karl	Sotenäs	Vma	1684	1741
Kungshamn	Södra Sotenäs	Åkerbo	GoB	1785	1787
Kungsholm or Ulrika Eleonora	Kungsholm	Stockholm	Sto	1672	1689
Kungs-Husby	Södra Trögd	Trögd	Upp	1715	1765
Kungslena	Dimbo	Vartofta	Ska	1680	1688
Kungsåra	Kungsåra	Siende	Vma	1627	1693
Kungsäter	Kungsäter	Mark	Älv	1689	1798
Kungsör	Kung Karl	Åkerbo	Vma		1822
Kungälv	Kungälv	Kungälv	GoB	1696	1803
Kvarsebo	Kolmården	Östkind	Öst	1698	1714
Kvenneberga	Hjortberga	Allbo	Kro	1775	1752
Kverrestad	Smedstorp	Ingelstad	Kri	1690	1779
Kvibille	Kvibille	Halmstad	Hal	1698	1753
Kvidinge	Kvidinge	Södra Åsbo	Kri	1720	1803
Kviinge	Knislinge	Östra Göinge	Kri	1646	1815
Kvikkjokk	Jokkmokk	Jokkmokks lappmark	Nbt	1784	1781
Kville	Kville	Kville	GoB	1860	1860
Kvillinge	Kvillinge	Bråbo	Öst	1667	1713
Kvinnestad	Vårgårda	Gäsene	Älv	1722	1784
Kvistbro	Svartå	Edsberg	Öre	1683	1800
Kvistofta	Vallåkra	Luggude	Mal	1689	1792
Kvänum	Kvänum	Skåning	Ska	1850	1782
Kymbo	Dimbo	Vartofta	Ska	1691	1695
Kyrkheddinge	Staffanstorp	Bara	Mal	1736	1824
Kyrkhult	Kyrkhult	Lister	Ble	1865	1865
Kyrkoköpinge	Gislöv	Skytt	Mal	1689	1801
Kyrkås	Lit	Lit och Rödön	Jäm	1693	1805
Kyrkås	Essunga	Barne	Ska	1689	1799
Kågeröd	Kågeröd	Luggude	Mal	1689	1773
Kållands-Åsaka	Kållands-Råda	Kålland	Ska	1686	1752
Kållered	Kållered	Askim	GoB	1737	1792
Kållerstad	Reftele	Västbo	Jön	1714	1751
Källstad	Östgöta-Dal	Dal	Öst	1688	1804
Kånna	Hammeda	Sunnerbo	Kro	1743	1794
Kårböle	Färila-Kårböle	Ljusdal	Gäv		1812
Kårsta	Össeby	Långhundra	Sto	1711	1766
Källa	Ölands-Åkerbo	Åkerbo	Kal	1695	1734
Källby	Husaby	Kinnefjärding	Ska	1694	1689
Källeryd	Gnosjö	Mo	Jön	1679	1717
Källna	Östra Ljungby	Norra Åsbo	Kri	1689	1814
Källsjö	Ullared	Faurås	Hal	1688	1812
Källs-Nöbbelöv	Teckomatorp	Onsjö	Mal	1749	1799
Källstad	Östgöta-Dal	Dal	Öst	1688	1804

Name of Parish Before 1952	After 1952	Name of District	County	Earliest year of Parish register	Clerical survey record
Källstorp	Klagstorp	Vemmenhög	Mal	1680	1813
Källunga	Gäsene	Gäsene	Älv	1706	1820
Källunge	Dalhem	Norra	Got	1710	1765
Kälvene	Vartofta	Vartofta	Ska	1687	1775
Kälvsten, see Västra	Stenby				
Kärda	Forsheda	Östbo	Jön	1689	1754
Käringön	Morlanda	Orust västra	GoB	1795	1787
Kärna	Kärna	Hanekind	Öst	1695	1807
Kärnbo	Mariefred	Selebo	Söd	1667	1689
Kärrbo	Kungsåra	Siende	Vma	1631	1727
Kärråkra	Hökerum	Ås	Älv	1688	1777
Kättilstad	Norra Kinda	Kinda	Öst	1693	1719
Kävlinge	Kävlinge	Harjager	Mal	1685	1811
Kävsjö	Gnosjö	Östbo	Jön	1688	1734
Köinge	Vessigebro	Fauräs	Hal	1688	1795
Köla	Köla	Jösse	Vär	1664	1694
Kölaby	Redväg	Redväg	Älv	1706	1774
Kölingared	Redväg	Redväg	Älv	1721	1792
Köping	Köpingsvik	Slättbo	Kal	1652	1777
Köping					
Stads		Åkerbo och Fellingsbro	Vma	1688	1731
Lands		Åkerbo och Fellingsbro	Vma	1688	1732
Köpinge	Vä	Gärd	Kri	1752	1811
Lackalänga	Furulund	Torna	Mal	1682	1826
Lagga	Knivsta	Långhundra	Sto	1698	1752
Lagmansered	Bjärke	Bjärke	Älv	1692	1768
Laholm					
Stads		Laholm	Hal	1697	1803
Lands		Laholm	Hal	1697	1806
Landa	Löftadalen	Fjäre	Hal	1683	1751
Landa	Vårgårda	Kulling	Älv	1748	1768
Landeryd	Landeryd	Hanekind	Öst	1635	1789
Landskrona					
Stads		Landskrona	Mal	1686	1778
Garnisons		Landskrona	Mal	1773	1819
Lands		Torna	Mal	1852	1813
Sankt Ibb		Landskrona	Mal	1709	1813
Landvetter	Landvetter	Sävedal	GoB	1687	1750
Lane-Ryr	Lane-Ryr	Lane	GoB	1711	1812
Lannaskede	Lannaskede	Östra	Jön	1733	1790
Larv	Larv	Laske	Ska	1688	1803
Laske-Vedum	Vedum	Laske	Ska	1710	1779
Lau	Ljugarn	Södra	Got	—	1796
Lavad	Örslösa	Kålland	Ska	1695	1738
Laxarby	Lelång	Vedbo	Älv	1703	1711
Ledberg	Kärna	Valkebo	Öst	1635	1755
Ledsjö	Husaby	Kinne	Ska	1688	1824
Lekaryd	Alvesta	Allbo	Kro	1688	1694
Lekeryd	Lekeryd	Tveta	Jön	1682	1718
Leksand	Leksand	Nedansiljans	Kop	1668	1672
Leksberg	Mariestad	Vadsbo	Ska	1688	1731
Lekvattnet	Fryksände	Frykdals	Vär	—	1851
Lekås	Essunga	Barne	Ska	1689	1799
Lemmeströ	Anderslöv	Vemmenhög	Mal	1689	
Lemnhult	Korsberga	Östra	Jön	1732	1753
Lena	Vattholma	Norunda	Upp	1683	1744
Lena	Vårgårda	Kulling	Älv	1705	1741

Name of Parish Before 1952	After 1952	Name of District	County	Earliest year of Parish register	Clerical survey record
Lenhovda	Lenhovda	Uppvidinge	Kro	1689	1690
Lerbo	Sköldinge	Oppunda	Söd	1666	1734
Lerbäck	Lerbäck	Kumla	Öre	1716	1780
Lerdal	Högsäter	Valbo	Älv	1724	1756
Lerdala	Timmersdala	Vadsbo	Ska	1630	1733
Lerum	Lerum	Vättle	Älv	1744	1813
Levene	Levene	Viste	Ska	1688	1746
Levide	Hemse	Södra	Got	1788	1784
Liared	Redväg	Redväg	Älv	1721	1792
Lid	Rönö	Rönö	Söd	1687	1689
Liden	Indals-Liden	Indal	Vno	1688	1736
Lidhult	Lidhult	Sunnerbo	Kro	1733	1788
Lidingö	Lidingö	Lidingö	Sto	1770	1741
Lidköping	Lidköping	Lidköping	Ska	1675	1738
Lilla Beddinge	Klagstorp	Vemmenhög	Mal	1680	1813
Lilla Edet	Lilla Edet	Flundre	Älv	1688	1781
Lilla Harrie	Harrie	Harjager	Mal	1720	1813
Lilla Isie	Klagstorp	Vemmenhög	Mal	1764	1793
Lilla Malma	Malmköping	Villåttinge	Söd	1666	1736
Lilla Mellösa, see Mellösa					
Lilla Slågarp	Alstad	Skytt	Mal	1729	1825
Lillhärad	Dingtuna	Tuhundra	Vma	1703	1835
Lillhärdal	Lillhärdal	Sveg	Jäm	1691	1808
Lillkyrka	Södra Trögd	Trögd	Upp	1688	1730
Lillkyrka	Glanshammar	Glanshammar	Öre	1694	1744
Lillkyrka	Åkerbo	Åkerbo	Öst	1667	1739
Lima	Lima	Malung	Kop	1631	1690
Lindberga	Lindberga	Himle	Hal	1691	1806
Linde	Hemse	Södra	Got		1785
Linderås	Linderås	Norra Vedbo	Jön	1651	1789
Linderöd	Tollarp	Gärd	Kri	1755	1833
Lindesberg					
Stads		Lindesberg	Öre	1632	1688
Bergs		Lindesberg	Öre	1632	1688
Lindome	Lindome	Fjäre	Hal	1688	1762
Lindärva	Vinninga	Kinnefjärding	Ska	1648	1776
Linköping					
Stads		Linköping	Öst	1664	1783
Sankt Lars		Linköping	Öst	1633	1789
Linneryd	Linneryd	Konga	Kro	1721	1692
Linsäll	Sveg	Sveg	Jäm	1807	1811
Listra	Västra Rekarne	Västerrekarne	Söd	1726	1745
Listerby	Listerby	Medelstad	Ble	1713	1801
Lit	Lit	Lit och Rödön	Jäm	1694	1739
Litslena	Norra Trögd	Trögd	Upp	1694	1719
Ljuder	Ljuder	Konga	Kro	1672	1699
Ljung	Ljungskile	Inlands Fräkne	GoB	1747	1805
Ljung	Vreta Kloster	Gullberg	Öst	1694	1791
Ljungarum	Jönköping	Jönköping	Jön	1708	1720
Ljungby	Vinberg	Faurås	Hal	1689	1784
Ljungby	Ljungbyholm	Södra Möre	Kal	1635	1771
Ljungby	Ljungby	Sunnerbo	Kro	1752	1781
Ljunghem	Värsås	Gudhem	Ska	1663	1782
Ljungsarp	Dalstorp	Kind	Älv	1699	1752
Ljur	Vårgårda	Gäsene	Älv	1722	1785
Ljusdal	Ljusdal	Västra Hälsingland	Gäv	1680	1767
Ljushult	Lysjö	Kind	Älv	1692	1837
Ljusnarsberg	Ljusnarsberg	Nya Kopparberg	Öre	1635	1708

Name of Parish Before 1952	After 1952	Name of District	County	Earliest year of Parish register	Clerical survey record
Ljusnedal	Tännäs	Hede	Jäm	1749	1816
Ljusterö	Ljusterö	Åker	Sto	1679	1773
Ljustorp	Hässjö	Njurunda, Skön och Ljustorp	Vno	1688	1803
Lockarp	Oxie	Oxie	Mal	1688	1799
Locketorp	Binneberg	Vadsbo	Ska	1688	1773
Lockne	Brunflo	Revsund, Brunflo och Näs	Jäm	1777	1695
Locknevi	Locknevi	Södra Tjust	Kal	1633	1790
Lofta	Gamleby	Norra Tjust	Kal	1633	1768
Loftahammar	Loftahammar	Norra Tjust	Kal	1684	1779
Lohärad	Lyhundra	Lyhundra	Sto	1688	1756
Lojsta	Hemse	Södra	Got		1785
Lokrume	Tingstäde	Norra	Got		1799
Lomma	Lomma	Bara	Mal	1684	1780
Lommaryd	Hullaryd	Norra Vedbo	Jön	1633	1723
Lommeland	Vette	Vette	GoB	1708	1811
Long	Levene	Barne	Ska	1704	1770
Los	Los	Västra Hälsingland	Gäv	1748	1748
Loshult	Loshult	Östra Göinge	Kri	1647	1780
Lovö	Ekerö	Färentuna	Sto	1665	1688
Ludgo	Rönö	Jönåker	Söd	1684	1750
Ludvika	Ludvika	Ludvika	Kop	1773	1785
Lugnås	Lugnås	Kinne	Ska	1688	1747
Luleå	Luleå	Luleå	Nbt	1687	1736
Lummelunda	Tingstäde	Norra	Got	1665	1695
Lund					
Stads		Lund	Mal	1671	1810
Lands		Lund	Mal	1671	1813
Lunda	Skepptuna	Seminghundra	Sto	1688	1765
Lunda	Jönåker	Jönåker	Söd	1685	1722
Lundby	Västerås	Västerås	Vma	1628	1628
Lungsund	Ullvättern	Färnebo	Vär	1687	1733
Lur	Tanum	Tanum	GoB	1719	1759
Luttra	Frökind	Vartofta	Ska	1726	1796
Lyby	Östra Frosta	Frosta	Mal	1688	1800
Lycke	Hermansby	Inlands Södre	GoB	1760	1791
Lyckeby	Lyckeby	Östra	Ble	1695	1808
Lycksele	Lycksele	Lycksele	Vbn	1702	1742
Lye	Ljugarn	Södra	Got	1835	1840
Lyngby	Genarp	Bara	Mal	1697	1772
Lyngsjö	Everöd	Gärd	Kri	1752	1811
Lyrestad	Lyrestad	Vadsbo	Ska	1625	1837
Lyse	Lysekil	Stångenäs	GoB	1703	1834
Lysekil	Lysekil	Lysekil	GoB	1703	1834
Lysvik	Lysvik	Frykdal	Vär	1692	1765
Långared	Bjärke	Kulling	Älv	1705	1736
Långaryd	Hylte	Västbo	Jön	1686	1717
Långaröd	Långaröd	Färs	Mal	1792	1826
Långasjö	Älmeboda	Konga	Kro	1698	1699
Långelanda	Myckleby	Orust östra	GoB	1688	1816
Långemåla	Högsby	Handbörd	Kal	1734	1752
Långlöt	Gärdslösa	Runsten	Kal	1680	1799
Långsele	Långsele	Sollefteå	Vno	1732	1805
Långserud	Svanskog	Gillberg	Vär	1693	1733
Långtora	Lagunda	Lagunda	Upp	1692	1687
Låssa	Upplands-Bro	Bro	Upp	1693	1765
Låstad	Ullervad	Vadsbo	Ska	1688	1785
Läby	Norra Hagunda	Ulleråker	Upp	1686	1766
Länghem	Länghem	Kind	Älv	1690	1807

Name of Parish		Name of		Earliest year of	
Before 1952	After 1952	District	County	Parish register	Clerical survey record
Längjum	Larv	Laske	Ska	1688	1805
Längnum	Grästorp	Viste	Ska	1721	1721
Länna	Roslags-Länna	Frötuna och Länna	Sto	1682	1699
Länna	Åker	Åker	Söd	1701	1689
Lännäs	Asker	Asker	öre	1686	1762
Lärbro	Lärbro	Norra	Got	1737	1737
Lästringe	Tystberga	Rönö	Söd	1714	1763
Löddeköpinge	Löddeköpinge	Harjager	Mal	1724	1787
Löderup	Löderup	Ingelstad	Kri	1684	1750
Lögdö bruk	Hässjö	Njurunda, Skön och Ljustorp	Vno	1734	1750
Lönneberga	Lönneberga	Aspeland	Kal	1688	1788
Lönsås	Boberg	Boberg	öst	1763	1788
Lösen	Lyckeby	östra	Ble	1695	1808
Löt	Köpingsvik	Runsten	Kal	1689	1790
Löt	Norra Trögd	Trögd	Upp	1678	1765
Löt	Norrköping	Memming	öst	1683	1773
Lövestad	östra Färs	Färs	Mal	1709	1813
Lövånger	Lövånger	Nysätra	Vbn	1691	1705
Madesjö	Madesjö	Södre Möre	Kal	1677	1728
Maglarp	Skegrie	Skytt	Mal	1688	1809
Maglehem	Degeberga	Gärd	Kri	1687	1796
Magra	Bjärke	Bjärke	Älv	1688	1780
Malexander	Södra Göstring	Göstring	öst	1633	1719
Malingsbro	Söderbärke	Västerbergslag	Kop	1675	1684
Malma	Essunga	Viste	Ska	1708	1721
Malma	Kolsva	Åkerbo	Vma	1656	1742
Malmbäck	Malmbäck	Västra	Jön	1689	1753
Malmköping	Malmköping	Villåttinge	Söd		1871
Malmö					
Caroli		Malmö	Mal	1688	1813
Garnison		Malmö	Mal	1710	1819
Hospital		Malmö	Mal	1786	1874
Sankt Petri		Malmö	Mal	1698	1891
Slott		Malmö	Mal	1745	
Malsta	Lyhundra	Lyhundra	Sto	1689	1736
Malung	Malung	Malung	Kop	1775	1803
Malå	Malå	Norsjö och Malå	Vbn		1862
Mangskog	Brunskog	Jösse	Vär	1706	1760
Marby	Hallen	Sunne, Oviken och Hallen	Jäm	1764	1770
Marbäck	Bredestad	Norra Vedbo	Jön	1639	1789
Marbäck	Åsunden	Kind	Älv	1723	1811
Maria	Maria	Stockholm	Sto	1668	1737
Marieby	Brunflo	Revsund, Brunflo och Näs	Jäm	1689	1807
Mariefred	Mariefred	Mariefred	Söd	1667	1689
Mariestad	Mariestad	Mariestad	Ska	1688	1702
Marka	Vilske	Vilske	Ska	1695	1788
Markaryd	Markaryd	Sunnerbo	Kro	1688	1770
Markim	Vallentuna	Seminghundra	Sto	1670	1772
Marstrand	Marstrand	Marstrand	GoB	1685	1715
Martebo	Tingstäde	Norra	Got	1665	1688
Marum	Ardala	Skåning	Ska	1688	1746
Matteröd	Tyringe	Västra Göinge	Kri	1690	1798
Mattmar	Mörsil	Undersåker och Otterdal	Jäm	1689	1749
Medelplana	Kinnekulle	Kinne	Ska	1688	1746
Medåker	Medåker	Åkerbo	Vma	1650	1685

Name of Parish Before 1952	After 1952	Name of District	County	Earliest year of Parish register	Clerical survey record
Mellan-Grevie	Malmö	Oxie	Mal	1690	1813
Mellby	Höreda	Södra Vedbo	Jön	1685	1762
Mellby	Kållands-Råda	Kålland	Ska	1686	1695
Mellerud, see Holm					
Mellösa	Mellösa	Villåttinge	Söd	1726	1733
Millesvik	Värmlandsnäs	Näs	Vär	1688	1700
Mistelås	Moheda	Allbo	Kro	1752	1731
Misterhult	Misterhult	Tunalän	Kal	1633	1812
Mjäldrunga	Gäsene	Gäsene	Älv	1711	1802
Mjällby	Mjällby	Lister	Ble	1723	1803
Mjöbäck	Högvad	Kind	Älv	1712	1818
Mjölby	Mjölby	Mjölby	öst	1771	1789
Mo	Söderala	Ala	Gäv	1694	1743
Mo	Bullaren	Bullaren	GoB	1843	1759
Mo	Moholm	Vadsbo	Ska	1688	1764
Mo	Mo	Ångermanlands norra	Vno	1827	1827
Mo	Tössbo	Tössbo	Älv	1703	1786
Mockfjärd	Gagnef	Leksand och Gagnef	Kop	1693	1820
Mofalla	Värsås	Kåkind	Ska	1705	1818
Mogata	Stegeborg	Hammarkind	öst	1693	1799
Moheda	Moheda	Allbo	Kro	1688	1751
Molla	Gäsene	Gäsene	Älv	1688	1808
Mollösund	Morlanda	Orust västra	GoB	1711	1794
Mora	Mora	Mora	Kop	1662	1667
Morkarla	Dannemora	Oland	Upp	1708	1765
Morlanda	Morlanda	Orust västra	GoB	1711	1787
Mortorp	Mortorp	Södra Möre	Kal	1700	1785
Morup	Morup	Fauräs	Hal	1752	1763
Mosjö	Mosjö	örebro	öre	1672	1697
Mossebo	Tranemo	Kind	Älv	1663	1774
Motala					
Stads		Motala	öst	1632	1779
Lands		Aska	öst	1632	1779
Mularp	Vartofta	Vartofta	Ska	1687	1796
Mulseryd	Norra Mo	Mo	Jön	1711	1780
Multrå	Sollefteå	Sollefteå	Vno	1688	1773
Munka-Ljungby	Munka-Ljungby	Norra Ljungby	Kri	1688	1819
Munkarp	Norra Frosta	Frosta	Mal	1795	1819
Munktorp	Munktorp	Snevringe	Vma	1681	1691
Munsö	Ekerö	Färentuna	Sto	1691	1711
Murum	Hökerum	Ås	Älv	1688	1766
Muskö	Västerhaninge	Sotholm	Sto	1677	1726
Myckleby	Myckleby	Orust östra	GoB	1688	1791
Myresjö	Lannaskede	östra	Jön	1684	1739
Myssjö	Oviken	Sunne, Oviken och Hallen	Jäm	1688	1779
Målilla	Målilla	Aspeland	Kal	1632	1788
Månsarp	Månsarp	Tveta	Jön	1688	1721
Månstad	Länghem	Kind	Älv	1728	1811
Mårdaklev	Kindaholm	Kind	Älv	1710	1772
Mästerby	Klintehamn	Södra	Got	1744	1787
Möja	Djurö	Värmdö	Sto	1726	1746
Möklinta	Möklinta	övertjurbo	Vma	1650	1656
Mölleberga	Staffanstorp	Bara	Mal	1719	1784
Mölltorp	Mölltorp	Vadsbo	Ska	1689	1768
Mölndal	Mölndal	Mölndal	GoB	1737	1794
Möne	Hökerum	Ås	Älv	1747	1766
Mönsterås	Mönsterås	Stranda	Kal	1634	1783

Name of Parish Before 1952	After 1952	Name of District	County	Earliest year of Parish register	Clerical survey record
Mörarp	Mörarp	Luggude	Mal	1689	1811
Mörbylånga	Mörbylånga	Algutsrum	Kal	1728	1778
Mörkö	Hölö	Hölebo	Söd	1719	1765
Mörlunda	Mörlunda	Aspeland	Kal	1694	1787
Mörrum	Mörrum	Lister	Ble	1696	1813
Mörsil	Mörsil	Undersåker och Otterdal	Jäm	1688	1695
Nacka	Nacka	Svartlösa	Sto	1698	1702
Naum	Ryda	Barne	Ska	1859	1792
Naverstad	Bullaren	Bullaren	GoB	1688	1690
Nederkalix	Nederkalix	Nederkalix	Nbt	1656	1732
Nederluleå	Nederluleå	Nederluleå	Nbt	1696	1708
Nedertorneå	Nedertorneå	Torneå	Nbt	1707	1818
(before 1814=Alatornio, Lappi county, Finland)					
Nedre Ullerud	Ullerud	Kil	Vär	1671	1733
Nevishög	Staffanstorp	Bara	Mal	1773	1825
Nianfors	Njutånger	Enånger	Gäv	1799	1799
Nicolai, see Nyköping					
Nittorp	Dalstorp	Kind	Älv	1699	1750
Njurunda	Njurunda	Njurunda, Skön och Ljustorp	Vno	1643	1758
Njutånger	Njutånger	Enånger	Gäv	1710	1712
Nor	Nor	Grums	Vär	1779	1781
Nora	Noraström	Ångermanlands södra	Vno	1711	1701
Nora	Nora	Våla	Vma	1679	1738
Nora	Nora	Nora	Öre	1700	1703
Norberg	Norberg	Gamla Norberg	Vma	1628	1628
Norderö	Hallen	Sunne, Oviken och Hallen	Jäm	1692	1693
Nordingrå	Nordingrå	Ångermanlands södra	Vno	1688	1741
Nordmaling	Nordmaling	Nordmaling och Bjurholm	Vbn	1701	1704
Nordmark	Värmlandsberg	Färnebo	Vär	1731	1733
Normlösa	Boberg	Vifolka	Öst	1633	1757
Norn	Hedemora	Hedemora	Kop	1673	1730
Norra Björke	Södra Väne	Väne	Älv	1688	1813
Norra Finnskoga	Finnskoga-Dalby	Älvdal	Vär	1841	1837
Norra Fågelås	Fågelås	Kåkind	Ska	1674	1789
Norrahammar	Norrahammar	Tveta	Jön	1734	1729
Norra Hestra	Södra Mo	Mo	Jön	1735	1776
Norra Härene	Vinninga	Kinnefjärding	Ska	1699	1792
Norra Kedum	Örslösa	Kålland	Ska	1695	1738
Norra Kyrketorp	Skultorp	Kåkind	Ska	1690	1702
Norrala	Norrala	Ala	Gäv	1674	1747
Norra Ljunga	Sävsjö	Västra	Jön	1705	1730
Norra Lundby	Valle	Valle	Ska	1688	1778
Norra Mellby	Sösdala	Västra Göinge	Kri	1690	1818
Norra Möckleby	Torslunda	Möckleby	Kal	1647	1772
Norra Ny	Norra Ny	Älvdal	Vär	1686	1745
Norra Nöbbelöv	Torn	Torna	Mal	1679	1794
Norra Råda	Norra Råda	Älvdal	Vär	1725	1783
Nora Rörum	Norra Frosta	Frosta, Västra Göinge	Mal (Kri)	1695	1751
Norra Sandby	Stoby	Västra Göinge	Kri	1778	1827
Norra Sandsjö	Norra Sandsjö	Västra	Jön	1690	1717

Name of Parish Before 1952	After 1952	Name of District	County	Earliest year of Parish register	Clerical survey record
Norra Skrävlinge	Teckomatorp	Onsjö	Mal	1689	1804
Norra Solberga	Solberga	Södra Vedbo	Jön	1635	1783
Norra Strö	Araslöv	östra Göinge	Kri	1690	1771
Norra Säm	Gäsene	Gäsene	Älv	1706	1820
Norra Unnaryd	Södra Mo	Mo	Jön	1688	1776
Norra Vi	Ydre	Ydre	öst	1634	1713
Norra Ving	Valle	Valle	Ska	1661	1795
Norra Vram	Billesholm	Luggude	Mal	1690	1806
Norra Vånga	Kvänum	Skåning	Ska	1688	1737
Norra Åkarp	Bjärnum	Västra Göinge	Kri	1690	1806
Norra Åsarp	Redväg	Redväg	Älv	1687	1774
Norra Åsum	Kristianstad	Gärd	Kri	1751	1753
Norrbo	Bjuråker	Delsbo	Gäv	1688	1748
Norrby	Tärna	Simtuna	Vma	1641	1687
Norrbyås	Stora Mellösa	Sköllersta	öre	1667	1748
Norrbärke	Norrbärke	Västerbergslag	Kop	1661	1671
Norrköping					
Hedvig		Norrköping	öst	1662	1776
Norrköpings norra		Norrköping	öst		1885
Sankt Johannes		Norrköping	öst	1640	1693
Sankt Olai		Norrköping	öst	1639	1690
Norrlanda	Dalhem	Norra	Got		1773
Norrsunda	Märsta	Ärlinghundra	Sto	1748	1798
Norrtälje	Norrtälje	Norrtälje	Sto	1689	1735
Norrvidinge	Teckomatorp	Onsjö och Harjager	Mal	1742	1797
Norsjö	Norsjö	Norsjö och Malå	Vbn	1811	1811
Norum	Stenungsund	Inlands Nedre	GoB	1690	1795
Nosaby	Nosaby	Villand	Kri	1678	1793
Nottebäck	Nottebäck	Uppvidinge	Kro	1683	1738
Ny	Älgå	Jösse	Vär	1688	1711
Nydala	Vrigstad	Västra	Jön	1805	1776
Nye	Nye	östra	Jön	1696	1717
Nyed	Nyed	Nyed	Vär	1699	1776
Nyhem	Bräcke	Revsund, Brunflo och Näs	Jäm		1858
Nykil	Södra Valkebo	Valkebo	öst	1634	1789
Nykyrka	Mullsjö	Vartofta	Ska	1674	1759
Nykyrka	Stigtomta	Jönåker	Söd	1795	1794
Nyköping					
Västra stads		Nyköping	Söd		1770
östra stads		Nyköping	Söd		1769
Nicolai lands		Nyköping	Söd	1707	1734
Nymö	Fjälkinge	Villand	Kri	1747	1783
Nyskoga	Vitsand	Älvdal	Vär		1880
Nysund	Svartå	Edsberg	Öre	1687	1751
Nysätra	Lagunda	Lagunda	Upp	1689	1689
Nysätra	Nysätra	Nysätra	Vbn	1688	1720
Nårunga	Vårgårda	Gäsene	Älv	1713	1763
Nås	Nås	Nås	Kop	1674	1690
Nämdö	Djurö	Sotholm	Sto	1772	1772
När	Stånga	Södra	Got	1686	1761
Närtuna	Skepptuna	Långhundra	Sto	1608	1744
Näs	Havdhem	Södra	Got	1840	1786
Näs	Näs	Revsund, Brunflo och Näs	Jäm	1691	1817
Näs	Vartofta	Vartofta	Ska	1721	1788
Näsby	Vetlanda	östra	Jön	1679	1717
Näsby	Frövi	Fellingsbro	öre	1674	1694
Näshult	Nye	östra	Jön	1681	1691

Name of Parish		Name of		Earliest year of	
Before 1952	After 1952	District	County	Parish register	Clerical survey record
Näshulta	Husby-Rekarne	Österrekarne	Söd	1691	1743
Näsinge	Vette	Vette	GoB	1708	1811
Näskott	Rödön	Lit och Rödön	Jäm	1688	1711
Nässja	Östgöta-Dal	Dal	Öst	1641	1748
Nässjö	Nässjö	Nässjö	Jön	1641	1779
Näsum	Näsum	Villand	Kri	1700	1775
Nätra	Nätra	Ångermanlands södra	Vno	1809	1810
Nättraby	Nättraby	Medelstad	Ble	1729	1814
Nävelsjö	Björkö	Östra	Jön	1680	1753
Nävlinge	Vinslöv	Västra Göinge	Kri	1691	1750
Nöbbele	Linneryd	Konga	Kro	1688	1688
Nöbbelöv	Simrishamn	Järrestad	Kri	1689	1811
Nödinge	Nödinge	Ale	Älv	1688	1790
Nössemark	Dals-Ed	Vedbo	Älv	1748	1811
Nösslinge	Himledalen	Himle	Hal	1712	1795
Nöttja	Annerstad	Sunnerbo	Kro	1689	1749
Od	Gäsene	Gäsene	Älv	1688	1808
Odarslöv	Torn	Torna	Mal	1706	1803
Odensala	Märsta	Ärlinghundra	Sto	1680	1760
Odensjö	Lidhunt	Sunnerbo	Kro	1701	1788
Odensvi	Odensvi	Tjust södra	Kal	1633	1713
Odensvi	Munktorp	Åkerbo	Vma	1680	1700
Odensåker	Ullervad	Vadsbo	Ska	1688	1779
Oderljunga	Perstorp	Norra Åsbo	Kri	1680	1831
Offerdal	Offerdal	Undersåker och Offerdal	Jäm	1642	1690
Okome	Vessigebro	Faurås	Hal	1688	1791
Onslunda	Onslunda	Ingelstad	Kri	1692	1780
Onsala	Onsala	Fjäre	Hal	1737	1810
Oppeby	Norra Kinda	Kinda	Öst	1676	1792
Oppmanna	Oppmanna	Villand	Kri	1693	1817
Ore	Ore	Rättvik	Kop	1670	1690
Orkesta	Vallentuna	Seminghundra	Sto	1719	1737
Orlunda	Aska	Aska	Öst	1680	1776
Ormesberga	Moheda	Norrvidinge	Kro	1722	1748
Ornunga	Vårgårda	Gäsene	Älv	1722	1784
Ornö	Österhaninge	Sotholm	Sto	1728	1861
Orsa	Orsa	Orsa	Kop	1672	1680
Osby	Osby	Östra Göinge	Kri	1647	1781
Oskar	Mortorp	Södra Möre	Kal	1797	1805
Ottarp	Vallåkra	Luggude	Mal	1698	1792
Otterstad	Norra Kålland	Kålland	Ska	1684	1778
Ottravad	Dimbo	Vartofta	Ska	1658	1747
Ova	Husaby	Kinnefjärding	Ska	1664	1772
Ovansjö	Ovansjö	Gästriklands västra	Gäv	1671	1700
Ovanåker	Ovanåker	Bollnäs	Gäv	1772	1767
Oviken	Oviken	Sunne, Oviken och Hallen	Jäm	1688	1726
Oxie	Oxie	Oxie	Mal	1687	1813
Pajala	Pajala	Pajala och Korpilombolo	Nbt	1728	1761
Partille	Partille	Sävedal	GoB	1687	1771
Pelarne	Sevede	Sevede	Kal	1688	1821
Persnäs	Ölands-Åkerbo	Åkerbo	Kal	1657	1737
Perstorps köping	Perstorp	Norra Åsbo	Kri	1680	1841
Piteå Stads		Piteå		1703	1811

Name of Parish		Name of		Earliest year of	
Before 1952	After 1952	District	County	Parish register	Clerical survey record
Lands		Piteå och Älvsby	Nbt	1656	1720
Pjätteryd	Göteryd	Sunnerbo	Kro	1677	1722
Rackeby	Norra Kålland	Kålland	Ska	1690	1788
Ragunda	Ragunda	Ragunda	Jäm	1818	1782
Ramdala	Ramdala	Östra	Ble	1662	1802
Ramkvilla	Bäckaby	Västra	Jön	1688	1688
Ramnäs	Ramnäs	Snevringe	Vma	1633	1697
Ramsberg	Ramsberg	Linde och Ramsberg	Öre	1679	1664
Ramsele	Ramsele	Ramsele och Resele	Vno	1685	1767
Ramsjö	Ramsjö	Västra Hälsingland	Gäv	1853	1853
Ramsta	Södra Hagunda	Hagunda	Upp	1683	1766
Ramsåsa	Tomelilla	Ingelstad	Kri	1689	1683
Ramundeboda	Laxå	Grimsten	Öre	1736	1767
Ransberg	Mölltorp	Vadsbo	Ska	1689	1746
Ransäter	Munkfors	Kil	Vär	1681	1776
Rappestad	Norra Valkebo	Valkebo	Öst	1656	1797
Rasbo	Rasbo	Rasbo	Upp	1686	1709
Rasbokil	Rasbo	Rasbo	Upp	1688	1685
Raus	Hälsingborg	Hälsingborg	Mal	1698	1790
Ravlunda	Brösarp	Albo	Kri	1701	1779
Rebbelberga	Ängelholm	Bjäre	Kri	1738	1812
Redslared	Axelfors	Kind	Älv	1714	1799
Reftele	Reftele	Västbo	Jön	1676	1717
Regna	Hävla	Finspångalän	Öst	1637	1793
Remmarlöv	Harrie	Harjager	Mal	1737	1808
Remmene	Herrljunga	Kulling	Älv	1718	1766
Rengsjö	Rengsjö	Ala	Gäv	1694	1741
Resele	Resele	Ramsele och Resele	Vno	1689	1769
Reslöv	Marieholm	Onsjö	Mal	1680	1802
Resmo	Mörbylånga	Algutsrum	Kal	1716	1762
Resteröd	Ljungskile	Inlands Fräkne	GoB	1752	1813
Revesjö	Axelfors	Kind	Älv	1750	1789
Revinge	Södra Sandby	Torna	Mal	1830	1790
Revsund	Revsund	Jämtlands östra	Jäm	1688	1729
Riala	Roslags-Länna	Åker	Sto	1722	1749
Riddarholmen	Riddarholmen	Stockholm	Sto	1636	1689
Rimbo	Sjuhundra	Sjuhundra	Sto	1643	1698
Ringamåla	Asarum	Bräkne	Ble	1883	1875
Ringarum	Ringarum	Hammarkind	Öst	1671	1774
Rinkaby	Fjälkinge	Villand	Kri	1690	1813
Rinkaby	Glanshammar	Glanshammar	Öre	1719	1775
Rinna	Folkunga	Göstring	Öst	1650	1788
Ripsa	Rönö	Rönö	Söd	1689	1692
Riseberga	Riseberga	Norra Åsbo	Kri	1689	1810
Risekatslösa	Billesholm	Luggude	Mal	1753	1813
Risinge	Finspång	Finspånga	Öst	1633	1788
Roasjö	Lysjö	Kind	Älv	1685	1809
Robertsfors	Bygdeå	Nysätra	Vbn	1799	1815
Rogberga	Tenhult	Tveta	Jön	1666	1752
Rogslösa	Östgöta-Dal	Dal	Öst	1633	1789
Rogsta	Hälsingtuna	Bergsjö och Forsa	Gäv	1688	1751
Rolfstorp	Himledalen	Himle	Hal	1695	1750
Roma	Romakloster	Norra	Got	1687	1737
Romelanda	Romelanda	Inlands södra	GoB	1812	1815
Romfartuna	Skultuna	Norrbo	Vma	1631	1684
Rommele	Flundre	Flundre	Älv	1687	1722
Rone	Hemse	Södra	Got	1675	1765
Ronneby					
Stads		Ronneby	Ble	1646	1806
Lands		Medelstad	Ble	1862	1753

Name of Parish Before 1952	Name of Parish After 1952	Name of District	County	Earliest year of Parish register	Earliest year of Clerical survey record
Roslags-Bro	Lyhundra	Bro och Vätö	Sto	1688	1705
Roslags-Kulla	Roslags-Länna	Åker	Sto	1689	1767
Rudskoga	Visnum	Visnum	Vär	1689	1729
Rumskulla	Sevede	Sevede	Kal	1650	1789
Runsten	Gärdslösa	Runsten	Kal	1713	1769
Runtuna	Rönö	Rönö	Söd	1688	1756
Rute	Fårösund	Norra	Got	1854	1860
Rya	Örkelljunga	Norra Åsbo	Kri	1688	1797
Ryd	Skövde	Kåkind	Ska	1690	1702
Ryda	Ryda	Barne	Ska	1696	1818
Rydaholm	Rydaholm	Östbo	Jön	1694	1763
Ryssby	Ryssby	Norra Möre	Kal	1640	1770
Ryssby	Ryssby	Sunnerbo	Kro	1676	1738
Rystad	Åkerbo	Åkerbo	Öst	1629	1788
Ryttern	Kolbäck	Snevringe	Vma	1639	1680
Råbelöv	Nosaby	Villand	Kri	1747	1797
Råby-Rekarne	Hällby	Västerrekarne	Söd	1697	1784
Råby-Rönö	Rönö	Rönö	Söd	1688	1688
Råda	Råda	Askim	GoB	1737	1792
Råda	Kållands-Råda	Kålland	Ska	1686	1695
Rådene	Skultorp	Gudhem	Ska	1647	1779
Rådmansö	Frötuna	Frötuna och Länna	Sto	1697	1760
Råggärd	Högsäter	Valbo	Älv	1687	1751
Råneå	Råneå	Råneå	Nbt	1693	1693
Rångedala	Toarp	Ås	Älv	1688	1749
Rämmen	Rämmen	Färnebo	Vär	1785	1785
Räng	Räng	Skytts	Mal	1677	1813
Rännelanda	Högsäter	Valbo	Älv	1656	1753
Ränneslöv	Oskarström	Hök	Hal	1704	1815
Räpplinge	Gärdslösa	Slättbo	Kal	1664	1786
Rätan	Rätan	Berg	Jäm	1695	1827
Rättvik	Rättvik	Rättvik	Kop	1628	1600
Rävinge	Getinge	Halmstad	Hal	1819	1854
Rö	Sjuhundra	Sjuhundra	Sto	1684	1749
Rödbo	Kungälv	Västra Hising	GoB	1696	1800
Röddinge	Östra Färs	Färs	Mal	1689	1810
Rödeby	Rödeby	Östra	Ble	1660	1755
Rödene	Alingsås	Alingsås	Älv	1698	1736
Rödön	Rödön	Lit och Rödön	Jäm	1688	1711
Rök	Alvastra	Lysing	Öst	1674	1781
Röke	Tyringe	Västra Göinge	Kri	1647	1810
Rölanda	Dals-Ed	Vedbo	Älv	1717	1788
Rönnäng	Tjörn	Tjörn	GoB	1797	1801
Rönö	Östra Vikbolandet	Rönö	Öst	1680	1803
Röra	Tegneby	Orusts västra	GoB	1860	1833
Rörum	Kivik	Albo	Kri	1777	1813
Röstånga	Röstånga	Onsjö	Mal	1647	1750
Sal	Grästorp	Åse	Ska	1771	1779
Sala					
Stads		Sala	Vma	1747	1680
Lands		Övertjurbo	Vma		
Saleby	Saleby	Skåning	Ska	1688	1735
Salem	Salem	Svartlösa	Sto	1665	1718
Sanda	Klintehamn	Södra	Got	1744	1787
Sandby	Torslunda	Möckleby	Kal	1661	1821
Sandhem	Mullsjö	Vartofta	Ska	1674	1759
Sandhult	Sandhult	Veden	Älv	1688	1766
Sandseryd, see Norrahammar					
Sandvik	Burseryd	Västbo	Jön	1708	1717
Sankt Anna	Stegeborg	Björkekind	Öst	1653	1795

Name of Parish Before 1952	After 1952	Name of District	County	Earliest year of Parish register	Clerical survey record
Gertrud, see Stockholm					
Sankt Ibb, see Landskrona					
Sankt Ilian	Västerås	Västerås	Vma	1622	1697
Sankt Johannes, see Norrköping					
Sankt Lars	Linköping	Linköping	öst	1633	1789
Sankt Nikolai, see Stockholm					
Sankt Olai, see Norrköping					
Sankt Olof	Kivik	Albo	Kri	1801	1813
Sankt Peder	Lödöse	Ale	Älv	1688	1822
Sankt Per	Vadstena	Dal	öst	1751	1790
Sankt Peters Kloster	Torn	Torna	Mal	1689	1794
Sankt Sigfrid	Ljungbyholm	Södra Möre	Kal	1857	1857
Sanne	Sörbygden	Sörbygden	GoB	1688	1789
Saxtorp	Dösjebro	Harjager	Mal	1691	1795
Segersta	Hanebo	Bollnäs	Gäv	1678	1774
Segerstad	Ottenby	Gräsgård	Kal	1690	1739
Segerstad	Stenstorp	Gudhem	Ska	1688	1740
Segerstad	Nor	Grums	Vär	1746	1765
Seglora	Seglora	Mark	Älv	1681	1750
Selånger	Selånger	Medelpads västra	Vno	1682	1707
Senäte	Norra Kålland	Kålland	Ska	1684	1825
Sevalla	Tillberga	Yttertjurbo	Vma	1673	1693
Sexdrega	Lysjö	Kind	Älv	1684	1809
Sibbarp	Tvååker	Fauräs	Hal	1687	1676
Sidensjö	Nätra	Ångermanlands norra	Vno	1689	1730
Siene	Vårgårda	Kulling	Älv	1700	1774
Sigtuna (Including Sankt Olof and Sankt Per)	Sigtuna	Sigtuna	Sto	1688	1743
Sil	Götene	Kinne	Ska	1688	1747
Silbodal	Årjäng	Nordmark	Vär	1709	1753
Sillerud	Sillerud	Nordmark	Vär	1683	1757
Sillhövda	Fridlevstad	Medelstad	Ble	1835	1846
Silte	Havdhem	Södra	Got	1755	1737
Silvberg	Gustafs	Falu Södra	Kop	1748	1729
Silvåkra	Veberöd	Torna	Mal	1680	1790
Simlinge	Gislöv	Vemmenhög	Mal	1734	1803
Simonstorp	Kvillinge	Bråbo	öst	1662	1792
Simris	Simrishamn	Järrestad	Kri	1690	1811
Simrishamn	Simrishamn	Simrishamn	Kri	1724	1800
Simtuna	Fjärdhundra	Simtuna	Vma	1687	1709
Singö	Häverö	Väddö och Häverö	Sto	1734	1734
Sireköpinge	Rönneberga	Rönneberg	Mal	1646	1809
Sjonhem	Romakloster	Norra	Got	1790	1778
Själevad	Själevad	Ångermanlands norra	Vno	1681	1791
Sjögerstad	Skultorp	Gudhem	Ska	1647	1777
Sjögestad	Norra Valkebo	Valkebo	öst	1801	1797
Sjörup	Ljunits	Ljunits	Mal	1698	1776
Sjösås	Braås	Uppvidinge	Kro	1705	1732
Sjötofta	Tranemo	Kind	Älv	1663	1797
Skabersjö	Bara	Bara	Mal	1688	1767
Skaftö	Skaftö	Orust västra	GoB		1888
Skagershult	Svartå	Edsberg	öre		1871
Skallmeja	Ardala	Skåning	Ska	1686	1746
Skallsjö	Skallsjö	Vättle	Älv	1689	1813
Skalunda	Norra Kålland	Kålland	Ska	1771	1790
Skanör	Skanör med Falsterbo	Skanör	Mal	1664	1811

Name of Parish Before 1952	After 1952	Name of District	County	Earliest year of Parish register	Clerical survey record
Skara					
Stads		Skara	Ska	1692	1746
Hospital		Skara	Ska	1736	1779
Lands		Skåning	Ska	1692	1746
Skarstad	Ryda	Barne	Ska	1667	1791
Skartofta	Bjärsjölagård	Färs	Mal	1707	1799
Skatelöv	Skatelöv	Allbo, Kinnevald	Kro	1680	1760
Skattunge	Orsa	Orsa	Kop		1870
Skeby	Husaby	Kinnefjärding	Ska	1694	1691
Skeda	Vårdnäs	Hanekind	Öst	1640	1747
Skede	Alseda	Östra	Jön	1763	1758
Skederid	Sjuhundra	Sjuhundra	Sto	1691	1722
Skedevi	Hävla	Finspångalän	Öst	1616	1792
Skedvi	Hallstahammar	Åkerbo	Vma	1676	1677
Skee	Vette	Vette	GoB	1693	1811
Skeglinge	Skarhult	Frosta	Mal	1688	1804
Skegrie	Skegrie	Skytt	Mal	1688	1813
Skellefteå	Skellefteå	Skellefteå	Vbn	1699	1720
Skepparslöv	Vä	Gärd	Kri	1734	1809
Skepperstad	Bäckaby	Västra	Jön	1703	1730
Skepplanda	Skepplanda	Ale	Älv	1688	1763
Skeppsholmen	Skeppsholmen	Stockholm	Sto	1711	1770
Skeppshult	Fritsla	Mark	Älv	1681	1758
Skeppsås	Boberg	Boberg	Öst	1695	1806
Skepptuna	Skepptuna	Seminghundra	Sto	1698	1645
Skerike	Västerås	Norrbo	Vma	1633	1708
Skillingmark	Järnskog	Nordmark	Vär	1688	1757
Skinnskatteberg	Skinnskatteberg	Skinnskatteberg	Vma	1623	1663
Skirö	Nye	Östra	Jön	1695	1717
Skivarp	Vemmenhög	Vemmenhög	Mal	1779	1809
Skofteby	Vinninga	Kinnefjärding	Ska	1704	
Skog	Skog	Ala	Gäv	1693	1737
Skog	Noraström	Ångermanlands södra	Vno	1688	1701
Skogsbygden	Vårgårda	Kulling	Älv	1713	1763
Skogs-Tibble	Norra Hagunda	Hagunda	Upp	1758	1740
Skokloster	Håbo	Håbo	Upp	1661	1786
Skorped	Anundsjö	Ångermanland norra	Vno	1779	1804
Skrea	Falkenberg	Årstad	Hal	1689	1756
Skredsvik	Skredsvik	Lane	GoB	1689	1756
Skultuna	Skultuna	Norrbo	Vma	1607	1681
Skummeslöv	Karup	Hök	Hal	1716	1788
Skurup	Skurup	Vemmenhög	Mal	1650	1785
Skuttunge	Balinge	Balinge	Upp	1603	1690
Skå	Färingsö	Färentuna	Sto	1750	1799
Skållerud	Skållerud	Nordal	Älv	1718	1739
Skånela	Märsta	Seminghundra	Sto	1672	1724
Skånes-Fagerhult	Skånes Fagerhult	Norra Åsbo	Kri	1732	1808
Skånings-Åsaka	Valle	Skånings	Ska	1686	1768
Skårby	Ljunits	Ljunits	Mal	1689	1782
Skäfthammar	Oland	Oland	Upp	1679	1749
Skällinge	Himledalen	Himle	Hal	1713	1795
Skällvik	Stegeborg	Hammarkind	Öst	1666	1788
Skälvum	Husaby	Kinnefjärding	Ska	1685	1815
Skänninge	Skänninge	Skänninge	Öst	1634	1747
Skärkind	Norsholm	Skärkind	Öst	1633	1739
Skärstad	Skärstad	Vista	Jön	1679	1727
Skärum	Redväg	Redväg	Älv	1695	1721
Skärv	Valle	Valle	Ska	1686	1795
Sköldinge	Sköldinge	Oppunda	Söd	1690	1691

Name of Parish Before 1952	After 1952	Name of District	County	Earliest year of Parish register	clerical survey record
Sköllersta	Sköllersta	Sköllersta	öre	1641	1721
Skölvene	Gäsene	Gäsene	Älv	1706	1820
Skön	Skön	Njurunda, Skön och Ljustorp	Vno	1707	1803
Skönberga	Söderköping	Hammarlund	öst	1635	1767
Skörstorp	Dimbo	Vartofta	Ska	1702	1824
Skövde	Skövde	Skövde	Ska	1690	1701
Slaka	Kärna	Hanekind	öst	1633	1788
Slimminge	Rydsgård	Vemmenhög	Mal	1736	1795
Slite	Slite	Norra	Got	1723	1788
Slädene	Levene	Viste	Ska	1715	1801
Släp	Särö	Fjäre	Hal	1718	1754
Slätthög	Moheda	Allbo	Kro	1691	1719
Slättåkra	Kvibille	Halmstad	Hal	1698	1819
Slöinge	Årstad	Årstad	Hal	1690	1790
Slöta	Vartofta	Vartofta	Ska	1715	1764
Smedby	Ottenby	Gräsgård	Kal	1652	1732
Smedstorp	Smedstorp	Ingelstad	Kri	1690	1779
Smula	Redväg	Redväg	Älv	1692	1793
Snavlunda	Lerbäck	Sundbo	öre	1689	1769
Snårestad	Ljunits	Ljunits	Mal	1688	1804
Snöstorp	Simlångsdalen	Tönnersjö	Hal	1694	1785
Sofia	Jönköping	Jönköping	Jön	1726	1718
Solberga	Kode	Inlands Nordre	GoB	1659	1786
Solberga	Rydsgård	Vemmenhög	Mal	1771	1813
Solberga	Redväg	Redväg	Älv	1697	1774
Sollefteå	Sollefteå	Sollefteå	Vno	1688	1762
Sollentuna	Sollentuna	Sollentuna	Sto	1659	1714
Sollerön	Sollerön	Mora	Kop	1661	1642
Solna	Solna	Danderyd	Sto	1670	1735
Solna (Karlberg)	Solna	Danderyd	Sto	1792	1793
Solna (Ulriksdal)	Solna	Danderyd	Sto	1823	
Sorsele	Sorsele	Lycksele	Vbn	1762	1778
Sorunda	Sorunda	Sotholm	Sto	1704	1735
Spannarp	Tvååker	Himle	Hal	1766	1769
Sparlösa	Levene	Viste	Ska	1687	1770
Sparrsätra	Åsunda	Åsunda	Upp	1699	1700
Spekeröd	Stenungsund	Inlands nordre	GoB	1690	1787
Spelvik	Rönö	Rönö	Söd	1684	1773
Spjutstorp	Onslunda	Ingelstad	Kri	1688	1790
Sproge	Klintehamn	Södra	Got	1723	1737
Stafsinge	Morup	Faurås	Hal	1689	1762
Stala	Tegneby	Orusts östra	GoB	1839	1849
Stamnared	Lindberga	Himle	Hal	1693	1789
Starby	Ausås	Södra Åsbo	Kri	1692	1813
Starrkärr	Starrkärr	Ale	Älv	1688	1775
Stavby	Oland	Oland	Upp	1659	1695
Stavnäs	Stavnäs	Gillberg	Vär	1687	1734
Stehag	Bosarp	Onsjö och Harjager	Mal	1731	1808
Sten, see Västra Stenby					
Stenberga	Nye	Östra	Jön	1665	1715
Stenbrohult	Stenbrohult	Allbo	Kro	1676	1695
Steneby	Steneby	Vedbo	Älv	1688	1799
Stenestad	Kågeröd	Luggude	Mal	1689	1775
Stengårdshult	Södra Mo	Mo	Jön	1681	1749
Steninge	Harplinge	Halmstad	Hal	1685	1813
Stenkumla	Stenkumla	Södra	Got	1677	1761
Stenkvista	Ärla	Österrekarne	Söd	1730	1734
Stenkyrka	Tingstäde	Norra	Got	1683	1721

Name of Parish Before 1952	After 1952	Name of District	County	Earliest year of Parish register	clerical survey record
Stenkyrka	Tjörn	Tjörn	GoB	1779	1807
Stensele	Stensele	Lycksele	Vbn	1816	1817
Stenstorp	Stenstorp	Gudhem	Ska	1673	1746
Stenum	Valle	Valle	Ska	1645	1795
Stenåsa	Mörbylånga	Möckleby	Kal	1833	1791
Stiby	Tommarp	Järrestad	Kri	1742	1790
Stigsjö	Säbrå	Ångermanlands södra	Vno	1670	1708
Stigtomta	Stigtomta	Jönåker	Söd	1723	1726
Stjärnorp	Vreta Kloster	Gullberg	Öst	1760	1811
Stjärnsund	Husby	Hedemora	Kop	1809	1726
Stoby	Stoby	Västra Göinge	Kri	1778	1827
Stockaryd	Hjälmseryd	Västra	Jön	1689	1789
Stockholm					
Adolf Fredrik		Stockholm	Sto	1741	1693
Allmänna barnbördshuset		Stockholm	Sto	1847	1775
Barnhuset		Stockholm	Sto	1697	1753
Brännkyrka		Svartlösa	Sto	1761	1772
Bromma		Sollentuna	Sto	1721	1779
Centralfängelset		Stockholm	Sto	1827	
Finska		Stockholm	Sto	1664	1783
Finska gardesregementet		Stockholm	Sto	1774	1774
Fransk-lutherska (French)		Stockholm	Sto	1690	
Göta livgarde		Stockholm	Sto	1810	1811
Hedvig Eleonora		Stockholm	Sto	1668	1730
Holländska (Dutch)		Stockholm	Sto	1693	
Hov (Royal Court)		Stockholm	Sto	1648	1692
Jakob		Stockholm	Sto	1643	1672
Johannes		Stockholm	Sto	1643	1672
Katarina		Stockholm	Sto	1654	1707
Klara		Stockholm	Sto	1680	1787
Kungsholm		Stockholm	Sto	1672	1689
Livgardet		Stockholm	Sto	1810	
Livgardet till häst		Stockholm	Sto	1792	1832
Livregementet		Stockholm	Sto	1774	
Maria		Stockholm	Sto	1678	1737
Riddarholmen		Stockholm	Sto	1636	1689
Sabbatsbergs fattighus		Stockholm	Sto	1808	
Sankt Gertrud		Stockholm	Sto	1639	
Sankt Nikolai		Stockholm	Sto	1609	1667
Skeppsholmen		Stockholm	Sto	1714	1770
Spånga		Sollentuna	Sto	1702	1710
Storkyrko, see Sankt Nikolai					
Svea artilleri		Stockholm	Sto	1720	1713
Svea livgarde		Stockholm	Sto	1790	1791
Svea livgardets grenadjärbataljon		Stockholm	Sto	1717	
Svea livgardets livbataljon		Stockholm	Sto	1706	1858
Svea livgardets norra bataljon		Stockholm	Sto	1697	1772
Svea livgardets södra bataljon		Stockholm	Sto	1694	1735
Svenska gardesregementet		Stockholm	Sto	1791	1791
Tyska (German), see Sankt Gertrud					
Ulrika Eleonora, see Kungsholm					
Stockholm-Näs	Upplands-Bro	Bro	Upp	1703	1767
Stora Hammar	Räng	Skytts	Mal	1677	1813
Stora Harrie	Harrie	Harjager	Mal	1730	1809
Stora Herrestad	Herrestad	Herrestad	Mal	1717	1792
Stora Kil	Stora Kil	Kil	Vär	1672	1735
Stora Kopparberg					
Stads		Falu norra	Kop	1683	1749
Lands		Falu norra	Kop	1683	1749

Name of Parish Before 1952	After 1952	Name of District	County	Earliest year of Parish register	clerical survey record
Stora Köpinge	Herrestad	Herrestad	Mal	1680	1764
Stora Lundby	Stora Lundby	Laske	Älv	1689	1819
Stora Malm	Stora Malm	Oppunda	Söd	1691	1711
Stora Mellby	Bjärke	Albo	Älv	1688	1768
Stora Mellösa	Stora Mellösa	Asker	Öre	1660	1749
Stora Råby	Lund	Torna	Mal	1689	1792
Stora Skedvi	Stora Skedvi	Hedemora	Kop	1650	1668
Stora Slågarp	Alstad	Skytt	Mal	1729	1825
Stora Tuna	Stora Tuna	Falu södra	Kop	1641	1663
Stora Åby	Ödeshög	Lysing	Öst	1693	1790
Storkyrko	Storkyrko	Stockholm	Sto	1609	1667
Storsjö	Övre Ljungadalen	Hede	Jäm	1750	1808
Strå	Östgöta-Dal	Dal	Öst	1687	1713
Stråvalla	Värö	Viske	Hal	1673	1739
Strängnäs					
Stads		Strängnäs	Söd	1666	1685
Lands		Åker	Söd	1666	1684
Strängsered	Redväg	Redväg	Älv	1692	1790
Strö	Norra Kålland	Kålland	Ska	1753	1786
Ström	Ström	Hammerdal	Jäm	1695	1780
Strömstad	Strömstad	Strömstad	GoB	1713	1770
Strövelstorp	Ausås	Södra Åsbo	Kri	1646	1813
Stugun	Stugun	Ragunda	Jäm	1689	1692
Sturkö	Sturkö	Östra	Ble	1701	1813
Styra	Aska	Aska	Öst	1691	1704
Styrnäs	Boteå	Boteå	Vno	1756	1808
Styrstad	Norrköping	Lösing	Öst	1662	1713
Styrsö	Styrsö	Askim	GoB	1686	1799
Stånga	Stånga	Södra	Got	1801	1796
Stångby	Torn	Torna	Mal	1689	1798
Stävie	Furulund	Torna	Mal	1682	1826
Stöde	Stöde	Medelpads västra	Vno	1688	1689
Sund	Ydre	Ydre	Öst	1658	1788
Sundals-Ryr	Brålanda	Sundal	Älv	1779	1774
Sundborn	Sundborn	Falu norra	Kop	1680	1680
Sundby	Kafjärden	Österrekarne	Söd	1695	1748
Sundre	Hoburg	Södra	Got	1841	1827
Sundsjö	Revsund	Revsund, Brunflo och Näs	Jäm	1688	1758
Sundsvall	Sundsvall	Sundsvall	Vno	1860	1714
Sunne	Hackås	Sunne ,Oviken och Hallen	Jäm	1691	1754
Sunne	Stora Sunne	Fryksdal	Vär	1680	1708
Sunnemo	Norra Råda	Älvdal	Vär	1725	1817
Sunnersberg	Norra Kålland	Kålland	Ska	1688	1802
Suntak	Dimbo	Vartofta	Ska	1691	1695
Sura	Sura	Snevringe	Vma	1656	1688
Surteby-Kattunga	Västra Mark	Mark	Älv		1855
Svalöv	Svalöv	Rönneberg	Mal	1690	1778
Svabensverk	Alfta	Bollnäs	Gäv	1844	1844
Svanshals	Alvastra	Lysing	Öst	1694	1694
Svanskog	Svanskog	Gillberg	Vär	1684	1758
Svarteborg	Svarteborg	Tunge	GoB	1688	1756
Svartnäs	Svärdsjö	Falu norra	Kop		1841
Svartrå	Vessigebro	Faurås	Hal	1688	1795
Svarttorp	Lekeryd	Tveta	Jön	1720	1743
Svea artilleri		Stockholm	Sto	1720	1713
Svea livgarde		Stockholm	Sto	1790	1791

Name of Parish Before 1952	After 1952	Name of District	County	Earliest year of Parish register	Clerical survey record
Svea Gardesregemente		Stockholm	Sto	1791	1791
Svea livgardets grenadiärbataljon		Stockholm	Sto	1717	
Svea livgardets livbataljon		Stockholm	Sto	1706	1858
Svea livgardes norra bataljon		Stockholm	Sto	1697	1772
Svea livgardes södra bataljon		Stockholm	Sto	1694	1735
Svedala	Svedala	Oxie	Mal	1688	1806
Svedvi	Hallstahammar	Snevringe	Vma	1676	1677
Sveg	Sveg	Sveg	Jäm	1636	1791
Svenarum	Vrigstad	Västra	Jön	1689	1789
Sveneby	Kville	Kville	GoB		1860
Sveneby	Moholm	Vadsbo	Ska	1688	1764
Svenljunga	Svenljunga	Kind	Älv	1721	1801
Svennevad	Sköllersta	Sköllersta	Öre	1663	1763
Svensköp	Östra Frosta	Frosta	Mal	1690	1697
Svenstorp	Vemmenhög	Vemmenhög	Mal	1688	1780
Sventorp	Värsås	Kåkind	Ska	1701	1776
Svinhult	Ydre	Ydre	Öst	1633	1789
Svinnegarn	Åsunda	Åsunda	Upp	1695	1687
Svärdsjö	Svärdsjö	Falu norra	Kop	1677	1676
Svärta	Svärta	Rönö	Söd	1681	1758
Sya	Vifolka	Vifolka	Öst	1688	1789
Synnerby	Ardala	Skåning	Ska	1686	1775
Sånga	Färingsö	Färentuna	Sto	1687	1771
Sånga	Boteå	Boteå	Vno	1756	1819
Säbrå	Säbrå	Ångermanlands södra	Vno	1722	1727
Säby	Tranås	Norra Vedbo	Jön	1633	1759
Säby	Härslöv	Rönneberg	Mal	1721	1787
Säby	Kolbäck	Snevringe	Vma	1631	1690
Säffle	Säffle	Näs	Vär		1884
Säfsnäs	Säfsnäs	Nås	Kop	1736	1744
Sällstorp	Veddige	Viske	Hal	1689	1787
Särestad	Grästorp	Åse	Ska	1688	1767
Särna	Särna	Särna och Idre	Kop	1682	1743
Särslöv	Staffanstorp	Oxie	Mal	1692	1813
Säter					
Stads		Säter	Kop	1664	1689
Lands		Hedemora tingslag	Kop	1664	1689
Säter	Binneberg	Vadsbo	Ska	1688	1719
Säterbo	Arboga	Åkerbo	Vma	1678	1725
Sätila	Sätila	Mark	Älv	1681	1792
Sättersta	Tystberga	Rönö	Söd	1673	1687
Sättna	Selånger	Medelpads västra	Vno	1682	1713
Sätuna	Gudhem	Gudhem	Ska	1703	1800
Sävar	Sävar	Umeå	Vbn	1823	1823
Sävare	Vinninga	Kinnefjärding	Ska	1648	1775
Säve	Säve	Västra Hising	GoB	1821	1795
Söderala	Söderala	Ala	Gäv	1695	1708
Söderbärke	Söderbärke	Västerbergslag	Kop	1675	1673
Söderby-Karl	Lyhundra	Lyhundra	Sto	1680	1720
Söderfors	Söderfors	Örbyhus	Upp	1689	1743
Söderhamn	Söderhamn	Söderhamn	Gäv	1721	1733
Söderköping	Söderköping	Söderköping	Öst	1660	1663
Södertälje					
Stads		Södertälje	Sto	1719	1737
Lands		Öknebo	Sto	1805	1749
Södervidinge	Teckomatorp	Harjager	Mal	1682	1805
Söderåkra	Söderåkra	Södra Möre	Kal	1704	1790
Södra Björke	Gäsene	Gäsene	Älv	1717	1760

Name of Parish Before 1952	After 1952	Name of District	County	Earliest year of Parish register	Clerical survey record
Södra Finnskoga	Finnskoga-Dalby	Älvdal	Vär	1831	1829
Södra Fågelås	Fågelås	Kåkind	Ska	1811	1810
Södra Hestra	Burseryd	Västbo	Jön	1684	1717
Södra Härene	Vårgårda	Kulling	Älv	1748	1768
Södra Kedom	Ryda	Barne	Ska	1686	1841
Södra Kyrketorp	Stenstorp	Gudhem	Ska	1673	1746
Södra Ljunga	Hamneda	Sunnerbo	Kro	1671	1757
Södra Lundby	Vedum	Laske	Ska		1805
Södra Mellby	Kivik	Albo	Kri	1703	1818
Södra Möckleby	Ottenby	Gräsgård	Kal	1688	1732
Södra Ny	Värmlandsnäs	Näs	Vär	1738	1775
Södra Råda	Visnum	Visnum	Vär	1685	1736
Södra Rörum	Östra Frosta	Frosta	Mal	1795	1820
Södra Sallerup	Malmö	Oxie	Mal	1740	1816
Södra Sandby	Södra Sandby	Torna	Mal	1745	1759
Södra Sandsjö	Södra Sandsjö	Konga	Kro	1732	1770
Södra Solberga	Korsberga	Västra	Jön	1690	1792
Södra Säm	Åsunden	Kind	Älv	1724	1813
Södra Unnaryd	Unnaryd	Västbo	Jön	1679	1703
Södra Vi	Södra Vi	Sevede	Kal	1697	1788
Södra Ving	Hökerum	Ås	Älv	1704	1777
Södra Vram	Billesholm	Luggude	Älv	1688	1805
Södra Vånga	Hökerum	Ås	Mal		1838
Södra Åby	Klagstorp	Vemmenhög	Mal	1688	1822
Södra Åkarp	Månstorp	Oxie	Mal	1690	1813
Södra Åsarp	Limmared	Kind	Älv	1720	1807
Södra Åsum	Sjöbo	Färs	Mal	1689	1803
Sölvesborg					
Stads		Sölvesborg	Ble	1752	1768
Lands		Lister	Ble	1858	1861
Söndrum	Söndrum	Halmstad	Hal	1688	1806
Söne	Örslösa	Kålland	Ska	1710	1752
Söraby	Rottne	Norrvidinge	Kro	1693	1749
Sörby	Vinslöv	Västra Göinge	Kri	1649	1821
Sörby	Vilske	Vilske	Ska	1695	1788
Sövde	Blentarp	Södra Färs	Mal	1693	1812
Sövestad	Herrestad	Herrestad	Mal	1690	1810
Tannåker	Forsheda	Västbo	Jön	1688	1789
Tanum	Tanum	Tanum	GoB	1719	1760
Tarsled	Herrljunga	Kulling	Älv	1718	1790
Taxinge	Mariefred	Selebo	Söd	1734	1693
Teda	Åsunda	Åsunda	Upp	1682	1762
Tegelsmora	Vendel	Oland	Upp	1741	1712
Tegnaby	Östra Torsås	Konga	Kro	1777	1790
Tegneby	Tegneby	Orust västra	GoB	1860	1841
Tengene	Grästorp	Viste	Ska	1688	1721
Tensta	Vattholma	Norunda	Upp	1671	1760
Tiarp	Vartofta	Vartofta	Ska	1687	1796
Tibro	Tibro	Kåkind	Ska	1704	1771
Tidavad	Ullervad	Vadsbo	Ska	1688	1789
Tidersrum	Västra Kinda	Kinda	Öst	1634	1789
Tierp	Tierp	Örbyhus	Upp	1723	1774
Tillberga	Tillberga	Siende	Vma	1668	1650
Tillinge	Åsunda	Åsunda	Upp	1681	1741
Timmele	Redväg	Redväg	Älv	1689	1808
Timmersdala	Timmersdala	Vadsbo	Ska	1630	1773
Timrå	Timrå	Njurunda, Skön och Ljustorp	Vno	1783	1803
Tingsås	Tingsryd	Konga	Kro	1696	1729

Name of Parish Before 1952	After 1952	Name of District	County	Earliest year of Parish register	Clerical survey record
Tingstad	Norrköping	Lösing	Öst	1625	1770
Tingstäde	Tingstäde	Norra	Got	1682	1786
Tirup	Svalöv	Rönneberg	Mal	1703	1830
Tisselskog	Steneby	Vedbo	Älv	1688	1798
Tived	Tiveden	Vadsbo	Ska	1848	1847
Tjureda	Rottne	Norrvidinge	Kro	1718	1718
Tjällmo	Tjällmo	Finspångalän	Öst	1687	1793
Tjärby	Veinge	Hök	Hal	1679	1790
Tjärnö	Tjärnö	Vette	GoB	1689	1812
Tjärstad	Norra Kinda	Kinda	Öst	1634	1800
Tjörnarp	Sösdala	Västra Göinge	Kri	1783	1818
Toarp	Toarp	Ås	Älv	1688	1767
Tofta	Stenkumla	Södra	Got	1730	1722
Tofta	Rönneberga	Rönneberg	Mal	1736	1791
Tofteryd	Klevshult	Östbo	Jön	1698	1717
Tolfta	Tierp	Örbyhus	Upp	1688	1773
Tolg	Rottne	Norrvidinge	Kro	1718	1719
Tolånga	Östra Färs	Färs	Mal	1695	1763
Torbjörntorp	Gudhem	Gudhem	Ska	1726	1798
Torekov	Västra Bjäre	Bjäre	Kri	1738	1813
Torestorp	Svansjö	Mark	Älv	1785	1784
Toresund	Stallarholmen	Selebo	Söd	1675	1694
Torhamn	Jämjö	Östra	Ble	1701	1791
Torp	Myckleby	Orust östra	GoB	1688	1791
Torp	Torp	Medelpads västra	Vno	1688	1706
Torp	Ödeborg	Valbo	Älv	1720	1793
Torpa	Lindberga	Himle	Hal	1691	1806
Torpa	Annerstad	Sunnerbo	Kro	1690	1717
Torpa	Kung Karl	Åkerbo	Vma	1688	1694
Torpa	Borås	Kind	Älv	1642	1736
Torpa	Ydre	Ydre	Öst	1665	1783
Torrlösa	Marieholm	Onsjö	Mal	1689	1804
Torrskog	Lelång	Vedbo	Älv	1707	1758
Torsby	Hermansby	Inlands södra	GoB	1760	1785
Torshälla					
Stads	Torshälla	Torshälla	Söd	1674	1716
Lands	Hällby	Västerrekarne	Söd	1674	1750
Torskinge	Forsheda	Västbo	Jön	1700	1757
Torslanda	Torslanda	Västra Hising	GoB	1684	1793
Torslunda	Torslunda	Algutsrum	Kal	1681	1800
Torstuna	Fjärdhundra	Torstuna	Vma	1710	1710
Torsvi	Södra Trögd	Trögd	Upp	1719	1765
Torsåker	Torsåker	Gästriklands västra	Gäv	1689	1693
Torsåker	Tystberga	Rönö	Söd	1769	1766
Torsåker	Ytterlännäs	Boteå	Vno	1688	1741
Torsång	Stora Tuna	Falu södra	Kop	1629	1712
Torsås	Torsås	Södra Möre	Kal	1670	1752
Torsö	Hasslerör	Vadsbo	Ska	1690	1796
Tortuna	Tillberga	Yttertjurbo	Vma	1638	1734
Torup	Torup	Halmstad	Hal	1668	1799
Torö	Ösmo	Sotholm	Sto	1689	1706
Tossene	Tossene	Sotenäs	GoB	1664	1705
Tostared	Västra Mark	Mark	Älv		1858
Tosterup	Glemmingebro	Ingelstad	Kri	1826	1818
Tottarp	Staffanstorp	Bara	Mal	1661	1791
Tranemo	Tranemo	Kind	Älv	1663	1795
Trankil	Holmedal	Nordmark	Vär	1790	1782
Transtrand	Transtrand	Malung	Kop	1665	167[illegible]
Tranum	Örslösa	Kålland	Ska	1695	173[illegible]

Name of Parish: Before 1952	Name of Parish: After 1952	Name of District	County	Earliest year of Parish register	Earliest year of Clerical survey record
Tranås	Onslunda	Ingelstad	Kri	1692	1780
Traryd	Traryd	Sunnerbo	Kro	1689	1769
Trehörna	Alvastra	Lysing	Öst	1652	1789
Trehörningsjö	Trehörningsjö	Ångermanlands norra	Vno		1865
Trelleborg	Trelleborg	Trelleborg	Mal	1688	1809
Trolle-Ljungby	Fjälkinge	Villand	Kri	1818	1825
Trollenäs	Bosarp	Onsjö	Mal	1647	1799
Trollhättan, (see also Gärdhem)	Trollhättan	Trollhättan	Älv		1813
Trosa	Trosa	Trosa	Söd	1688	1761
Trosa	Vagnhärad	Trosa	Söd	1701	1701
Tryde	Tomelilla	Ingelstad	Kri	1688	1790
Tryserum	Tjust-Ed	Norra Tjust	Kal	1634	1809
Tråvad	Larv	Laske	Ska	1688	1805
Träkumla	Stenkumla	Södra	Got	1771	1785
Träne	Träne	Gärd	Kri	1692	1813
Träslöv	Träslöv	Himle	Hal	1686	1755
Trässberg	Saleby	Skåning	Ska	1692	1756
Trästena	Moholm	Vadsbo	Ska	1695	1810
Trävattna	Vilske	Vilske	Ska	1690	1816
Trökörna	Grästorp	Viste	Ska	1688	1721
Trönninge	Eldsberga	Tönnersjö	Hal	1694	1785
Trönö	Norrala	Ala	Gäv	1671	1730
Tullstorp	Klagstorp	Vemmenhög	Mal	1688	1780
Tumberg	Vårgårda	Kulling	Älv	1688	1768
Tumbo	Hällby	Västerrekarne	Söd	1697	1696
Tun	Tun	Åse	Ska	1672	1744
Tuna	Tuna	Tunalän	Kal	1686	1788
Tuna	Jönåker	Jönåker	Söd	1680	1746
Tuna	Oland	Oland	Upp	1661	1693
Tuna	Tuna	Medelpads västra	Vno	1688	1688
Tunaberg	Tunaberg	Jönåker	Söd	1680	1688
Tunge	Lödöse	Ale	Älv	1694	1822
Turinge	Turinge	Öknebo	Sto	1702	1779
Tutaryd	Ryssby	Sunnerbo	Kro	1857	1717
Tuve	Tuve	Östra Hising	GoB	1693	1753
Tveta	Mörlunda	Aspeland	Kal	1683	1787
Tveta	Östertälje	Öknebo	Sto	1688	1689
Tveta	Säffle	Näs	Vär	1687	1747
Tving	Tving	Medelstad	Ble	1711	1786
Tvååker	Tvååker	Himle	Hal	1766	1768
Tvärred	Åsunden	Kind	Älv	1724	1811
Tydje	Tössbo	Tössbo	Älv	1688	1757
Tygelsjö	Bunkeflo	Oxie	Mal	1694	1816
Tynderö	Hässjö	Medelpad, Njurunda, Skön och Ljustorp	Vno	1688	1745
Tyngsjö	Malung	Malung	Kop	1855	1855
Tyresö	Tyresö	Sotholm	Sto	1634	1688
Tysslinge	Tysslinge	Örebro	Öre	1700	1725
Tystberga	Tystberga	Rönö	Söd	1666	1705
Tåby	Västra Vikbolandet	Björkekind	Öst	1665	1779
Tådene	Örslösa	Kålland	Ska	1695	1738
Tångeråsa	Viby	Edsberg	Öre	1695	1694
Tånnö	Bor	Östbo	Jön	1749	1861
Tåsjö	Tåsjö	Fjällsjö	Vno	1773	1768
Tåssjö	Munka-Ljungby	Norra Ljungby	Kri	1690	1813
Tåstarp	Hjärnarp	Bjäre	Kri	1763	1822
Täby	Täby	Danderyd	Sto	1710	1748

Name of Parish Before 1952	After 1952	Name of District	County	Earliest year of Parish register	Clerical survey record
Täby	Mosjö	Örebro	Öre	1672	1751
Tämta	Fristad	Veden	Älv	1688	1767
Täng	Grästorp	Viste	Ska	1688	1788
Tännäs	Tännäs	Hede	Jäm	1749	1805
Tärby	Fristad	Ås	Älv	1689	1738
Tärendö	Tärendö	Pajala och Korpilombolo	Nbt		1882
Tärna	Tärna	Lycksele	Vbn	1854	1854
Tärna	Tärna	Simtuna	Vma	1717	1761
Tävelsås	Mellersta Kinnevald	Kinnevald	Kro	1705	1706
Töcksmark	Töcksmark	Nordmark	Vär	1717	1754
Töftedal	Dals-Ed	Vedbo	Älv	1706	1791
Töllsjö	Bollebygd	Bollebygd	Älv	1681	1746
Tölö	Tölö	Fjäre	Hal	1687	1762
Tönnersjö	Eldsberga	Tönnersjö	Hal	1765	1760
Töreboda	Töreboda	Vadsbo	Ska	1745	1806
Törnevalla	Åkerbo	Åkerbo	Öst	1633	1793
Törnsfall	Gladhammar	Södra Tjust	Kal	1688	1786
Törringe	Månstorp	Oxie	Mal	1688	1767
Tösse	Tössbo	Tössbo	Älv	1695	1757
Ucklum	Stenungsund	Inlands Nordre	GoB	1714	1816
Uddevalla	Uddevalla	Uddevalla	GoB	1698	1812
Ugglum	Gudhem	Gudhem	Ska	1721	1762
Ukna	Uknadalen	Norra Tjust	Kal	1680	1713
Ullared	Ullared	Fauräs	Hal	1688	1784
Ullasjö	Axelfors	Kind	Älv	1716	1798
Ullene	Vilske	Vilske	Ska	1682	1792
Ullervad	Ullervad	Vadsbo	Ska	1691	1775
Ullstorp	Tomelilla	Ingelstad	Kri	1689	1813
Ullånger	Ullånger	Ångermanlands södra	Vno	1733	1777
Ulricehamn	Ulricehamn	Ulricehamn	Älv	1688	1818
Ulrika	Södra Valkebo	Valkebo	Öst	1737	1788
Ulriksdal	Solna	Danderyd	Sto	1823	
Umeå					
Stads		Umeå	Vbn	1725	1737
Lands		Umeå	Vbn	1721	1720
Undenäs	Undenäs	Vadsbo	Ska	1689	1782
Undersvik	Arbrå	Väster Hälsingland	Gäv	1706	1747
Undersåker	Undersåker	Undersåker och Offerdal	Jäm	1688	1784
Ununge	Häverö	Näringhundra	Sto	1698	1779
Upphärad	Flundre	Flundre	Älv	1688	1772
Uppsala Domkyrko	Uppsala	Uppsala	Upp	1693	1728
Uppsala-Näs	Södra Hagunda	Ulleråker	Upp	1662	1694
Uppåkra	Staffanstorp	Bara	Mal	1712	1768
Urshult	Urshult	Kinnevald	Kro	1643	1726
Uråsa	Väckelsång	Konga	Kro	1696	1741
Utby	Ullervad	Vadsbo	Ska	1688	1747
Utvängstorp	Mullsjö	Vartofta	Ska	1696	1774
Utö	Österhaninge	Sotholm	Sto	1657	1776
Uvered	Järpås	Kålland	Ska	1648	1688
Vad	Tidan	Vadsbo	Ska	1688	1764
Vada	Össeby	Vallentuna	Sto	1725	1745
Vadensjö	Härslöv	Rönneberg	Mal	1693	1809
Vadsbro	Bettna	Oppunda	Söd	1667	1752
Vadstena					
Stads		Vadstena	Öst	1642	1713
Hospital		Vadstena	Öst	1735	1814

Name of Parish Before 1952	After 1952	Name of District	County	Earliest year of Parish register	Clerical survey record
Vagnhärad	Vagnhärad	Hölebo	Söd	1668	1708
Vaksala	Vaksala	Vaksala	Upp	1704	1779
Valbo	Valbo	Gästriklands östra	Gäv	1688	1709
Valbo-Ryr	Öreborg	Valbo	Älv	1702	1793
Valdemarsvik	Valdemarsvik	Hammarkind	Öst		1881
Valdshult	Södra Mo	Mo	Jön	1687	1780
Valinge	Lindberga	Himle	Hal	1690	1795
Vall	Stenkumla	Södra	Got	1782	1752
Valla	Tjörn	Tjörn	GoB	1691	1783
Vallby	Hammenhög	Järrestad	Kri	1756	1815
Vallby	Kafjärden	Österrekarne	Söd	1774	1778
Vallby	Södra Trögd	Trögd	Upp	1701	1701
Vallda	Särö	Fjäre	Hal	1706	1755
Valleberga	Löderup	Ingelstad	Kri	1678	1804
Vallentuna	Vallentuna	Vallentuna	Sto	1640	1719
Vallerstad	Boberg	Boberg	Öst	1634	1694
Vallkärra	Torn	Torna	Mal	1689	1798
Vallsjö	Sävsjö	Västra	Jön	1690	1717
Vallstena	Dalhem	Norra	Got	1861	1792
Valstad	Dimbo	Vartofta	Ska	1691	1695
Valtorp	Stenstorp	Gudhem	Ska	1688	1740
Valö	Östhammar	Frösåker	Sto	1727	1751
Vamlingbo	Hoburg	Södra	Got	1768	1756
Vankiva	Bjärnum	Västra Göinge	Kri	1690	1808
Vanstad	Östra Färs	Färs	Mal	1695	1763
Vansö	Vårfruberga	Åker	Söd	1702	1707
Vapnö	Söndrum	Halmstad	Hal	1688	1807
Vara	Vara	Barne	Ska	1667	1775
Varberg					
Stads		Varberg	Hal	1690	1785
Slotts		Varberg	Hal	1718	1763
Varnhem	Valle	Valle	Ska	1694	1779
Varnum	Kristinehamn	Ölme	Vär	1645	1756
Varnum	Hökerum	Ås	Alv	1688	1737
Varola	Värsås	Kåkind	Ska	1671	1782
Vartofta-Åsaka	Vartofta	Vartofta	Ska	1687	1753
Varv	Dimbo	Vartofta	Ska	1680	1704
Varv	Aska	Aska	Öst	1639	1704
Vassunda	Knivsta	Ärlinghundra	Sto	1702	1744
Vassända-Naglum	Vänersborg	Väne	Älv	1693	1819
Vaxholm					
Stads		Vaxholm	Sto	1699	1736
Lands		Vaxholm	Sto		1861
Veberöd	Veberöd	Torna	Mal	1736	1810
Veckholm	Södra Trögd	Trögd	Upp	1669	1765
Vedby	Klippan	Norra Åsbo	Kri	1782	1818
Veddige	Veddige	Viske	Hal	1770	1779
Vedevågs bruk	Lindesberg	Linde och Ramsberg	Öre		1688
Vederslöv	Mellersta Kinnevald	Kinnevald	Kro	1688	1740
Veinge	Veinge	Hök	Hal	1679	1790
Velinga	Hökensås	Vartofta	Ska	1680	1771
Vellinge	Vellinge	Skytt	Mal	1756	1786
Vemdalen	Hede	Hede	Jäm	1777	1808
Vena	Vena	Sevede	Kal	1633	1788
Vendel	Vendel	Örbyhus	Upp	1683	1750
Venjan	Venjan	Mora	Kop	1682	1684
Ventlinge	Ottenby	Gräsgård	Kal	1837	1809
Verum	Vittsjö	Västra Göinge	Kri	1647	1780
Vesene	Gäsene	Gäsene	Älv	1707	1780
Vessige	Vessigebro	Årstad	Hal	1690	1767

Name of Parish		Name of		Earliest year of	
Before 1952	After 1952	District	County	Parish register	Clerical survey record
Vessmantorp	Sösdala	Västra Göinge	Kri		1834
Veta	Vifolka	Vifolka	Öst	1658	1727
Vetlanda	Vetlanda	Vetlanda	Jön	1726	1727
Viby	Viby	Grimsten	Öre	1694	1748
Viby	Vifolka	Vifolka	Öst	1658	1789
Vibyggerå	Ullånger	Ångermanlands södra	Vno	1688	1778
Vickleby	Mörbylånga	Algutsrum	Kal	1703	1767
Vidbo	Skepptuna	Seminghundra	Sto	1719	1763
Vika	Vika	Falu norra	Kop	1677	1664
Viken	Väsby	Luggude	Mal	1689	1775
Viker, see Nora	Noraskog	Nora och Hjulsjö	Öre		1872
Vikingstad	Norra Valkebo	Valkebo	Öst	1633	1737
Viklau	Romakloster	Norra	Got	1706	1852
Viksjö	Säbrå	Ångermanlands södra	Vno	1753	1801
Viksta	Björklinge	Norunda	Upp	1716	1743
Vilhelmina	Vilhelmina	Vilhelmina	Vbn	1786	1780
Villberga	Norra Trögd	Trögd	Upp	1737	1737
Villie	Rydsgård	Ljunit	Mal	1670	1807
Villstad	Villstad	Västbo	Jön	1688	1717
Vilske-Kleva	Vilske	Vilske	Ska	1682	1792
Vimmerby					
Stads	Vimmerby	Vimmerby	Kal	1673	1753
Lands	Sevede	Sevede	Kal	1824	1752
Vinberg	Vinberg	Faurås	Hal	1688	1762
Vinköl	Ardala	Skåning	Ska	1690	1773
Vinnerstad	Motala	Aska	Öst	1699	1814
Vinslöv	Vinslöv	Västra Göinge	Kri	1647	1750
Vintrosa	Tysslinge	Örebro	Öre	1686	1727
Vireda	Hullaryd	Norra Vedbo	Jön	1689	1789
Virestad	Virestad	Allbo	Kro	1738	1771
Virke	Harrie	Harjager	Mal	1843	1809
Virserum	Virserum	Aspeland	Kal	1673	1788
Visby					
Stads		Visby	Got	1661	1709
Lands		Norra	Got	1678	1811
Visingsö	Visingsö	Vista	Jön	1693	1719
Visnum	Visnum	Visnum	Vär	1689	1733
Visnums-Kil	Visnum	Visnum	Vär	1688	1743
Vislanda	Vislanda	Allbo	Kro	1688	1688
Vissefjärda	Vissefjärda	Södra Möre	Kal	1696	1802
Visseltofta	Vittsjö	Västra Göinge	Kri	1690	1733
Vist	Ulricehamn	Redväg	Älv	1807	1817
Vist	Vårdnäs	Hanekind	Öst	1640	1792
Vistorp	Vartofta	Vartofta	Ska	1696	1760
Vitaby	Kivik	Albo	Kri	1703	1818
Vitsand	Vitsand	Fryksdal	Vär	1824	1824
Vittaryd	Berga	Sunnerbo	Kro	1689	1740
Vittinge	Vittinge	Torstuna	Vma	1688	1721
Vittsjö	Vittsjö	Västra Göinge	Kri	1690	1806
Vittskövle	Degeberga	Gärd	Kri	1688	1825
Vollsjö	Vollsjö	Färs	Mal	1729	1813
Vomb	Veberöd	Färs	Mal	1689	1810
Voxna	Ovanåker	Bollnäs	Gäv	1759	1779
Voxtorp	Bor	Östbo	Jön		1861
Voxtorp	Södermöre	Södra Möre	Kal	1714	1758
Vrena	Bettna	Oppunda	Söd	1763	1763
Vreta Kloster	Vreta Kloster	Gullberg	Öst	1633	1751

Name of Parish Before 1952	After 1952	Name of District	County	Earliest year of Parish register	Clerical survey record
Vrigstad	Vrigstad	Västra	Jön	1688	1727
Vrå	Lidhult	Sunnerbo	Kro	1701	1788
Våmb	Skövde	Kåkind	Ska	1690	1702
Våmhus	Våmhus	Mora	Kop	1661	1667
Vånga	Oppmanna	Villand	Kri	1690	1817
Vånga	Skärblacka	Finspångalän	Öst	1659	1714
Vårdinge	Järna	Öknebo	Sto	1665	1709
Vårdnäs	Vårdnäs	Kinda	Öst	1661	1781
Vårdsberg	Askeby	Bankekind	Öst	1656	1788
Vårfrukyrka	Åsunda	Åsunda	Upp	1663	1769
Vårkumla	Frökind	Frökind	Ska	1713	1825
Vårvik	Lelång	Vedbo	Älv	1685	1748
Våthult	Gislaved	Västbo	Jön	1697	1717
Våxtorp	Våxtorp	Hök	Hal	1692	1760
Vä	Vä	Gärd	Kri	1687	1809
Väckelsång	Väckelsång	Konga	Kro	1687	1729
Väddö	Väddö	Väddö och Häverö	Sto	1719	1694
Väderstad	Folkunga	Göstring	Öst	1645	1790
Väla	Örslösa	Kålland	Ska	1710	1752
Välinge	Kattarp	Luggude	Mal	1688	1813
Välluv	Mörarp	Luggude	Mal	1698	1790
Vänersborg	Vänersborg	Vänersborg	Älv	1690	1810
Vänersnäs	Västra Tunhem	Åse	Älv	1714	1827
Väne-Ryr	Vänersborg	Väne	Älv	1743	1810
Väne-Åsaka	Södra Väne	Väne	Älv	1688	1813
Vänga	Fristad	Veden	Älv	1688	1767
Vänge	Romakloster	Halla	Got	1710	1761
Vänge	Norra Hagunda	Ulleråker	Upp	1658	1766
Vännäs	Vännäs	Umeå	Vbn	1829	1825
Väring	Binneberg	Vadsbo	Ska	1688	1773
Värmdö	Värmdö	Värmdö	Sto	1679	1704
Värmskog	Stavnäs	Gillberg	Vär	1679	1775
Värna	Björsäter	Bankekind	Öst	1714	1802
Värnamo	Värnamo	Värnamo	Jön	1825	1861
Värsås	Värsås	Kåkind	Ska	1772	1782
Värö	Värö	Viske	Hal	1673	1739
Väsby	Väsby	Luggude	Mal	1689	1775
Väse	Väse	Väse	Vär	1678	1723
Väskinde	Tingstäde	Norra	Got	1667	1764
Västanfors	Fagersta	Gamla Norberg	Vma	1662	1668
Västerbitterna	Vedum	Laske	Ska	1710	1762
Västerfärnebo	Västerfärnebo	Vagnsbro	Vma	1646	1690
Västergarn	Klintehamn	Södra	Got	1744	1787
Västerhaninge	Västerhaninge	Sotholm	Sto	1668	1690
Västerhejde	Stenkumla	Södra	Got	1771	1785
Västerlanda	Inlands Torpe	Inlands Torpe	GoB	1686	1792
Västerljung	Vagnhärad	Hölebo	Söd	1713	1749
Västerlösa	Norra Valkebo	Vifolka	Öst	1631	1778
Västerlövsta	Västerlövsta	Simtuna	Vma	1685	1698
Västermo	Västra Rekarne	Västerrekarne	Söd		1755
Västerplana	Kinnekulle	Kinne	Ska	1688	1751
Västerstad	Bjärsjölagård	Färs	Mal	1736	1771
Västervik	Västervik	Västervik	Kal	1655	1724
Västervåla	Ramnäs	Gamla Norberg	Vma	1628	1690
Västeråker	Södra Hagunda	Hagunda	Upp	1692	1773
Västerås	Västerås	Västerås	Vma	1622	1697
Västerås-Barkarö	Dingtuna	Tuhundra	Vma	1647	1663
Västland	Västland	Örbyhus	Upp	1688	1768
Västra Alstad	Alstad	Skytt	Mal	1688	1816

Name of Parish Before 1952	After 1952	Name of District	County	Earliest year of Parish register	Clerical survey record
Västra Broby	Åstorp	Södra Åsby	Kri	1689	1812
Västra Ed	Tjust-Ed	Norra Tjust	Kal	1625	1722
Västra Eneby	Västra Kinda	Kinda	Öst	1633	1797
Västra Fågelvik	Töcksmark	Nordmark	Vär	1717	1754
Västra Frölunda	Göteborg	Askim	GoB	1737	1813
Västra Gerum	Ardala	Skåning	Ska	1686	1797
Västra Harg	Vifolka	Vifolka	Öst	1797	1800
Västra Hoby	Torn	Torna	Mal	1724	1812
Västra Husby	Aspveden	Hammarkind	Öst	1637	1713
Västra Ingelstad	Månstorp	Oxie	Mal	1755	1805
Västra Karaby	Dösjebro	Harjager	Mal	1688	1795
Västra Karup	Västra Bjäre	Bjäre	Kri	1689	1790
Västra Klagstorp	Bunkeflo	Oxie	Mal	1753	1818
Västra Kärrstorp	Månstorp	Oxie	Mal	1686	1811
Västra Ny	Godegård	Aska	Öst	1695	1789
Västra Nöbbelöv	Vemmenhög	Ljunit	Mal	1779	1809
Västra Ryd	Upplands-Bro	Bro	Upp	1705	1758
Västra Ryd	Ydre	Ydre	Öst	1633	1789
Västra Sallerup	Harrie	Harjager	Mal	1757	1808
Västra Skedvi	Medåker	Åkerbo	Vma	1672	1659
Västra Skrukeby	Mjölby	Göstring	Öst	1712	1789
Västra Skrävlinge	Malmö	Oxie	Mal	1688	1815
Västra Stenby	Aska	Aska	Öst	1662	1816
Västra Strö	Bosarp	Onsjö	Mal	1684	1814
Västra Sönnarslöv	Klippan	Södra Åsbo	Kri	1720	1813
Västra Tollstad	Alvastra	Lysing	Öst	1673	1713
Västra Tommarp	Skegrie	Skytt	Mal	1688	1813
Västra Torsås	Västra Torsås	Allbo	Kro	1680	1773
Västra Torup	Tyringe	Västra Göinge	Kri	1690	1824
Västra Tunhem	Västra Tunhem	Väne	Älv	1688	1813
Västra Vemmenhög	Vemmenhög	Vemmenhög	Mal	1688	1812
Västra Vemmerlöv	Skegrie	Skytt	**Mal**	1691	1821
Västra Vingåker	Västra Vingåker	Oppunda	Söd	1666	1757
Västra Vram	Tollarp	Gärd	Kri	1688	1805
Västra Ämtervik	Stora Sunne	Frykdal	Vär	1690	1804
Västrum	Gladhammar	Södra Tjust	Kal	1765	1700
Väte	Klintehamn	Södra	Got		1785
Vättak	Dimbo	Vartofta	Ska	1691	1695
Vättlösa	Götene	Kinne	Ska	1793	1807
Vätö	Lyhundra	Bro och Vätö	Sto	1652	1688
Väversunda	Östgöta-Dal	Dal	Öst	1693	1790
Växjö					
Stads		Växjö	Kro	1724	1716
Lands		Konga	Kro	1807	1802
Hospital		Växjö	Kro		1866
Yllestad	Vartofta	Vartofta	Ska	1694	1760
Ysane	Gammalstorp	Lister	Ble	1689	1790
Ysby	Oskarström	Hök	Hal	1704	1815
Ystad					
Garnisons		Ystad	Mal	1852	1852
Sankt Maria		Ystad	Mal	1677	1800
Sankt Petri		Ystad	Mal	1689	1783
Ytterby	Ytterby	Inlands Södra	GoB	1696	1800
Ytterenhörna	Enhörna	Selebo	Söd	1695	1780
Yttergran	Håbo	Håbo	Upp	1738	1778
Ytterhogdal	Hogdal	Sveg	Jäm	1681	1741
Ytterjärna	Järna	Öknebo	Sto	1737	1776
Ytterlännäs	Ytterlännäs	Boteå	Vno	1688	1777
Ytterselö	Stallarholmen	Selebo	Söd	1640	1703
Yxnerum	Björsäter	Skärkind	Öst	1689	1816

Name of Parish Before 1952	After 1952	Name of District	County	Earliest year of Parish register	Clerical survey record
Å	Västra Vikbolandet	Björkekind	Öst	1650	1793
Åby	Läckeby	Norra Möre	Kal	1645	1771
Ådals-Liden	Ådals-Liden	Ramsele och Resele	Vno	1751	1811
Åhus	Åhus	Villand	Kri	1706	1814
Åker	Klevshult	Östbo	Jön	1682	1717
Åker	Åker	Åker	Söd	1676	1696
Åkerby	Bälinge	Bälinge	Upp	1679	1696
Ål	Ål	Leksand och Gagnef	Kop	1648	1712
Åland	Norra Hagunda	Hagunda	Upp	1685	1738
Ålem	Ålem	Stranda	Kal	1654	1755
Åmot	Ockelbo	Gästriklands västra	Gäv	1798	1797
Åmål					
Stads	Åmål	Åmål	Älv	1718	1764
Lands	Tössbo	Tössbo	Älv	1718	1764
Ånimskog	Tössbo	Tössbo	Älv	1711	1736
Ånsta-Längbro	Örebro	Örebro	Öre	1693	1707
Årdala	Sparreholm	Villåttinge	Söd	1682	1747
Åre	Åre	Undersåker och Offerdal	Jäm	1689	1765
Årjäng, see Silbodal					
Årstad	Årstad	Årstad	Hal	1813	1786
Årsunda	Årsunda	Gästriklands östra	Gäv	1704	1708
Åryd	Hällaryd	Bräkne	Ble	1704	1813
Ås	Veddige	Viske	Hal	1689	1805
Ås	Rödön	Lit och Rödön	Jäm	1727	1707
Ås	Reftele	Västbo	Jön	1666	1752
Ås	Ottenby	Gräsgård	Kal	1759	1806
Ås	Grästorp	Åse	Ska	1771	1795
Åsarne	Övre Ljungadalen	Berg	Jäm		1861
Åsbo	Södra Göstring	Göstring	Öst	1633	1789
Åsbräcka	Flundre	Flundre	Älv	1688	1776
Åseda	Åseda	Uppvidinge	Kro	1688	1737
Åsele	Åsele	Åsele	Vbn	1701	1772
Åsenhöga	Gnosjö	Mo	Jön	1642	1756
Åsle	Vartofta	Vartofta	Ska	1659	1796
Åtvid	Åtvidaberg	Bankekind	Öst	1683	1790
Älekulla	Svansjö	Mark	Älv	1668	1784
Älgarås	Hova	Vadsbo	Ska	1688	1793
Älghult	Älghult	Uppvidinge	Kro	1679	1747
Älgå	Älgå	Jösse	Vär	1687	1726
Älmeboda	Älmeboda	Konga	Kro	1690	1728
Älvdalen	Älvdalen	Älvdalen	Kop	1659	1719
Älvestad	Boberg	Boberg	Öst	1695	1783
Älvkarleby	Älvkarleby	Örbyhus	Upp	1730	1736
Älvros	Sveg	Sveg	Jäm	1798	1829
Älvsbacka	Nyed	Nyed	Vär	1731	1779
Älvsby	Älvsby	Piteå och Älvsby	Nbt	1808	1809
Älvsered	Högvad	Kind	Älv	1712	1818
Älvsåker	Tölö	Fjäre	Hal	1688	1762
Ängelholm					
Stads		Ängelholm	Kri	1689	1812
Garnisons		Ängelholm	Kri	1845	1838
Ängersjö	Hogdal	Sveg	Jäm		
Ängsö	Kungsåra	Yttertjurbo	Vma	1668	1662
Äppelbo	Äppelbo	Malung	Kop	1630	1698
Ärentuna	Vattholma	Norunda	Upp	1685	1770
Ärla	Ärla	Österrekarne	Söd	1674	1719
Ärtemark	Lelång	Vedbo	Älv	1688	1785
Äspered	Toarp	Ås	Älv	1689	1749

Name of Parish		Name of		Earliest year of	
Before 1952	After 1952	District	County	Parish register	Clerical survey record
Äsphult	Träne	Gärd	Kri	1755	1813
Äspinge	Östra Frosta	Frosta	Mal	1655	1819
Äspö	Klagstorp	Vemmenhög	Mal	1677	1818
Öckerö	Öckero	Västra Hising	GoB	1684	1800
Ödeborg	Ödeborg	Valbo	Älv	1688	1761
Ödeby	Glanshammar	Glanshammar	Öre	1685	1769
Ödenäs	Hemsjö	Kulling	Älv	1688	1732
Ödeshög	Ödeshög	Lysing	Öst	1660	1766
Ödestugu	Tenhult	Västra	Jön	1680	1687
Ödsköl	Bäckefors	Vedbo	Älv	1688	1749
Ödsmål	Stenungsund	Inlands Nordre	GoB	1714	1785
Öggestorp	Tenhult	Tveta	Jön	1670	1751
Öglunda	Valle	Valle	Ska	1758	1780
Öja	Hoburg	Södra	Got	1714	1783
Öja	Bergunda	Kinnevald	Kro	1696	1740
Öja	Herrestad	Herrestad	Mal	1679	1794
Öja	Västra Rekarne	Västerrekarne	Söd	1688	1755
Öjaby	Bergunda	Kinnevald	Kro	1693	1751
Ökna	Alseda	Östra	Jön	1721	1717
Öljehult	Hallabro	Bräkne	Ble	1860	1856
Ölme	Väse	Ölme	Vär	1674	1747
Ölmevalla	Löftadalen	Fjäre	Hal	1683	1751
Ölmstad	Skärstad	Vista	Jön	1666	1697
Ölserud	Värmlandsnäs	Näs	Vär	1754	1777
Ölsremma	Dalstorp	Kind	Älv	1736	1748
Öm	Skövde	Kåkind	Ska	1690	1702
Önnarp	Anderslöv	Vemmenhög	Mal	1749	1813
Önnestad	Araslöv	Göinge	Kri	1695	1797
Önum	Ryda	Barne	Ska	1667	1775
Ör	Moheda	Allbo	Kro	1688	1785
Ör	Kroppefjäll	Nordal	Älv	1647	1779
Öra	Gäsene	Gäsene	Älv	1736	1808
Öraby	Glemmingebro	Ingelstad	Kri	1684	1813
Örberga	Östgöta-Dal	Dal	Öst	1633	1781
Örby	Örby	Mark	Älv	1762	1791
Örebro	Örebro	Örebro	Öre	1659	1697
Öregrund	Öregrund	Öregrund	Sto	1783	1783
Öreryd	Södra Mo	Mo	Jön	1681	1782
Örja	Härslöv	Rönneberg	Mal	1693	1809
Örkelljunga	Örkelljunga	Norra Åsby	Kri	1722	1790
Örkened	Örkened	Östra Göinge	Kri	1721	1772
Örnsköldsvik	Örnsköldsvik	Örnsköldsvik	Vno		1859
Örsjö	Madesjö	Södra Möre	Kal		
(made parish in	1893)				
Örsjö	Rydsgård	Vemmenhög	Mal	1698	1807
Örslösa	Örslösa	Kålland	Ska	1705	1752
Örsås	Axelfors	Kind	Älv	1684	1799
Örtofta	Harrie	Harjager	Mal	1720	1814
Örtomta	Askeby	Bankekind	Öst	1603	1712
Örträsk	Örträsk	Lycksele	Vbn	1850	1849
Ösmo	Ösmo	Sotholm	Sto	1662	1689
Össeb-Garn	Össeby	Vallentuna	Sto	1694	1749
Össjö	Östra Ljungby	Norra Åsbo	Kri	1689	1813
Östad	Stora Lundby	Ale	Älv	1672	1803
Österbitterna	Vedum	Laske	Ska	1731	1775
Österbybruk	Dannemora	Oland	Upp	1791	1765
Österfärnebo	Österfärnebo	Gästriklands östra	Gäv	1688	1692
Östergarn	Romakloster	Norra	Got	1717	1783
Österhaninge	Österhaninge	Sotholm	Sto	1665	1746

Name of Parish Before 1952	After 1952	Name of District	County	Earliest year of Parish register	Clerical survey record
Österlövsta	Österlövsta	Oland	Upp	1661	1771
Österplana	Kinnekulle	Kinne	Ska	1732	1740
Österslöv	Nosaby	Villand	Kri	1690	1749
Östersund	Östersund	Östersund	Jäm	1789	1795
Österunda	Fjärdhundra	Torstuna	Vma	1688	1768
Östervallskog	Töcksmark	Nordmark	Vär	1716	1778
Östervåla	Östervåla	Våla	Vma	1684	1748
Österåker	Österåker	Åker	Sto	1676	1683
Österåker	Julita	Oppunda	Söd	1665	1791
Östhammar	Östhammar	Östhammar	Sto	1731	1773
Östmark	Östmark	Fryksdal	Vär	1765	1773
Östra Broby	Broby	Östra Göinge	Kri	1647	1812
Östraby	Bjärsjölagård	Färs	Mal	1656	1771
Östra Ed	Tjust-Ed	Norra Tjust	Kal	1687	1701
Östra Eneby	Norrköping	Norrköping	Öst	1690	1761
Östra Frölunda	Kindaholm	Kind	Älv	1728	1811
Östra Fågelvik	Östra Fågelvik	Väse	Vär	1688	1728
Östra Gerum	Dimbo	Vartofta	Ska	1702	1824
Östra Grevie	Månstorp	Oxie	Mal	1755	1805
Östra Harg	Åkerbo	Åkerbo	Öst	1635	1763
Östra Herrestad	Hammenhög	Ingelstad	Kri	1806	1823
Östra Hoby	Borrby	Ingelstad	Kri	1777	1808
Östra Husby	Östra Vikbolandet	Östkind	Öst	1633	1716
Östra Ingelstad	Hammenhög	Ingelstad	Kri	1806	1823
Östra Karaby	Marieholm	Onsjö	Mal	1680	1802
Östra Karup	Karup	Hök	Hal	1716	1788
Östra Klagstorp	Klagstorp	Vemmenhög	Mal	1677	1818
Östra Kärrstorp	Bjärsjölagård	Färs	Mal	1774	1683
Östra Ljungby	Östra Ljungby	Norra Åsbo	Kri	1689	1814
Östra Ny	Östra Vikbolandet	Björkekind	Öst	1634	1790
Östra Nöbbelöv	Simrishamn	Järrestad	Kri	1689	1813
Östra Ryd	Österåker	Danderyd	Sto	1671	1732
Östra Ryd	Aspveden	Skärkind	Öst	1688	1790
Östra Sallerup	Långaröd	Frosta	Mal	1690	1826
Östra Skrukeby	Åkerbo	Åkerbo	Öst	1630	1745
Östra Stenby	Västra Vikbolandet	Östkind	Öst	1671	1694
Östra Strö	Skarhult	Frosta	Mal	1688	1794
Östra Sönnarslöv	Everöd	Gärd	Kri	1692	1802
Östra Tollstad	Vifolka	Vifolka	Öst	1634	1796
Östra Tommarp	Tommarp	Järrestad	Kri	1663	1806
Östra Torp	Klagstorp	Vemmenhög	Mal	1764	1793
Östra Torsås	Östra Torsås	Konga	Kro	1712	1688
Östra Tunhem	Gudhem	Gudhem	Ska	1721	1762
Östra Vemmenhög	Vemmenhög	Vemmenhög	Mal	1714	1812
Östra Vemmerlöv	Tommarp	Järrestad	Kri	1733	1813
Östra Vingåker	Stora Malm	Oppunda	Söd	1670	1756
Östra Vram	Tollarp	Gärd	Kri	1718	1805
Östra Ämtervik	Stora Sunne	Fryksdal	Vär	1706	1774
Östuna	Knivsta	Långhundra	Sto	1698	1727
Öttum	Kvänum	Skåning	Ska	1688	1793
Öved	Bjärsjölagård	Färs	Mal	1773	1799
Överenhörna	Enhörna	Selebo	Söd	1703	1765
Övergran	Håbo	Håbo	Upp	1703	1718
Överhogdal	Hogdal	Sveg	Jäm	1681	1808
Överjärna	Järna	Öknebo	Sto	1688	1780
Överkalix	Överkalix	Överkalix	Nbt	1689	1697
Överluleå	Överluleå	Överluleå	Nbt	1831	1831
Överlännäs	Boteå	Boteå	Vno	1756	1818
Överselö	Stallarholmen	Selebo	Söd	1670	1757

Name of Parish		Name of		Earliest year of	
Before 1952	After 1952	District	County	Parish register	Clerical survey record
Övertorneå	Övertorneå	Torneå	Nbt	1718	1781
Överum	Överum	Norra Tjust	Kal		
(Made parish in 1931)					
Övraby	Enslöv	Halmstad	Hal	1821	1814
Övraby, see Öraby					
Övre Ullerud	Ullerud	Kil	Vär	1670	1738
Öxabäck	Svansjö	Mark	Älv	1668	1782
Öxnevalla	Horred	Mark	Älv	1763	1762

APPENDIX D

Word List

This word list contains both Swedish and Latin expressions found in the genealogical records mentioned in this book. The Latin words or abbreviations are indicated by (L).

Abiit	(L)	moved out
abs(ens)	(L)	absent
abs		absolved (mother after illegitimate child birth)
accessit	(L)	came, moved in
adm(onitus)	(L)	confirmed
aetas	(L)	age
afg(ången)		moved to, departed to
afs(kedad)		discharged (from military service)
agnatus	(L)	related through the male line
allmoge(man)		the farming estate, farmer
alumnus	(L)	foster child, student
anm(ärkning)		remark, note, annotation
antal		number
antavla		pedigree chart
a(nte) n(uptius)	(L)	before the marriage
arbetare		worker
arrendator		farmer, tenant farmer
arv		inheritance
arvlåtare		person leaving an inheritance
arvskifte		dividing of death estate
arvtagare		heir
attest		certificate
avliden, avlidne		deceased
b(ergsman)		miner, owner of miner's homestead
b(onde)		farmer
b(rukare)		farmer
b(ar) b(arnet)		carried, or held, the child at christening
backe		hill, mound
backstugusittare		crofter
bagare		baker
banco		monetary system
bank		bank
barn		child
barnlös		childless
barnmorska		midwife
beatus, beata, beati	(L)	bury, buried
begrava, begravd		bury, buried
begravning(sbok)		burial (record)
benämnd		called, named, christened
berg		mountain
bergsman		miner, owner of miner's homestead
betyg		certificate
bevaka		protect
beväring(skarl)		(conscript) soldier
bo(et)		place, nest, estate
bok		book, record
bokhållare		bookkeeper
bonde		farmer
boning(sställe)		residence
borg		castle
borgare		burgher, freeman, citizen
borgmästare		mayor

boskap		cattle
boställe		farm, residence
bouppteckning		probate, recording of inventory
bro		bridge
broder		brother
bror		brother
brorsdotter		niece
brorson		nephew
brovakt		bridge toll-man
brud		bride
brudgum		bride groom
brudpar		bridal couple
bruk		mill
brukare		farmer
bruksarbetare		mill worker
bröder		brothers, brethren
bröstarvinge		direct heir
by		village
båtsman		boats-man, sailor, soldier
bäck		stream, creek
capplan		minister
clerus	(L)	minister
cognatus	(L)	related
conjugati	(L)	married
cop(ulatus)	(L)	married
copulerad		married
cr(ono)		crown owned
cr(ono) h(emman)		crown owned farm
d(otter)		daughter
d(räng)		farm hand
dag		day
dag(a)karl		day laborer
dagsverksarbetare		day laborer
dal		valley, vale
damm		dam
danneman		farmer
defunctus	(L)	dead
deja		maid servant
denatus	(L)	dead
diakon		deacon
dies	(L)	day
dies sequens	(L)	the following day
djup		deep
djur		animal
dom		sentence, judgment
domare		judge
dombok		court record
dominus	(L)	Mr., Lord, knight, minister, priest
domstol		court
doplängd		christening or baptism record
dopnamn		first name, Christian name
dotter		daughter
dr		daughter
dr(äng)		farm hand
dragon		dragoon (cavalryman)
död		death, dead
död utan bröstarvinge		died without issue
dödfödd		stillborn
dödslängd		death record
dödsorsak		cause of death
döpa		baptize, christen
dött		died
döttrar		daughters

ed		oath
ejusd(em)	(L)	same (day, month, etc.)
eod(em) die		the same day
extinctus	(L)	deceased, murdered
f(ader)		father
f(adder)		sponsor, godfather, godmother, etc.
f(ilius) (ilia)	(L)	son, daughter
fabrik		factory, mill, shop
fabriksarbetare		factory worker
fadder		sponsor, godfather, godmother, etc.
fader		father
fall		waterfall
farbror		uncle
farfar		grandfather (father's father)
farmor		grandmother
fartyg		ship, vessel, steamer
faster		aunt
fattighjon		pauper
fattighus		poor house
fiskare		fisherman
fiskläge		fishing village
fjärd		bay, inlet
fjärdingsman		sheriff, parish constable
fl(icka)		girl
fl.b. (flyttningsbetyg)		certificate of moving
flytta		move
f(ödelse)o(rt)		birth place
fogde		marshall, foreman
fors		rapid
fr(ater)	(L)	brother
frånskild		divorced
frälse		nobility
frälsegård		tax exempt farm
främling		stranger
född		born
födelselängd		birth record
förfäder		forefathers
förmyndare		guardian
förrätta		perform
församling		parish, congregation
förstfödd		firstborn
förstärkningskarl		soldier
föräldrar		parents
gammal, gamle, gamla		old
garde		guard (regiment)
gardessoldat		soldier at the Guard (King's)
garvare		tanner
ges(äll)		apprentice
gift		married, poison
giftoman		sponsor of bride
gl. (gammal)		old
g:ne (gemene, menig)		private (soldier)
gosse		boy
gren		branch
grenadjär		grenadier, soldier
gruva		mine
gudfader		godfather
gård		farm, estate
göl		lake, pool
H(err)		Mr., lord
h(ustru)		wife
hammarsmed		forging smith

han, hans		he, his
hd, h:d, (härad)		district
handskmakare		glove maker
hav		sea
h:n, hem, (hemman)		farm, homestead
hemmansbrukare		farmer
hemort		residence
herrgård		manorial or large estate
henne, hennes		her, hers
hjälte		hero
holm(e)		islet (on land or in water)
hon		she
hovrätt		court of appeal
hujus	(L)	this, in this month
hus		house
husförhör		house examination, clerical survey
husman		crofter
hustru		wife
hydda		cottage
härad		district
häradsrätt		district court
hög, högt		mound, hill, high
höst		autumn, fall
ibid(em)	(L)	same, the same place
inflyttning(sbetyg)		moving in (certificate)
infra	(L)	below
inhyses		farmer
innehållsförteckning		table of content, index, register
inre		inner
jord		earth, soil, land
jordbruk(are)		farm(er)
jordebok		land record
jordebokssocken		civil parish
jordegumma		midwife
jordtorpare		farming crofter
jungfru		Miss, maiden
juni		June
kallas		called, named, christened
kallelse		call, appointment
karl		man, male
karta		map
katekismilängd		communion record
klensmed		smith (of smaller products)
kläder		clothes
klädespersedlar		clothes
kn, kommun		parish
knekt		soldier
kolare		charcoal burner (person's occupation)
kommun		parish
konfirmation		confirmation, partaking of communion for the first time
krigsarkiv		war archive
krono		belonging to the crown (government)
krögare		innkeeper
kung(lig)		king(ly), royal
kvarter		block
kvinna		woman
kyrka		church
kyrkobok		parish register
kyrkogång		introduction into the church after childbirth
kyrkoherde		parish minister
kyrkosocken		ecclesiastical parish

kyrkotagen		introduced into the church after childbirth
kyrkvärd		church or parish warden
kär(a)		dear, beloved
kärr		lake, pool, bog
kökspiga		kitchen maid, servant
l(ägra) (ägermål)		about a man having illicit relations
l(oco)		place, locality, here
lag		law, area within which a law was valid in olden days
land		land, country, farm, soil, homestead
landsarkiv		provincial archive
landskap		province
lilla		little, small
liten		little, small
litt(eratur)	(L)	literate, able to read
livgardist		soldier at the King's Guard
ljung		heather
loco	(L)	place, locality, here
lund		grove
lysning(sbok)		banns, record of banns
län		county
längd		roll, book, record
länskalender		county directory
länsstyrelse		county commission
lärare		teacher
m(oder)		mother
m(åg)		son-in-law
maka		wife
make		husband
man		man, male, husband
mantal		measure of size of farm
mantalslängd		census record, tax list
mellan		middle, between
mellersta		middle
ministerialbok		parish register
morbror		uncle, mother's brother
morfar		mother's father, grandfather
morgongåva		morning gift
mormor		mother's mother, grandmother
mortuus, mortua, mortui	(L)	dead
mosse		pool, bog
moster		aunt, mother's sister
månad		month
nattvard(sgång)		communion
natus	(L)	name
nedre		lower
nomen	(L)	name
norr(a), nord		north
nuptiae	(L)	wedding
ny, nytt, nya		new
närvarande		present
näs		point, peninsula
nöddop		emergency baptism
obiit		dead, died
ogift		unmarried
okänd		unknown
omkring		about
omyndig		minor, not of age
ort(er)		place(s)
oä(kta)		illegitimate child

p(agina) pag	(L)	page
p(arentes) par	(L)	parents
parochia	(L)	parish
pastor		parish minister
pastorat		clerical district (one or more parishes)
pastorsämbete		parish office
personakt		personal record
piga		maid, maid servant
pilt		boy
pojke		boy
posth(umus)	(L)	born after father's death
präst		priest, minister
prästgård		parsonage
protokoll		minutes (records)
puella	(L)	girl
puer	(L)	boy
pupillus	(L)	motherless, fosterchild
q(uinna)		woman
r(yttare)		soldier (on horse)
reg(emente)		regiment
renatus	(L)	baptized
r. hr. (ryttarhustru)		soldier's wife
Riddarhuset		House of Nobility
riksarkiv		national archives
riksdaler		dollar (monetary unit)
rote		district or ward of parish or city
rotehjon		person (pauper) supported by a "rote"
rotesoldat		soldier for a "rote"
rulla		record, roll
rusth. rusth:t, rusthåll		farm(s) equipping a soldier (cavalryman)
ryttartorp		soldier's croft
rådhusrätt		city court
rådman		councilman
rådstugurätt		city court
räkenskapslängd		account record
rätt		court, right, correct
s(alig)		deceased
s(on)		son
saltpetersjudare		salt (nitrate) boiler (trade)
samhälle		community (not a record keeping unit)
sankt		saint
sepultus	(L)	buried
sexman		parish custodian or caretaker
s:hu(stru)		daughter-in-law, soldier's wife
sjuk(dom)		sick(ness)
sjö		sea, lake
sjöman		sailor
sk. hem. (skättehemman)		farm on which taxes were paid
skeppslag		district
skog		forest
skol(lärare)		school (teacher)
skomakare		shoemaker
skräddare		tailor
skuld		debt
slätt		plain
slåtter		hay mowing
smed		smith, black smith
s:n, sochn, socken		parish
snickare		carpenter
sockenman		man in parish with right to vote
soldat		soldier
sommar		summer

sondotter		granddaughter
sonson		grandson
s:r, s(oro)	(L)	sister
sponsor	(L)	godfather, witness at baptism
sponsus, sponsa	(L)	groom, bride
spädbarn		infant
s:ska, svägerska		sister-in-law
stad(sarkiv)		city (archive)
stamfader		progenitor
stamtavla		pedigree
statare		cotter, farm-servant (in nearly all cases married) receiving pay in cash and kind
stor, stort, stora		large, big, great
ström		stream, creek
stuga		cottage, house
styvson		stepson
stöld		theft
supra	(L)	above
susceptor, susceptrix	(L)	godfather or godmother who carried the child
sven		young man, apprentice
svärson		son-in-law
syskon		brothers(s) and sisters(s), siblings
syster		sister
systerson		sister's son, nephew
söder, södra		south
testis	(L)	godfather, witness
testamente		will
tillgångar		assets
ting		court
tingslag		district
tjuvnad		stealing
tjänare		servant
tjärn		little lake, tarn
torp(are)		croft, crofter
trädgårdsmästare		gardener
trumslagare		drummer
undantagsman		previous farmowner living on "pension" from a former farm
undertecknad		undersigned
urtima		special, extra (of court session)
uteluckt		excommunicated
utesluten		excommunicated
utflyttning		moving out
utvandrare		emigrant
vide	(L)	see
vigsel(längd)		marriage (record)
vik		bay, gulf
vinter		winter
vittne		witness
vår		spring, our
välsignelse		blessing
värderingsman		appraiser
väster, västra, västlig		west
yngst		youngest
ytter, yttre		outer
åbo		farmer
ålder		age
år (åhr)		year
äga, ägor		estate, piece of land
äga (verb)		own
ägare		owner

äkta	legitimate, real
äldst	oldest
äldste	elder
äng	meadow
änka	widow
änkeman	widower
änkling	widower
öster, östra, östlig	east
över, övre	upper

APPENDIX E

Bibliography

Among general bibliographies we would like to mention two:

Svensk Bokförteckning published by Bibliografiska institutet at the Royal Library in Stockholm (Kungl. Biblioteket) and

Handbok i Släkt — och personforskning by Bengt Hildebrand, published by Wahlström and Widstrand, Stockholm.

Chapter 1. **Swedish Simplified,** Hugo's Language Institute, London.
Teach Yourself Swedish by R. J. McClean, London.
Modern Swedish Grammar by Im. Björkhagen, Stockholm.
Beginning Swedish by Walter Johnson, Philadelphia.
A Guide for Genealogical Research by Archibald F. Bennett, Salt Lake City.

Chapter 2. **Svensk Ortförteckning,** Kungliga Poststyrelsen, Stockholm.
Sweden, Gazeteer Number 72, U. S. Department of Interior, Washington.
Svenska Orter, Generalstabens Litografiska Anstalt, Stockholm.
Geografiskt-Statistiskt Handlexikon by C. M. Rosenberg, Stockholm
Nordisk Familjebok, AB Familjebokens förlag, Stockholm.
Svensk Uppslagsbok, Förlagshuset Norden AB, Malmö.
KAKs bilatlas, Kungliga Automobilklubben, Stockholm.
The Times, Atlas of the World, Vol. III, Boston
The National Geographic Atlas of the World, Washington.

Chapter 3. See Chapter 2.

Chapter 4. **Förslag till Namnlag,** Justitiedepartementet, Stockholm.
Svensk Namnbok by P. A. Kjöllerström, Ulricehamn, Sweden.
Svenska Dopnamn och Släktnamn by P. A. Kjöllerström, Wahlström och Widstrand, Stockholm.
Svenska Familjenamn vid början av 1900-talet by Erik and Adolf Noreen, Uppsala.
Sex kapitel om släktforskning by Ella Heckscher, Albert Bonnier, Stockholm.

Chapter 5. **Libraries and Archives in Sweden,** the Swedish Institute, Stockholm.
Svenska Bibliotek by J. Victor Johansson, Wahlström and Widstrand, Stockholm.

Chapter 6. **Genealogical Instruction Manual,** The Genealogical Society of the Church of Jesus Christ of Latter-day Saints, Inc., Salt Lake City.
Latin-English and English-Latin Dictionary, Cassell and Co., New York

Chapter 7. **Läsning av gamla handstilar** by Alf Åberg, Stockholm.
Svenska Skriftprov 1464-1828 by R. Svedlund and O. Svenonius, Uppsala.
Thus They Wrote by Carl-Erik Johansson, Provo, Utah.

Chapter 8. **History of the Scandinavian Mission** by Andrew Jenson, Salt Lake City
Encyclopedic History of the Church of Jesus Christ of Latter-day Saints by Andrew Jenson, Salt Lake City.
Latter-day Saint Biographical Encyclopedia by Andrew Jenson, Salt Lake City
Fundamentals of Genealogical Research by Laureen R. Jaussi and Gloria D. Chaston, Salt Lake City
Homeward to Zion by William Mulder, Minneapolis
Prelude to The Kingdom by Gustive O. Larson, Francestown, N. H.

Chapter 9. **Tracing your Swedish Ancestry** by Nils William Olsson, The Swedish Pioneer Historical Quarterly, October 1962, Chicago.

Source Materials on Emigration in the United States National Archives, With Particular Emphasis on Swedish Emigration to the United States by Nils William Olsson, The Swedish Pioneer Historical Quarterly, January 1961, Chicago.

Glimpses from the Activities of a Swedish Emigrant Agent by Olof Thörn, The Swedish Pioneer Historical Quarterly, January and April 1959, Chicago.

Genealogical Records in the National Archives, General Services Administration, Washington.

List of National Archives Microfilm Publications, General Services Administration, Washington.

Den Stora Utvandringen by Lars Ljungmark, Stockholm.

Along the Scandinavian Emigrant Trail, by Nils William Olsson, Ph. D. Lecture of World Conference on Records, Genealogical Society, Salt Lake City, 1969.

Swedish Settlements and Records in the United States, by Nils William Olsson, Ph. D, Lecture of World Conference on Records, Genealogical Society, Salt Lake City, 1969.

Chapter 10. **Finding you Forefathers**, Utrikesdepartementet, Stockholm.

Searching for Scandinavian Ancestors at the Genealogical Society Library, by Henry E. Christiansen, Lecture from World Conference on Records, Genealogical Society, Salt Lake City, 1969.

Chapter 11. See Chapter 10.

Swedish Genealogical Research Techniques Prior to 1750, by Sten C. O. Carlsson, Ph. D. Lecture from World Conference on Records, Genealogical Society, Salt Lake City, 1969.

Chapter 12. See Chapter 10.

Chapter 13. See Chapter 10.

The Court Records of Sweden — How Valuable Is Their Content as a Genealogical Source? by Birgitta Lager, Ph. D., Lecture of World Conference on Records, Genealogical Society, Salt Lake City, 1969.

Chapter 14. **Statistiskt Sammandrag av Svenska Indelningsverket** by C. Grill, Isaac Markus Printing, Stockholm 1857.

NOTE! Many of these books and articles may be used in connection with the study of several chapters, but they have only been mentioned once.